Praise for EMANCIPATORY POLITICS AND PRAXIS

Now more than ever we need a concerted vision of social justice, transformed into an academic pragmatism that can help stem the rising tide of oppressive governance, media-driven vitriol and the ubiquitous devastation of neoliberal capitalism. This incisive and illuminating collection of essays by David Scott (and co-authors), informed by decades of research and activism conducted by members of the European Group for the Study of Deviancy and Social Control, delivers a powerful message of defiance and hope, providing a pathway towards a 'real utopia' of inclusiveness, genuine equality and a humanitarian foundation for social order. While focussing largely on penal abolitionism, Scott deftly extends his arguments to provide a broader picture of the abuses of state power and the means of resistance to them, employing an accessible language that will inspire a readership hungry for change, and an even larger one as yet unaware of its appetite for a more just world.
Paddy Rawlinson, Associate Professor of International Criminology at Western Sydney University

Scott's anthology is a timely reminder of the crucial importance of critical criminology and its close bond with grass roots activism at a time when continuing penal expansion, austerity policies and exclusionary practices yet again define much of the states' approach to 'justice'. Engaging in a discussion of its theoretical underpinnings, the collection also shows how academic work grounded in critical criminological thought provides a powerful challenge to the exclusionary and often harmful order of contemporary societies. The book underlines how a collaborative, supportive and non-hierarchical academic space, such as that provided by the European Group for the Study of Deviance and Social Control, leads to the flourishing of critical ideas and innovative thinking about justice, equality, fairness, power and resistance in today's world. It is a message of which the increasingly 'corporate' contemporary academic institutions should also take heed.
Agnieszka Martynowicz, PhD candidate, Ulster University

David Scott's essays represent the very best in abolitionist thought. They are based on a critical combination of rigorous scholarship and activist interventionism. Taken together, they provide a searing indictment of the deadly and relentless power of the state to inflict pain and punishment on the poor and the powerless. His essays offer an alternative vision to this punitive degradation, underpinned as they are by a utopian commitment to a world based on the progressive ideals of social inclusion, social justice and democratic accountability.
Professor Joe Sim, Liverpool John Moores University

In this book, David Scott epitomises the core values and sentiments of the European Group. The collection of essays and reflections demonstrates the collaborative and collegial nature of critical criminologists working towards effectively challenging entrenched models of 'justice'. Scott provides a tribute to some of the most prolific and influential critical criminologists alongside a genealogy of the Group overall. The ideas put forth in the chapters offer valid alternatives to harmful and ineffectual criminal justice perspectives and practices based on the author's substantive empirical engagement with the justice system. It also demonstrates some of the challenges facing critical criminologists – new and established – working in (and against) an increasingly neoliberal, marketised higher educational system. This book is a must-read for anyone interested in crime, harm and social justice alternatives.

Dr Marian Duggan, Lecturer in Criminology, University of Kent

'Inclusivity' defines the development, consolidation and maintenance of critical analysis and its relevance beyond the conference hall or classroom. It requires open and accessible dialogue, with discussions and debates unlimited by 'tradition' (however recent), initiating collective participation unhindered by institutional status or formal standing. Too often, academic groups and conferences reflect the structural constraints of established institutions. They are hierarchical, often isolationist, and regularly intimidate those who enter within the lecture hall. Soon to reach its half century, the European Group for the Study of Deviance and Social Control has challenged academic orthodoxy in so many ways. It has promoted critical scholarship entwined with political intervention, critiquing mainstream criminological and penal theories, policies and practices. As an organisation inevitably marginalised by its proclaimed 'outsider' status, the European Group's existence has waxed and waned, regularly undermined by financial precariousness. In this engaging, reflective volume David Scott recalls his first involvement with the Group in Venice, 2001. Soon after, as attendance at the annual conference dwindled and our close friend and organiser, Karen Leander, died in tragic circumstances, the Group faced closure. David had other ideas and, with support, he became directly instrumental in the Group's revival and renewal as a primary, innovative forum for critical exchange. This book is an exemplar of his collaborative contribution to a process that has taken the European Group to a new and sustainable level without compromising its founding principles. It is testimony to his academic scholarship, to his political commitment and to his unswerving comradeship.

Professor Phil Scraton, School of Law, Queen's University, Belfast.

Reading *Emancipatory Politics and Praxis* the words that immediately jumped off the page were 'justice', 'vision' 'dedication' and the meaning of solidarity. We need all of this and each other ever more in these dangerous times.

Ann Singleton, Senior Research Fellow, Centre for the Study of Poverty and Social Justice, University of Bristol

As one would expect from Scott and fellow members of the European Group, this passionately written text overflows with compassion, wisdom and hope. The chapters are beautifully written and contain a mix of personal reflections, historical discussions and theoretically informed explorations. Their cumulative effect is to shed light on the violence contained within and inherent to the criminal justice system, and in doing so, this collection asks that the reader thinks more critically about harm and their social, political and economic consequences. Rather than simply accept the status quo, this collection of short chapters by Scott and others makes a strong case for working towards an alternative 'real utopia' which seeks to minimise harm and inequality, rather than the current criminal justice system which helps to perpetuate it. *Emancipatory Politics and Practice* should be a core text for anyone interested in the violent power of criminal justice systems and in the opportunities for resistance and social justice.
Dr Lisa White, Senior Lecturer, University of Lincoln

Emancipatory Politics and Praxis is a powerful collection of essays which provide a solid foundation for future directions in critical criminological research. Above all, the book makes clear that 'critical criminology' is about more than just critique – it requires a commitment to emancipatory knowledge, solidarity and the resistance of oppression in all its forms. It is essential reading for students, academics and activists alike.
Dr Joanna Gilmore, Lecturer in Law, University of York

The book is at once a tribute to the European Group's roots and a testament to its renewed vitality. The essays capture wonderfully the intellectual and political spirit of the collective and also canvass a number of key themes and concerns in a thorough and accessible manner. David Scott and colleagues have produced what deserves to be regarded as the essential primer to contemporary critical thinking about criminalisation, social harm and social justice.
Georgios Papanicolaou, Reader in Criminology, Teesside University

An informative and thoughtful book that provides deep insights into the evolution of critical criminology, and that of the European Group for the Study of Deviance and Social Control itself. Scott and his colleagues also provide inspiration for us in continuing this emancipatory work.
Maeve McMahon, Associate Professor, Department of Law and Legal Studies, Carleton University,

Dear Pauline,

It has been great to work with you over the last 3 years.

Wishing you all the best.

In friendship and solidarity.

David

17/08/2016

Emancipatory Politics and Praxis:

An anthology of essays written for the European Group
for the Study of Deviance and Social Control, 2013–16

David Scott

Emancipatory Politics and Praxis:

An anthology of essays written for the European Group for the Study of Deviance and Social Control, 2013–16

David Scott

with

Emma Bell, Joanna Gilmore, Helena Gosling, J.M. Moore and Faith Spear

EG Press Limited
London
2016

Published by the EG Press Limited,
London, England
www.egpress.org/

ISBN 978-1-911439-01-1

Dedication

This book is dedicated to the memory of
Barbara Hudson

All author's royalties have been donated to the European Group

Contents

Acknowledgements   i

Notes on contributors   ii

Dedication: Barbara Hudson: A torchbearer of justice   iii

Foreword: Turn the Tables: On the importance of   vii
       'Armchair Activism'
       Ida Nafstad and Per Jørgen Ystehede

Prologue   1

1.   Introduction: Emancipatory politics and praxis   7

Part A: Critical criminology and the utopian imagination

2.   Critical Criminology and the European Group   15
    for the Study of Deviance and Social Control
    (with *Joanna Gilmore* and *J.M. Moore*)

3.   Reawakening our Radical Imagination: Thinking   29
    realistically about utopias, dystopias and the non-penal
    (with *Emma Bell*)

4.   A Disobedient Visionary with an Enquiring Mind: 53
    An essay on the contribution of Stan Cohen

5.   Critical Criminology in the Corporate University: Results   63
    from a survey in England, Wales and the North of Ireland

Part B: Iatrogenic penal harms and visions of justice

6.   Beyond Criminal Justice: 'It's a long road to wisdom,   93
    but it is a short one to being ignored'
    (with *J.M. Moore*)

7.   Constance Lytton: Living for a cause   109
    (with *Faith Spear*)

8.   Speaking the Language of State Violence: 123
    An abolitionist perspective

9.   Against Criminal Injustice, For Social Justice: 143
    Reflections and possibilities

Part C: Abolitionist real utopia

10. Reimagining Citizenship: Justice, responsibility and   161
    non-penal real utopias
    (with *Emma Bell*)

11. Otherwise than Prisons, not Prisons Otherwise: 181
    Therapeutic communities as non-penal real utopias
    (with *Helena Gosling*)

12. Playing the 'Get Out of Jail Free' Card: 203
    Creating a new abolitionist-based consensus?

Epilogue   215

Appendices

1: Manifesto of the Working Group on Prisons, Detention   219
   and Punishment

2: G4S 2014 Annual General Meeting   225

3: G4S and Human Rights   229

4: Critical Criminology Survey Institutions   233

5: Critical Criminology Survey Respondent Details   235

6: Critical Criminology Survey Questionnaire   237

Acknowledgements

This book would not have been possible without the help and support of a great many people. First, a massive thank you to Emma Bell, Joanna Gilmore, Helena Gosling, J.M. Moore and Faith Spear for agreeing that our co-authored papers could be included as chapters in this book. Many thanks also to everyone who agreed to participate in the critical criminology survey that was undertaken in universities in England, Wales and the North of Ireland between March and May 2014. Much appreciation to Emma Bell and Jen Morgan for reading the final version of the manuscript. Thanks also to J.M. Moore and all involved in the production process at EG Press.

I would also like to thank all of my wonderful colleagues at *Liverpool John Moores University* (LJMU) for their support and encouragement. I have been very fortunate to work within such a brilliant team and all of the essays in the book were written in the three years I spent working for LJMU from 2013-2016. So a massive thank you to all and especially Chris Allen, Kym Atkinson, Giles Barrett, Helen Beckett-Wilson, Yulia Chistyakova, Yarin Eski, Jacinta Fleming, Sarah Greenhow, Katherine Harbord, Anne Hayes, Jim Hollinshead, Antoinette Huber, Will Jackson, Janet Jamieson, Laura Kelly, Steve Lawler, Sian Lincoln, Pauline Marne, Lindsey Metcalf, Pete Millward, Helen Monk, Shiobhan Rogers, Rizwaan Sabir, Carly Speed, Julie Shaw, Joe Sim, Sarah Tickle, Lucinda Thompson, Katie Tucker, David Tyrer and Steve Wakeman for making LJMU such a great place to work.

I would also like to say a special thank you to all my friends in *the European Group for the Study of Deviance and Social Control*. This anthology would not have possible without the enormous contributions of members of the group. For their support in a both a personal and professional capacity I would also like to say thank you Anne Alvesalo-Kuusi, Alana Barton, Anette Ballinger, Vanessa Barker, Andrea Beckmann, Monish Bhatia, Michelle Brown, Tony Bunyan, Victoria Canning, Bree Carlton, Eamonn Carrabine, Mick Cavadino, Kathryn Chadwick, Gilles Chantraine, Becky Clarke, Helen Codd, Roy Coleman, Deborah Coles, Vickie Cooper, Mary Corcoran, Tom Daems, Sacha Darke, Pamela Davies, James Deane, John Dennison, Anita Dockley, Andrew Douglas, Deborah Drake, Rod Earle, Anne Egelund, Samantha Fletcher, Billy Frank, Peter Francis, Stratos Georgoulas, Barry Goldson, Fabrice Guilbaud, Penny Green, Simon Hallsworth, William Harrison, Deena Haydon, Andrew Henley, Paddy Hillyard, Laura Margaret Kelly, Andrew Jefferson, Alessandro Maculan, Margaret Malloch, Agnieszka Martynowicz, Thomas Mathiesen, Simon Mackenzie, Maeve McMahon, Will McMahon, Brenda McWilliams, Linda Moore, Wayne Morrison, Bepe Mosconi, Ida Nafstad, Martin O'Brien, Christina Pantazis, Georgios Papanicolaou, Justin Piche, Scott Poynting, Paddy Rawlinson, Rebecca Roberts, Bill Rolston, Mick Ryan, Simone Santorso, Alvise Sbraccia, Holger Schmidt, Sebastian Scheerer, Phil Scraton, Ann Singleton,

Paula Skidmore, Ragnhild Sollund, Lizzy Stanley, Rene van Swaaningen, Steve Tombs, Waqas Tufail, Francesca Vianello, Reece Walters, Tony Ward, Lisa White, David Whyte, Richard Wild, Patrick Williams, Tunde Zak-Williams and Per Jørgen Ystehede.

Finally, many thanks are also due to my friends and family for their constant encouragement and helpful distractions, especially Ian Nickson, Emily Nickson, Kim Jones, Richard Wilbraham, Sue Wilbraham, Helen Maher, Ian Scott and Ben Scott.

Despite all of the help of the above, I take responsibility for any errors that lie within.

Notes on contributors

David Scott is senior lecturer in criminology at Liverpool John Moores University, England

Emma Bell is professor of British politics at the University of Savoie, France

Joanna Gilmore is lecturer in law at York University, England

Helena Gosling is senior lecturer in criminal justice at Liverpool John Moores University, England

J.M. Moore is senior lecturer in criminology at Newman University, England

Ida Nafstad is coordinator of the *European Group for the Study of Deviance and Social Control*, and a post-doctoral researcher in Department of the Sociology of Law, Lund University, Sweden

Faith Spear is chair of the Independent Monitoring Board, HMP Hollesley Bay Prison, England

Per Jørgen Ystehede is secretary of the *European Group for the Study of Deviance and Social Control*, and Senior Executive Officer in the Department of Criminology and Sociology of Law, University of Oslo, Norway

Dedication: Barbara Hudson: a torchbearer of justice

Barbara Hudson was a longstanding member of the *European Group for the Study of Deviance and Social Control*, who not only cherished, but lived, its principles and values. She was a PhD student of Stan Cohen in the early 1980s and his work inspired her to write on a number of topics, such as social control, the sociology of punishment and penal abolitionism. Ultimately, though, the leitmotiv running through her life work was an exploration of the meaning of justice: the failure of punishment and criminal processes to deliver justice; the importance of doing justice to difference/diversity in structurally unequal societies; the foundations and practices of 'restorative justice' and, in more recent times, developing and applying the idea of 'cosmopolitan justice'. An internationalist and socialist, who felt passionately about Europe and the need for strong commitments to human rights and social justice, her most well-known books are *Justice through Punishment* (Macmillan, 1987); *Penal Policy and Social Justice* (Macmillan, 1993); *Understanding Justice* (Open University Press, 1996); and, what many consider to be her magnum opus, *Justice in the Risk Society* (Sage, 2003).

Known for her integrity and scholarship, Barbara Hudson was an innovative and ground-breaking thinker who, by drawing upon moral and political philosophy and legal jurisprudence, alongside sociological, criminological and penological studies, opened up new avenues for critical analysis. She was a proud representative of the tradition known as 'critical criminology' and her own contributions brought into sharp relief the close relationships between penalisation and social inequalities. Throughout her body of work she placed *human* beings at the centre of her analysis and constantly challenged the demonisation, dehumanisation and monstering of the 'Other'. Alongside critiques of injustice and inhumanity, and charting contemporary threats to justice, her work was also characterised by the endeavour to present a modernist normative framework that could both protect and promote justice, reflecting our common humanity. Indeed, it was her dual emphasis on both the need for the *deconstruction* of existing capitalist, patriarchal and neocolonial structural inequalities and the in-depth exploration of possibilities of *reconstruction* that made her one of the most important criminological thinkers of our time.

Barbara Hudson engaged with the most pressing issues of the day. Her writings on 'just deserts' were produced at a time when the concept dominated both jurisprudence and penal policy. Recognising its limitations, she was motivated to write *Justice through Punishment* because she was unable to find an appropriate book-length treatise which engaged critically with the concept. Her recent work also engaged with the key issues of our time — risk consciousness and risk control; torture; hyper-incarceration; poverty; the detention of migrants and the promotion of global injustice. At times she seemed to present a lone voice on justice, and she felt that not only had the general public lost interest in justice, but perhaps also her 'fellow criminologists'. Barbara Hudson looked for balance and was always against domination, whether in wider society or the academy. For example, in the mid-1990s, she was concerned about the dominance of both the 'masculinities' thesis — primarily because it led us back, in effect, to the old criminological focus on delinquent working-class boys — and the Foucauldian-inspired governmentality perspective.

There was an openness in her writings and, through her extraordinarily rich analysis, she destroyed the myth that critical criminology has nothing new to say. There was consistency in her analysis and she is deservedly recognised as one of the most influential criminologists and 'European abolitionists' in recent years. Though a confirmed atheist and humanist, she often described the ethos underscoring her work as 'hate sin, but love the sinner'. Her writings are characterised by not only scholarship and interdisciplinary work but also understandability — she aimed to communicate rather than bamboozle readers with academic jargon. Her clarifications of complex and convoluted arguments made her work invaluable in the elaboration and advancement of critical criminology. As a result, her writings were accessible to a wide audience. This is perhaps nowhere more so than in her book *Understanding Justice*. This book, read primarily by students, can also be considered as an exercise in public criminology, for it is often overlooked that students are members of the public, too. In *Understanding Justice*, she influenced, therefore, not only the curricula in universities but also the views of literally tens of thousands of people.

Barbara Hudson was very proud of her intellectual heritage — Steven Box taught her MA level; her PhD was supervised by Stan Cohen; and her PhD external examiner was Antony Giddens. His first viva question for her was "what do you mean by truth?" which perhaps was appropriate for someone who had read philosophy before "anyone told [her] it was difficult". She was particularly well read in phenomenology, reading Jacques Derrida's *Writing and Difference* as early as the 1970s, for example. Stan Cohen had told her that she must "get those philosophical eagles off her shoulder" when she was doing her PhD, but that at some point "they would come home to roost". That this prediction proved accurate is evident in scholarship found in her last and perhaps her finest single-authored book: *Justice in the Risk Society*. She was also a 'renaissance woman' — well read in many different disciplines and schools of thought, whether it be academia, science or literature. Indeed, one of her favourite discussion areas concerned the differences between nuclear fusion and nuclear fission.

That Barbara Hudson took the values and principles of 'cosmopolitan justice' seriously could be seen in how this philosophy influenced her non-hierarchical relationships with others and her ability to relate to people from different social backgrounds, for she possessed not only a remarkable intellect but also a wonderful sense of compassion for and understanding of others. Her non-hierarchical approach can perhaps be summed up by one illustrative example. The day after appearing on a local north-west TV programme, she was very warmly welcomed by the cleaners where she worked in the Harris Building, Lancashire Law School. They were both delighted and surprised in equal measure to have seen her on television the previous evening for, though they had known her for a number of years, they had never realised that she was a professor.

Barbara Hudson carried the torch of justice for some thirty years and, in so doing, not only lit up critical criminology but also shed new light upon contemporary injustices and the meaning of justice itself. It is now time, sadly, for new torchbearers to journey down a path that she dedicated her life to illuminate.[1]

---

[1] An extended version of this obituary was published in the *European Group Newsletter* as 'Rehumanising the Other and the meaning of justice' in the November 2013 issue.

Foreword

Turn the Tables: On the importance of 'Armchair Activism'

Ida Nafstad & Per Jørgen Ystehede

A Seat at the Table

In his autobiography *Cadenza*,[1] Thomas Mathiesen tells about his experiences as a member of the Faculty Board at the Law Faculty in Oslo in the
early 1970's (Mathiesen, forthcoming). Back then the Faculty Board was
the most important body governing the Faculty and consisted of all the
professors. Mathiesen had just been appointed full professor and arrived
at his first meeting, not wanting to be late, a bit early and sat down at the
table. The dean arrived and sat down next to Mathiesen. When the
meeting started, he introduced Mathiesen in the following manner: "We
have a new young professor at our Faculty. Not only is he the only non-
legal scholar, he is a sociologist but that is OK. He has also chosen a very
prominent seat at the table" (Ibid.: 173). The dean's remark caused a
polite chuckle from the others sitting around the table. What Mathiesen
did not know, what no one had told him, was that at the Faculty Board
meetings – akin to the tradition in the Norwegian Supreme Court –
members sat in accordance of seniority. He did not change seat at this
meeting, but the next time, Mathiesen made sure to sit at the far end of
the table, the furthest away from the dean. This was not the only thing
Mathiesen found peculiar about the seating arrangement at the Faculty
Board meetings. The dean's chair was the only chair at the table with side
support for the arms. Mathiesen recounts, that for some reason he at the
time could not quite grasp, he started to get obsessed about this fact until
finally he decided to do an experiment – literally to become an armchair
activist. Prior to one of the meetings, he snuck into the room, stole the
dean's chair and replaced it with one identical to all the other chairs
lacking side support. The meeting started and adjourned and no one
mentioned that the dean's chair had been replaced, however, at the next
meeting, the dean's armchair had been put back where it used to be
(Ibid.).

---

[1] A cadenza is "a difficult part of a piece of classical music that is performed by only one
person near the end of the piece" (Merriam-Webster Dictionary)

These anecdotes from the Faculty Board, of course, speak volumes about symbolic and manifest power structures. We are also sure that many have experienced similar situations at school or university where they have faced ridicule, feeling stupid and/or humiliated by not having been informed and included in the social codes in a (formal) setting by your so called peers. The reason we wanted to start with these anecdotes is that they may be seen as the polar opposite, the antithesis to how David Scott in this anthology describes the ethos of the European Group. As he refers to his first meeting at the European Group:

> I was impressed by the level of collegiality, solidarity and friendship, and the general non-hierarchical ethos that permeated nearly all my interactions with members. It mattered not whether you were, as I was, a PhD student or world famous professor. It was what was said that was important, not the status of the speaker. (Scott, 2016: 2)

Emancipatory Politics and Praxis: An anthology of essays written for the European Group for the Study of Deviance and Social Control, 2013 – 2016 covers more than the 3 years referenced to in the title. In one respect, the work might be seen as documenting both part of Scott's involvement in the European Group over the last 15 years, but moreover some of his main research interest such as prisons, abolitionism, the work of Stan Cohen and his visions for critical criminology and libertarian socialism to mention a few. We will not try to comment on all of these themes except two: the question of real utopias and the history; the past, present and future of the European Group.

Real Utopias

A dictionary will explain utopia as an imagined place, or state of things in which everything is perfect. Examples of such utopias are heaven, Garden of Eden, nirvana, Valhalla or the Elysian Field. 'Utopia' is often used as a synonym for something impossible, imaginary – yes, *utopic*. According to Scott, however, a:

> ... real utopia is a form of emancipatory knowledge that entails the explicit intention of not just understanding individual and social problems, but generating information that can challenge human oppression and transform existing hierarchies of power. (Scott, 2016: 9)

Following Scott's definition there are arguably many real utopians out there, and utopias have become real. Nils Christie can be said to be one example of a scholar who was committed to real utopias, even if he didn't use those words about himself. Christie was dedicated to working towards social justice and a more humane society, where everyone has a place, is heard, and has the possibility to participate, striving towards emancipatory knowledge to reach these goals. His work has showed how utopias are real and how they may be part of the very fabric of a society. Christie's seminal article 'Conflict as Property' (Christie, 1977), achieved the aims of the abolitionist real utopia, as it is defined by Scott: "The aim of the abolitionist real utopia is to provide a vision of socially just interventions that are historically immanent" (Scott, 2016: 9-10), it further has to be: "realistic and pragmatic, whilst at the same time be[ing] consistent with idealistic and utopian visions" (Ibid: 182). Christie's main argument and vision in this article was that conflicts are important to a society and ideally we should have more of them, but we have to deal with them differently than we do now, we have to take them away from the possession of lawyers and out of the courtrooms. We have to give the conflicts and the solutions to them back to the community, back to the people who owns the conflicts, and solve them collectively. Christie draws up an ideal solution, a utopia, of how to solve conflicts. He was well aware of the limits to his utopia. But he believed that what is most important was to strive towards the ideals. And, in fact, Christie did not just provide the vision; he also contributed to the realisation of this vision, through the implementation of the main principles of his utopia. His article became the source of inspiration for the establishment of the Norwegian restorative justice program. Christie played a key-role as a mentor, consistently contributing to ensuring that this restorative justice institution could be a real alternative, and not an add-on to the traditional state systems of punishment. Utopias can be real, and Christie demonstrated it eloquently.

In chapter 11 in this book, Scott writes, together with Helena Gosling, about the abolitionist potential of therapeutic communities (TC) for substance-using lawbreakers:

> The TC, when promoted as part of wider strategy to tackle social inequalities and social injustice, may be an intervention that can help ameliorate, rather than exacerbate, some of the worst harms,

pains and injuries generated in advanced capitalist societies. (Scott and Gosling, 2016: 199)

Christie writes about a different sort of community in his work *Beyond Loneliness and Institutions* (Christie, 1989), which is also important to consider striving for emancipation, inclusion, and the reduction of social injustice and inequalities. Christie engaged with Camphill communities, villages for people with 'special needs', based on Rudolf Steiner's philosophy. Scott and Gosling are concerned with communities for drug users, while Christie focuses on communities for what he calls extraordinary people[2] – the first group criminalised, the second not, both with experiences of exclusion in mainstream society. There are huge discrepancies between the two groups, even though there are principal meeting points between the texts in regard to real utopias – the central one being the abolition of institutions, inclusion in communities, and through that reaching emancipation for vulnerable groups. The crucial point being that abolitionist utopias have importance not only for the prison institution, but any institution causing human suffering.

Another point of importance in regard to Scott's definition of real utopias is the centrality of knowledge – knowledge that reveals the naturalisation of power structures. Bourdieu (1977) called such naturalisations 'doxa', which describes the reproduction of power relations through all that is taken for granted in society in ways that make the "social world appear as self-evident" (Ibid: 164). The use of prison might be just one example. In opposition to 'doxa' stands heterodoxy which entails: "awareness and recognition of the possibility of different or antagonistic beliefs" (Ibid: 164). Promoting heterodoxy, revealing power structures, through knowledge would in itself contribute to emancipation, and from there real utopias, thus constituting one of the core tasks of an 'armchair activist'. Scott makes a great contribution to the task in this book. Heterodox knowledge is at the core of his concept of real utopias.

As Scott et al. show: making utopias real is a collective effort, it is a process. It is a process which has to consist of plurality and equality of voices and opinions, with a footing in the past and a vision for the future (see epilogue). This also mirrors the work of the European Group, with its emphasis on plurality and equality, characterised and shaped by its distinguished history, and with a determination for a better future.

---

[2] The extraordinary people are those often 'seen as "deficient" by the state classificatory system' (Christie, 1989:7).

Future and Present Pasts

This anthology provides information about the history of the European Group. Not only about the ups and downs of the last few decades, but also of the ideas of some of the original founders of the Group. We believe that it is important to continue the work started – the oral history project – to continue gathering stories from the European Group members throughout the world (Scott, 2016: 217). In addition to collecting these stories, it is also important to include not only autobiographical and 'hagiographical' accounts but histories thinking about the activities of the European Group within broader historical and social frameworks. It is all too easy and simplistic to 'reduce' the rise of the European Group to the context of 1968 and the radical social and political movements of the post-Second World War period. Broader historical analyses may also in part provide answers to the longevity of the European Group. If we consider *The European Group for the Study of Deviance and Social Control* - in the context of the history of criminology - this is by far the first interdisciplinary critical criminological forum. As early as the late 19th Century one will find Fabian socialists, feminists, libertarian socialists, anarchists and so on meeting to discuss criminal policy and social reforms. These groups are nowadays mostly forgotten by all except those with a special interest in historical criminology. What arguably makes the European Group different from these groups is that from the beginning it involved both practitioners of the field and also those who had felt on their bodies the punitive embrace of the modern state. Herein one may also perhaps find part of the reason why the group has continued to be relevant. The European Group was formed to create an alternative critical criminology forum more than 40 years ago. As one may read on the European Group's web pages:

> Recognising the dominant influence of Anglo-American criminology, this new forum was to be characterized by a distinct European focus. This sense of place was to be significant on a further level, linking the conference theme with the conference location and offering support to local political activists, for example through press releases and resolutions and sometimes even joining them on demonstrations.

The European Group has never been only for Europeans, but today includes members from throughout the world. This has also led to debates on whether one should keep the adjective European. Irrespective, we believe the adjective should invite reflections on: what does 'a sense of place' mean today? The issue of positionality is an important question when both considering narrating a history of the European Group's pasts as well as when narrating visions of the Groups futures. Scott writes that:

> The European Group for the Study of Deviance and Social Control must learn from its past: it must ensure that, in all its workings and organisation, it retains a commitment to dialogue, participatory democracy and non-hierarchical relations. It must also retain its commitment to emancipatory politics and praxis. (Scott 2016: 218)

We wholeheartedly agree with this and would like to add that we look forward to listening to a multitude of stories about the European Group's pasts and futures coming from all over the world.

As current coordinator and secretary we are fortunate to receive some of these as submissions to the monthly *European Group Newsletter*, and we are looking forward to receiving more in the following years. This anthology is also a testament to the importance of the Newsletter.

We would like to thank all the contributors to the European Group past, present and future – visionaries striving towards real utopias.

References

Bourdieu, P. (1977) *Outline of a Theory of Practice* Cambridge: Cambridge University Press

Christie, N. (1977) "Conflicts as Property" *The British Journal of Criminology*, Vol. 17, No. 1, p. 1-15

Christie, N. (1989) *Beyond Loneliness and Institution: Communes for Extraordinary People* Eugene, Oregon: Wipf & Stock Publishers

Mathiesen, T. (Forthcoming) *Cadenza* Oslo [publisher TBC]

Scott, D. (2016) "Introduction: emancipatory politics and praxis", David Scott et al: *Emancipatory Politics and Praxis: An anthology of essays written for the European Group for the Study of Deviance and Social Control, 2013-16* London: EG Press

Scott, D. and Gosling, H. (2016) "Otherwise than prions, not prisons otherwise: therapeutic communities as non-penal real utopias", David Scott et al: *Emancipatory Politics and Praxis: An anthology of essays written for the European Group for the Study of Deviance and Social Control, 2013-16* London: EG Press

Prologue

All academic writing is collaborative. It is collaborative in the sense that when we write academic discourse, we inevitably engage with the ideas of others who have previously written on our topic areas; that when we publish our work it has often — and largely invisibly — benefitted from formal and informal reviews, suggestions and helpful comments from colleagues and other peers; and often, what we write can be an indirect and serendipitous result of being part of an intellectual milieu where we are able to freely discuss issues and debates collectively and learn through a dialogue with like-minded people. Without such a collaborative ethos, academic discourse would be much the poorer and advances in scholarship much harder to come by. Those forums which facilitate collaboration should be treasured and their crucial contribution acknowledged.

This book, *Emancipatory Politics and Praxis*, is a collaborative effort on a number of levels. It engages with and builds upon the traditions of critical criminology, zemiology and penal abolitionism, taking this work in some new directions as well as reaffirming some long-held values, principles and assumptions about the problems of 'crime', harm and punishment. In so doing, this contribution stands on the shoulders of intellectual giants. The book takes personal and intellectual inspiration from the writings of such great critical thinkers as Stan Cohen, Stuart Hall, Phil Scraton, Joe Sim and Barbara Hudson, the latter being my former PhD supervisor and friend for many years. Many of the ideas and issues found in the book (and indeed in my work elsewhere over the last decade or so) were first explored in informal discussions with Barbara Hudson, and her intellectual influence can be seen in the sentiments of this book and direction it takes. Finally, the book is collaborative in a more direct and concrete sense, in that a number of the chapters have been co-authored with friends and colleagues in the *European Group for the Study of Deviance and Social Control* (European Group): notably, Emma Bell, Joanna Gilmore, Helena Gosling, J.M. Moore and Faith Spear. This book would not have been possible without their intellectual input and cooperation. Significantly, though, it is the European Group that has provided the intellectual milieu in which the ideas explored in the book have germinated and developed. All of the chapters in the book were first published in the three-year period 2013–2016, in either books about the European Group (Gilmore et al., 2013; Moore et al., 2014), the *European*

1

Group Newsletter or the European Group journal *Justice, Power and Resistance*.

The European Group, which had its serendipitous foundations when three European critical criminologists, Stan Cohen, Karl Schumann and Mario Simondi, shared an office in Berkley, California in 1970, is the institutionalisation of the intellectual tradition known as 'critical criminology' in Europe, and is increasingly relevant to the organisation of critical criminologies around the world. The European Group is a forum which allows critical thinkers, practitioners and activists to meet, share ideas and make friendships to facilitate critical academic discourses. It is a space which gives us the opportunity to learn together, share ideas and experiences and collaborate. In a world which today is largely hostile to the values, principles and politics of the critical criminologies, the European Group is an essential ingredient in the continued success of critical criminological knowledges and interventions. In this prologue, I wish to acknowledge the huge personal and intellectual debt that I have owed to the European Group for the last sixteen years. In so doing, I also explore some of the key values and principles of the group. At the end of the book, in an epilogue, I discuss how these values and principles may be best expressed as a means of securing the long-term prosperity and vitality of the group.

I attended my first European Group conference in Venice, Italy in September 2001. I had some indication of what to expect as Phil Scraton had been the supervisor of my MA thesis *Heavenly Confinement?* (Scott, 2011 [1996]) and I was, at that time, a PhD student of Barbara Hudson. The conference, though, excelled all expectations. In Venice, I had the opportunity to talk, make friends and share laughter and music with some of the leading critical criminologists in Europe. I was impressed by the level of collegiality, solidarity and friendship, and the generally supportive and non-hierarchical ethos that permeated nearly all my interactions with members. It mattered not whether you were, as I was, a PhD student or world-famous professor. It was what was said that was important, not the status of the speaker. One world-famous professor, Louk Hulsman, attended my first international conference paper 'Sympathy for the Devil' (published almost word for word eleven years later in *Criminal Justice Matters*, June 2012) and his supportive and kind words were all a PhD student needed to be motivated for the next twelve months. Louk Hulsman was a man filled with an enormous joy for life, and to meet him and spend time in his company and that of my new friends in the group was a very positive experience, and one not to be forgotten.

The European Group is a forum and unique intellectual space fostering confidence and self-motivation in new scholars, as well as providing opportunities to make connections with established critical researchers from around the globe. One of my strongest recollections of the Venice conference was the considerable depth and intellectual dynamism of the conference papers and subsequent discussions. The European Group was a place of learning and its informal atmosphere only enhanced understanding. Aided, perhaps, also by the beautiful scenery, the organisation, scope and general sense of camaraderie were very impressive. I immediately noted the importance of the National Representatives (national reps) in steering the ethos of the conference; the important role performed by the then coordinator Karen Leander in ensuring all went smoothly; and the strong commitment of members to democratic and participatory principles in the annual general meeting, where the conference theme for the following year was debated.

The few days I spent in Venice in September 2001 felt hugely significant. My positive experiences of the European Group conferences continued in the following years, attending stimulating and engaging conferences in Helsinki in 2003 and Bristol in 2004. These later conferences confirmed my overall impression of the importance of the forum as a pedagogical tool for critical and emancipatory thought. I was so motivated that I agreed to organise a British Irish Section conference of the European Group in Preston, Lancashire in April 2005. At this conference, there were keynotes from Steve Tombs, Michael Lavalette, Rene van Swaaningen, Janet Alder, Phil Scraton and Barbara Hudson, and more than forty conference papers.

I began to realise that the more a person participated in group activities, the stronger the sense of belonging, responsibility and commitment to the values of the group. Further conference attendance followed and, directly after the annual conference in Utrecht in 2007, I agreed to convene the 2009 European Group Annual Conference in Preston, Lancashire. Following the suggestion of Stan Cohen, we held a colloquium in honour of Louk Hulsman on the first day of the conference, who had sadly passed away in January 2009. Keynote speakers at the conference included Stan Cohen, Scott Poynting, Vincenzo Ruggiero, Barbara Hudson and Jehanne Hulsman, and there were more than sixty other papers delivered across the three days. When Stan Cohen spoke on the opening day of the conference, you could have heard a pin drop in the densely packed Greenback Lecture Theatre, University of Central

Lancashire — which I subsequently referred to as the 'Stan Cohen Lecture Theatre'.

The European Group has had its ups and downs during its forty-four-year history, and one of its recent low points was the period from 2007–2009/10. Conference numbers were down and many of the most committed people, including those who had been convenors of previous annual conferences, were no longer attending. There was much soul searching at that time and a number of initiatives were hatched in 2008/9 that, in only a few years, would see a great revival in the fortunes of the European Group. Towards the end of 2008, the European Group's website was completely reorganised and hosted by Manchester University, and in November 2008 the now enormously successful European Group Facebook page was established. The later part of the decade also saw the influx of a number of new people into the group, including J.M. Moore, Joanna Gilmore, Stratos Georgoulas and Emma Bell, who were all to perform important roles over the next few years. There was to be one further great loss to the group, when only a few days after the 2009 Preston annual conference, Karen Leander, who had been coordinator for twenty-five years, died unexpectedly. Her death sent shock waves through the group and left an enormous gap in terms of leadership and organisation. Karen had epitomised the spirit of the group and her strength of character and commitment was unquestionable. With her loss, the group once again fell into crisis.

Joanna Gilmore and I did our best to fill the vacuum and support the organisation of the 2010 annual conference in Lesvos. At that conference, we were confirmed in the roles of group secretary (Joanna) and coordinator (myself). After officially taking the role of coordinator, I spoke at length with Stan Cohen, who shared with me not only his extensive knowledge of the history of the group but also his original vision for it. For Stan Cohen, the principles of participatory democracy, 'fraternity'/solidarity, friendship, mutual aid and a spirit of openness and cooperation should underscore the practices of the group in all ways. Reinvigorating the group would mean returning it to its roots and, where possible, giving power and influence back to ordinary members. It meant listening to the voices of those with experience regarding how the group worked — such as Phil Scraton, Tony Bunyan, Paddy Hillyard and Ann Singleton who had all performed important roles in sustaining the group over many years — and giving new members opportunities to be involved in the organisation of group and thus feel like they belonged. It meant 'leading from behind'. When asked to rearticulate the core values of the group for the 2011 annual conference, I drew upon this original vision of the group (Scott, 2012b, 2012c). Stan Cohen had felt that the group continued to be a vital part of the success of critical criminology. A strong European Group would provide members with support as well as a platform from which to sustain its strong presence in the academy and beyond.

The Lesvos conference in 2010 was a great success and a clear indication that the group was moving in the right direction. The 2011 conference was organised by Emma Bell, who was to become the new coordinator of the group the following year, whilst the 2012 conference in Cyprus was a much more collectively organised event. The collective nature of conference organisation has continued in the last few years with the new working-group coordinators now taking responsibility for organising conference streams. The sharing of responsibilities has helped to prevent conveners becoming isolated, as well as building a greater pool of people with conference organisation experience.

With Emma Bell and Monish Bhatia elected as the new coordinator and secretary respectively in September 2012, the group went from strength to strength. Successful conferences, new working groups and further initiatives in social media were introduced under their tenure. Building on the twice-weekly email bulletins of 'European Group News', they also reintroduced the hugely successful monthly *European Group Newsletter*, the primary source of the chapters that follow. Alongside this, there was renewed interest in publishing European Group conference papers. From 1980 through to 1990, the European Group published ten volumes of its Working Papers in European Criminology, which brought together 163 conference papers delivered during this period (see Gilmore et al., 2013: 370–381). Although there was to be one further volume in 1996 bringing together a further fourteen papers (Ibid.: 382), there was a long period of time before European Group conference papers were to be published collectively again. Indeed, it was not until Stratos Georgoulas edited a book bringing together a number of the papers delivered in Lesvos 2010 that the tradition of bringing out an edited collection of working papers was revived and momentum built once again for a specific European Group outlet.

Joanna Gilmore, J.M. Moore and I helped the momentum by editing a book in 2013 to celebrate the 40th Conference of the European Group (Gilmore et al., 2013). Alongside this, J.M. Moore and I edited a further collection of papers in 2014 on penal abolitionism that had originally been published in the first ten Working Papers in European Criminology (Moore et al., 2014). This book was published by the European Group itself, the first time that this had happened since 1990. The group was placed in safe hands once again when Ida Nafstad and Per Jorgen Yesthede became the new coordinator and secretary respectively in September 2015, and a new era began when the foundation volume of the European Group Journal *Justice, Power and Resistance* was published by EG Press in September 2016. It is within this context — that is, being a part of the intellectual milieu of the *European Group for the Study of Deviance and Social Control* — that the papers drawn together in this anthology were conceived and written.

References

Gilmore, J., Moore, J.M. and Scott, D. (eds) (2013) *Critique and Dissent*. Ottawa: Red Quill Books

Moore, J.M., Rolston, W., Scott, D. and Tomlinson, M. (eds) (2014) *Beyond Criminal Justice*. Bristol: EG Press

Scott, D. (2011 [1996]) *Heavenly Confinement?* London: Lambert Academic Press

Scott, D. (2012a) 'Sympathy for the devil' in *Criminal Justice Matters* Volume 88, No 1 pp 8-9, June 2012

Scott, D. (2012b) 'The European Group for the Study of Deviance and Social Control' in Bell, E. (ed) (2012) *No Borders* Chambery: University of Savoie Press

Scott, D. (2012c) 'European Group Coordinator Opening Address, 2012' (see European Group YouTube) https://www.youtube.com/watch?v=YOBsQjQ5xus

Swaaningen, R. van (1997) *Critical Criminology* London: Sage

1

Introduction:

Emancipatory politics and praxis

This book brings together papers that have been published by the *European Group for the Study of Deviance and Social Control* (European Group) in the last three years. The rationale behind the book is that whilst the papers were all written separately, and often for specific reasons — such as the obituary for Stan Cohen in the *European Group Newsletter* in September 2013 — they all share a commitment to emancipatory knowledge. The aim of this introduction is to highlight some of the key ideas explored in the following eleven chapters, and to indicate the rationale behind the selection and overall objective of this collection of papers.

One of the central features underscoring the generation of emancipatory knowledge is the desire for human liberation and freedom from oppression. Such a desire for liberation, equitable social relationships, respect and recognition of human diversity are principles that have been present in critical criminologies since their modern formulation in the late 1960s and early 1970s (Tifft and Sullivan, 1980). More than thirty-five years ago, Larry Tifft and Dennis Sullivan (1980: 22) argued that contemporary mainstream criminologists were plagued by what they called a "warped spirituality". Rather than being 'scientists of the moral' looking to uncover moral laws and social equilibrium — as envisioned in early contributions to critical analysis on 'crime' and punishment (see for example the nineteenth-century socialist writings of P.J. Proudhon[1], Peter Kropotkin and Emile Durkheim) — criminologists today have become technicians of the state and the powerful, performing key roles in legitimating, mystifying and masking state repression, authoritarianism and domination.

---

[1] It is important that the ideas of Proudhon are strongly connected with the emancipatory logic of socialist feminism.

Further, for Tifft and Sullivan (1980), there can be no 'value freedom' or 'scientific objectivity' in criminological research, as positivist criminologists claim. Rather, the goal of those studying and researching issues around 'crime' and punishment must be to engage directly with people to understand their world view and facilitate social justice. For libertarian socialists such as Tifft and Sullivan (1980), the key areas of concern — that is, critique — for an emancipatory politics and praxis are hierarchies and elitism; domination and authoritarianism; dehumanised relationships, slavery and the negation of human spirituality; bureaucratic and managerial rationalisations; the coercion and violence of law and punishment; the creation of social harms, pain and human suffering; and the centralisation of power and the corruption of the powerful. But liberation also means *being for* something. Thus Tifft and Sullivan (1980) maintain that an emancipatory politics and praxis means promoting visions of justice grounded in participatory democracy; community values of inclusion, tolerance, diversity, autonomy and freedom; human flourishing and dignity; reciprocal awareness, mutuality and ethical responsibility; and social transformations facilitating a more equitable redistribution of wealth. As the fumes of injustice spread far and wide, beyond their direct victims, there can be no real justice for anyone unless there is justice for all (Proudhon, 1990 [1840]; Kropotkin, 1924).

In this book, the emancipatory logic of libertarian socialism[2] is explored primarily through the lens of penal abolitionism. Bringing together the 'red' (Marxist and Neo-Marxist socialism) and the 'black' (socialist anarchism), libertarian socialist visions of justice have undoubtedly been important in the development of penal abolitionism, but it is sometimes overlooked how significant penal abolitionism can be for contemporary libertarian socialism. Objections have been raised against libertarian socialism regarding the apparent necessity of coercion, the force of law and state punishment. Penal abolitionism is a perspective that aims specifically to question the inevitability of penalisation, thus offering important intellectual resources in defence of this broader ethico-political socialist project. This book aims to contribute to such an endeavour.

---

[2] This is a broad anti-authoritarian and anti-capitalist political ideology that promotes non-hierarchical and equitable social relations. My understanding of libertarian socialism draws extensively upon the key Neo-Marxist thinker Antonio Gramsci and the moral philosophers P.J. Proudhon and Peter Kropotkin. This understanding also reflects ideas found in the work of the contemporary Neo-Gramscian postcolonial philosopher Enrique Dussel, the ethical thinker Zygmunt Bauman and understandings of justice in contemporary socialist-feminist thought (Hudson, 2003).

Penal abolitionism has both a negative and a positive moment. In its *negative moment*, abolitionists maintain that rather than providing a solution to social problems, the penal law creates them (Swaaningen, 1997). Penal abolitionists have argued that prisons are places of *'iatrogenic penal harm'*. Iatrogenic harms refer to the injury, hurt or damage generated by institutions which, instead of facilitating positive outcomes, deliberately manufacture the opposite (Illich, 1974). For penal abolitionists, the prison place is a toxic environment, for all humans placed in such a degrading and damaging situational context are considered vulnerable to harm (Scott and Codd, 2010; Scott, 2015). Whilst there is hope and (isolated) acts of human kindness within prisons, most prisoners only just manage to cope with its mundane realities. Though at times prisons are places of frantic activities, paradoxically, at others they are empty, dull and motionless (Cope, 2003). This emptiness and estrangement from ordinary life means that prisons are always more likely to harm rather than help: boredom creates a need for substance usage; isolation and degradation exacerbates mental-health problems; and the institutionally structured violence of imprisonment generates suicidal ideation and death (Scott and Codd, 2010). This conscious wasting of life, the enforced passivity and the emptiness of time are sources of 'acute suffering' (Medlicott, 2001). As Sykes (1958), Mathiesen (1986) and Medlicott (2001) have so convincingly argued, prisons hurt so much because of the denial of personal autonomy, feelings of time consciousness, and the lack of an effective vocabulary to express the hardship of watching life slip away. This negation of the ability to control time and space is something which affects the wellbeing of *everyone* (Medlicott, 2001). Despite the continuous rhetoric of 'reform' and 'rehabilitation', pain infliction and suffering are the real products of the prison place.

But penal abolitionism also has a *positive moment*. Abolitionism can be a replacement, a counter-hegemonic discourse providing an alternative way of thinking about social problems, and promoting an alternative vision of morality and justice. In our current era of penal expansionism, we need more than ever radical visions that can transcend the punitive rationale and inspire people to mobilise effective resistance. Drawing upon the libertarian socialist writings of Erik Olin Wright (2010), this positive moment can be conceived of as an "abolitionist real utopia" (Scott, 2013). A real utopia is a form of emancipatory knowledge that entails the explicit intention of not just understanding individual and social problems, but generating information that can challenge human oppression and transform existing hierarchies of power. The aim of the abolitionist real utopia is to provide a vision of socially just interventions that are historically immanent. As such, an abolitionist real utopia looks to explore policies, practices and designs that could challenge poverty and social disadvantage, and provide different ways of handling social conflicts (Scott, 2013). It provides a libertarian socialist vision of justice that is immanent and possible in the here and now.

I have organised the following eleven chapters around the three key themes discussed above: the theoretical priorities of critical criminology; the prevalence of iatrogenic penal harms in prison; and the importance of conceiving abolitionist real utopian visions of social and transformative justice. Part A comprises four chapters, which first situate critical criminology within the intellectual milieu of the European Group (Chapter 2) and then provide a brief account the development of critical criminologies and the radical 'utopian imagination' since the 1960s (Chapter 3). Chapter 4 provides an in-depth account of one of the key thinkers in critical criminology — Stan Cohen, whilst Chapter 5 explores some of the key pressures facing the production of emancipatory and critical knowledge in the 'corporate university'. Part B also comprises four chapters, and starts with an account of some of the key debates on penal abolitionism that have been held in the European Group (Chapter 6) before moving on to further explore the nature and extent of iatrogenic penal harms: first through the personal examples of Lady Constance Lytton/Jane Warton (Chapter 7) and then by a broader critique of institutionally structured violence (Chapter 8). The final chapter in this section (Chapter 9) considers the problem of criminal injustice and the need for social justice.

Part C explores the theoretical underpinnings of the abolitionist real utopia (Chapter 10) and one historically immanent illustration of a non-penal real utopia — the Therapeutic Community (Chapter 11). The final chapter gives consideration to the continued relevance of the abolitionist strategy of 'attrition' as a means of releasing ourselves from the clutches of the penal state (Chapter 12). Following the epilogue are six appendices. They include the 2013 Manifesto of the Working Group on Prisons, Detention and Punishment;[3] a short account of the 2014 *Reclaim Justice*

---

[3] The Prison, Detention and Punishment working group of the *European Group for the Study of Deviance and Social Control* was re-established by myself in 2012. After standing down as coordinator of the European Group in September 2012 I became the Prisons, Detention and Punishment working group coordinator for its first year (2012-13) to help create its membership, mailing list and manifesto. This was the first working group to be

Network[4] interventions at the G4S annual general meeting and a follow up letter in May 2016; and details of the 2014 critical criminology questionnaire discussed in Chapter 5.

Six of the papers drawn together for this anthology were co-written, emphasising the collaborative nature of my writings for the European Group over the last three years. Where this is the case, the name(s) of my co-author(s) are indicated at the start of the chapter. Every chapter provides details of where and when the original paper was first published. Overall, I have tried to take a minimalistic approach to the editing, but some repetition has been removed and I have also added some further text or altered the order of the text in a few chapters. As a consequence, some of the chapters are slightly different from those papers first published by the European Group. I have not consolidated the references into a general bibliography, and so a number of my favourite sources and authors will become evident as they are repeated in the different chapters of the book. This 'self-contained' approach allows readers to engage with each chapter separately and/or to go directly to chapters of specific interest if they so wish.

Like all anthologies, bringing together papers written for different purposes means that, at times, the themes explored in the book are a little fragmented, although I do hope that the overall message remains clear. Where there is repetition between chapters, it indicates the centrality of these ideas to my thinking. When the chapters are read together, a picture emerges of what I consider to be key to contemporary debates regarding 'crime' and punishment: the emancipatory politics and praxis of libertarian socialism.

References

Cope, N. (2003) 'It's No 'Time or High Time': Young offenders' experiences of time and drug use in prison' in *The Howard Journal* Volume 42, No. 2 pp 158–175

Hudson, B. A. (2003) *Justice in the Risk Society* London: Sage

Illich, I. (1974) *Limits to Medicine: Medical Nemesis* London: Marion Boyars Publishers

---

reintroduced following a number of years of absence and the inspiration for the new working group came after reading the 1975 manifesto whilst compiling the anthology *Critique and Dissent*.

[4] The *Reclaim Justice Network* is a grouping of abolitionists in the United Kingdom. https://downsizingcriminaljustice.wordpress.com/

Kropotkin, P. (1924) *Ethics* New York: Dial Press

Mathiesen, T. (1986) 'The Politics of Abolition' in *Contemporary Crises* Volume 10, pp 81–94

Medlicott, D. (2001) *Surviving the Prison Place* Aldershot: Ashgate

Proudhon, P.J. (1990 [1840]) *What is Property?* Cambridge: Cambridge University Press

Scott, D. (2013) 'Visualising an Abolitionist Real Utopia: Principles, policy and praxis' in Malloch, M. and Munro, W. (eds) (2013) *Crime, Critique and Utopia* Basingstoke: Palgrave

Scott, D. (2015) 'Eating your Insides Out', *Prison Service Journal* September, No. 201 pp 68–72

Scott, D. and Codd, H. (2010) *Controversial Issues in Prisons* Buckingham: Open University Press

Swaaningen, R. van (1997) *Critical Criminology* London: Sage

Sykes, G. (1958) *Society of Captives* New Jersey: Princeton University Press

Tifft, L. and Sullivan, D. (1980) *The Struggle to be Human* Orkney: Cienfuegos Press

Wright, E.O. (2010) *Envisioning Real Utopias* Cambridge: Polity Press

Part A:

Critical Criminology
and
the Utopian Imagination

2.

Critical Criminology and the European Group for the Study of Deviance and Social Control

This chapter is an edited and revised version of chapters, which first appeared in August 2013, in the book Critique and Dissent: An Anthology to Mark 40 Years of the European Group for the Study of Deviance and Social Control. *The chapter is co-written with Joanna Gilmore and J.M. Moore.*

In 1970, three visiting scholars at the School of Criminology in the University of California at Berkeley — Stan Cohen, from Durham University, England; Karl Schumann from Bielefeld University in Germany; and Mario Simondi, from the University of Florence, Italy — were allocated the same office to share. As they exchanged ideas from their various parts of Europe, Stan Cohen (cited in McMahon and Kellough, 2013: 44) declared, "it's crazy that we have to come to Berkeley to see each other. Let's do something when we go back to Europe". The conversation led to the founding of the *European Group for the Study of Deviance and Social Control* (European Group). The intellectual origins of the European Group lie in a range of political developments and projects that occurred in a number of European countries in the late 1960s and early 1970s. These included various patients' and prisoners' movements; radical and social lawyers; the Arbeitsgruppe Junger Krimlnologen (AJK) in Germany; and the National Deviancy Conference (NDC) in Britain.

From its beginnings, the European Group has been explicitly political (Swaaningen, 1997; Gilmore et al., 2013). In an interview conducted in 1987 with McMahon and Kellough (2013), Stan Cohen talks at length about the emergence of radical criminology, placing it in the context of political and cultural developments and the influence of writers such as R.D. Laing, Herbert Marcuse, Franz Fanon, Ivan Illich and Michel Foucault. Although the original manifesto stated that the group was "Marxist", Stan Cohen has highlighted how, from its earliest days, the European Group had "a strong anarchistic and libertarian [socialist] ethos" (Cohen, personal correspondence with David Scott, 2010). As such, the European

Group has always been willing to take sides — siding consistently with the powerless and progressive forces.

Since its first conference in 1973, the European Group has been at the forefront of debates and creative developments in the emergence and consolidation of critical criminologies in Europe and beyond. Now, some forty-three years on from its first annual conference, the European Group remains a vibrant and relevant organisation. The conferences of the European Group have explored deviant behaviour, harm, power, social control, punishment and regulation from various philosophical viewpoints. Indeed, European Group conferences have been characterised by the absence of a uniform dogma. State punishment's function as an instrument of dominance has been repeatedly emphasised, together with explanations of 'crime' and criminality that perceives them as reflections of the societal structure. Within the group, there has been a desire to investigate how human/civil rights are being eroded through shifting political and State control. The European Group has, since its inception, sought to promote critical and radical criminology as a legitimate field of research and to provide a forum through which critical academics can connect with those outside the academy who are actively working for social justice.

The European Group was formed against the backdrop of the radical social movements of the 1960s and 70s — a period which saw student occupations, civil rights campaigns and industrial strikes erupt across Europe and beyond. Central to the development of the European Group has been the infusion of academic research and political activism. European Group members continue to play an active role in campaigns for social justice and civil rights, including prisoners' rights organisations, LGBTIQ liberation groups and campaigns against police violence. European Group conferences have provided a meeting place for academics, practitioners and activists who share critical perspectives on 'crime', deviance and criminal justice, and other social control institutions. For example, during the height of the 1984–5 miners' strike in Britain, striking miners and their supporters participated in the twelfth Annual European Group Conference in Cardiff, debating alongside academics the extraordinary expansion of the State's security and intelligence-gathering apparatus during the strike. Further, at the 40th Annual Conference in Cyprus in 2012, delegates joined striking hotel workers on picket lines and passed resolutions of solidarity to support their campaign for fair pay and welfare rights. In recent years, European Group conferences have passed motions condemning the violent policing of anti-'austerity' protests and racist immigration policies across Europe.

The group's founders sought to resist the predominance of what Nils Christie later termed "useful knowledge" — knowledge useful only to institutions of the State. Also arguing along such lines, Karl Schumann reminds us of the important relationship between mainstream criminology and State policy and practice. For Schumann (2013: 245), the State draws a distinction between "proper" criminologists, who advocate a "pseudo-science" of criminology, and "deviant" criminologists, who examine law in its social context. The latter are very much associated with the European Group, whereas Schumann suggests that the former category play a central role in legitimising the repressive practices of criminal justice institutions. Schumann dismisses claims to scientific objectivity prevalent within the positivist orientations of mainstream criminology as the work of "charlatan scientists". In doing so, he identifies various 'deceptive practices' adopted by criminologists in order to demonstrate legitimation, something which European Group scholars have always warned against. The claim that legitimate criminological research adopts the highest standards in research methodology has resulted in a fetishistic attachment to scientific research standards and the rejection of critical research which falls foul of the scientific model (Schumann, 2013). This leads to a growing patronage of criminological research by the State in terms of research funding and an access for loyalty bargain — an understanding that the researcher will not report on his or her observations in a way that will harm the institution studied. The impact of disloyalty by deviant criminologists' is the rejection of research findings and the denial of future research possibilities.

The problem is that the scientific criminological knowledge can be used to legitimate State-planning activities (Behr et al., 2013: 204). In other words, scientific 'experts' may be asked to perform the role of manufacturing stereotypes that can lead directly to discriminatory practices (Stalstrom, 2013). Such a "misuse of science" must be located within its wider social and political contexts. Behr et al. (2013) remind us that the "Interventionist State" carefully constructs its research projects, and that there may be a significant gap between what the researcher is being asked to do and how the knowledge derived from their study is then used by the patron. State research agendas can be separated into a number of small projects but then collated holistically to be used by the State. The division of academic labour means that those undertaking research for the State are powerless in the face of any such broader agenda, as they are merely tiny cogs in the machine working towards a State-orientated project. Whilst individual researchers may have some control over the research process itself, their independence is fatally undermined as they operate within the definitions of the State and have no control over how their findings may be used. Accepting State definitions of a given set of social circumstances rules in and rules out certain realities, thus shaping legitimate knowledge. Researchers financed by the State are free to perform tasks, but not the tasks of their own choosing. For forty-three years, the European Group has provided a forum allowing space for reflection upon the 'big picture' and the opportunity to create emancipatory knowledge that can be used to critique discriminatory and repressive policies and practices, rather than servicing the State machine.

Perhaps unsurprisingly, then, papers at European Group conferences have consistently explored critically the scope and applications of the criminal law in socially divided and divisive societies. Important questions have been proposed through the forum of the European Group, such as: *How has a social problem been formulated and defined? What is the knowledge base of criminologically informed interventions? Why has certain legislation been drafted and subsequently enacted?* and *What does the new law aim to achieve? Critique* means more than being just 'critical'. For the European Group, critical theory must be grounded within socio-economic and political contexts, linked with the work of grass-roots social movements (or interpreting their interventions) and intended to facilitate emancipatory change.

The European Group has always been committed to developing a theory that both grants 'deviant' actors agency and recognises that their acts take place in a social setting not of their own making. Although this approach was initially close to the Marxist paradigm, the European Group recognised "the problematic nature of that framework" and sought to avoid "a dogmatic stance within that debate" (EG Manifesto, 1975). Making connections between everyday struggles, lived experiences and social structures, firstly around class, but later around 'race', sexuality, gender, age and disability, the European Group has helped produce a new critical discourse for understanding conflicts, harms and troubles that are popularly referred to as 'crime'. The European Group has encouraged the embedding of a critical analysis exploring the relationship between *the individual* and *the social* through consideration of the boundaries placed upon everyday interactions, choices, meanings and motivations, by determining structural contexts (Sim et al., 1987; Scraton and Chadwick,

1991; Barton et al., 2006). Constructions of 'crime', deviance and social control have been located within the power-knowledge axis and social structures pertaining to our given historical conjuncture. This has ultimately led to the centrality of questions concerning power, inequality, justice and legitimacy.

There are undoubtedly considerable difficulties with the very framing of social problems through the language of 'crime' and the meaning and scope of the discipline of criminology itself. European Group members and radical scholars across Europe, such as Karl Schumann, Alessandro Baratta, Louk Hulsman, Nils Christie and Paddy Hillyard, have long presented us with the argument that we need to move both *beyond criminology* and *beyond criminal justice*. Whilst we continue to work within 'criminology' we will always be bound by the definitions of 'crime' and criminality dictated by the State.

Karl Schumann (2013) has questioned the claim that criminology is a unique and coherent subject which is able to explain 'crime'. Noting that the only consistent feature of all 'crimes' is that they are labelled as such by actors within the criminal justice system, Schumann dismisses these claims as an 'illusion' designed to obscure the partial application of criminal law by the State. As a discipline, criminology perpetuates myths about the nature and extent of 'criminal conduct', excludes many of the most harmful events, and provides legitimacy to existing power relations and the penal apparatus of the State. Hillyard (2013), for example, argues that the only effective strategy to challenge the discursive power of 'crime' is to establish a new separate discipline grounded in the study of harm that would provide a new language or counter-discourse to that of criminology. Hillyard refers to this approach as zemiology, the name of which arose from discussions at the 1998 European Group Annual Conference, which would locate inequality, poverty, disadvantage, racism and sexism at the centre of its approach. Unlike 'crime', Hillyard (2013) maintains that 'harms' can be counted and have a material and 'ontological reality'. By arguing for a focus on 'harm' rather than 'crime' or 'deviancy', zemiology facilitates a movement away from the often petty and relatively insignificant harms of street crime to the far more harmful acts of States and corporations (Hillyard and Tombs, 2004).

This spotlight on State-caused harms and political economy has led members of the European Group, from the date of its foundation, to reject the focus on the individual deviant actor that had previously dominated criminology and instead see "the exercise of social control as being its principal reference point" (Ciacci and Simondi, 2013: 66). The impact of this approach is highlighted by the approach of European Group members to white-collar crime, which Ciacci and Simondi (2013 :67) see as a radical departure from the tradition begun by Edwin Sutherland. Whereas previously work had seen crimes of the powerful "as a (rectifiable) incidence of the dysfunction of the social system", European Group members have instead highlighted how they are "the inevitable corollary of the management of power in a capitalist society". Yet the European Group has always encouraged a nuanced and sophisticated understanding of the role of social control. Rather than seeing the law as a crude instrument of capitalist oppressors, members have pointed to the contradictory nature of the law in capitalist societies: law enforcement and mechanisms of social control can both protect the general population, including vulnerable and/or impoverished individuals, whilst at the same time playing a decisive role in maintaining structural divisions.

Though there are continuities with an earlier interventionist social democratic 'welfare state' regarding the application of the criminal law — notably that it continues to target the 'crimes' of the poor whilst 'crimes' of the powerful are largely ignored — policies in neoliberal Britain have undoubtedly become more invasive and punitive. Not only have we witnessed a major expansion in the penal apparatus of the State — new surveillance technologies, extensive regulatory powers and the rise of out-of-court penalties — but there has also been an extension of punishment through welfare. In short, in recent times, a new 'security-industrial complex' has emerged (Bell, 2013). Central to it is the relationship between neoliberalism and State legitimacy. Neoliberalism, with its emphasis on the 'free market', has exacerbated social divisions and rendered the State impotent to intervene. This raises questions regarding the legitimate role of government under the logic of neoliberalism: the State can no longer intervene in the economy or promote progressive welfare interventions for those at the bottom of the social structure.

Further, neoliberalism has also demanded massive public-spending cuts and welfare retrenchment, acts that are likely to undermine public support and exacerbate social divisions. As Emma Bell (2013) has argued, this crisis of legitimacy has been accommodated on a number of levels. First, to appeal to the electorate, increasing emphasis has focused on the control of criminals and immigrants. Second, there has been a shift towards a more managerial approach; the reconstruction of welfare recipients as consumers and a transformation of the State from provider to facilitator of social services (Bell, 2013). Consequently, there has existed a 'correspondence of interests' between the neoliberal governments and the private sector, which has led to the privileging of market solutions and an increased emphasis on the privatisation of crime control. Yet accommodations to the neoliberal condition remain shot through with contradictions, erode civil liberties and fail to adequately address the most pressing social harms of our day. Rather than being effectively policed, the crisis is likely only to deepen, raising questions around authoritarianism, domination and political accountability (Bell, 2013).

The European Group has always looked to foster emancipatory changes grounded in the principles of democratic accountability. Marxists and Anarchists are considered as presenting a particular danger to the State (Sheerer, 2013). This is not because of the harm or instability wrought through political violence — the State has legislative power enough to contain this — but rather because (libertarian) socialists propose to *fulfil the principles and values* of democracy, justice, freedom and equality. The State is thus presented with a dilemma when dealing with socialist-inspired instances of direct action — repressive legislation may strengthen the internal powers of administrators and expand the remit of the penal apparatus of the State, but is unlikely to be effective in its stated aim of controlling political activists. Further, to abandon entirely its commitment to democracy would only increase the potency of socialist critique and further exacerbate the legitimation crises. Liberal democracies are therefore shackled by their need to pay at least lip service to the principles of democracy, thus leaving legal loopholes that can be exploited by pro-democracy campaigners. A shift towards more coercion, domination and authoritarianism could prove counterproductive for the State. Indeed, the more repressive State interventions are, the greater the attractiveness of socialisms and their critiques of actually existing democracy (Scheerer, 2013).

The European Group today[1]

Despite the troubling economic and political times and widespread attacks on intellectual autonomy across universities in Europe and beyond, the European Group continues to be an essential forum for students of deviance and social control. The European Group continues to attract membership from a broad range of people — local advocacy and

---

[1] See Scott (2012), 'Opening Address of 40th Annual Conference of the European Group'

21

activist groups, academics, researchers, students, practitioners — with an array of different philosophies — Anarchism, Marxism, Feminism, Anti-racism, Postcolonialism and Penal Abolitionism. European Group conferences continue to highlight the importance of understanding the political nature of private troubles and public issues: the essentially contested nature of 'crime', and how deviancy, normality and disorder must be located within the structural contexts of a given society. Further, by critically scrutinising the "organised ways in which society responds to behaviour and people it regards as deviant, problematic, worrying, threatening, troublesome or undesirable in some way or another" (Cohen, 1985: 1), manifestations of social control, such as migration and border controls, policing, the judiciary and detention, are placed firmly in the spotlight.

The European Group continues a critical tradition that challenges privilege, power and social and economic inequalities; exposes human suffering in its many different manifestations; provides a platform for those people whose voices are elsewhere denied; and works towards profound social transformations that can promote the genuine freedom and fulfilment of *humanity for all*. Whilst the critique and transformation of class hierarchies remains important to the European Group, its conferences also address a myriad of wider concerns regarding nationalism, heterophobia, racism, ability, ageism, heteronormativity and sexual divisions (Swaaningen, 1997). The European Group therefore aims to foster "emancipatory knowledge" (Wright, 2010) which has the explicit political and theoretical intention of not just understanding individual and social problems, but also challenging and transforming existing power relations.

The European Group remains rooted in a philosophy of anti-elitism and non-hierarchy — at conferences it makes no difference whether someone is a first-year PhD student or highly distinguished Professor, *all* are students of deviancy and social control who meet as equals. This non-hierarchical ethos continues to be central to the democratic and participatory workings of the European Group itself, with conferences deliberately organised in an informal manner that emphasises a sense of camaraderie and friendship. The European Group offers a radical alternative to the values and politics underscoring capitalist, patriarchal and neocolonial social relations, and the managerial ethos that seems to characterise many universities today. In terms of the core values of the European Group:

- rather than individualised competition, *the European Group looks to foster mutual support, cooperation and sisterly and brotherly warmth*;

- rather than false hierarchies and elitism, *the European Group aims to nurture comradeship, collegiality and solidarity with sufferers and the oppressed*;

- rather than become politically sterile through claims to scientific objectivity, neutrality and value freedom, *the European Group emphasises political commitments, direct engagement in struggle and compassion for fellow human beings in need*;

- rather than determining research agendas simply according to 'where the money is', or where the source and size of a research grant becomes more significant than the research itself, *the European Group promotes craftsmanship, intellectual autonomy and integrity*;

- and, rather than providing knowledge that can be used by the powerful to maintain the status quo, *the European Group endeavours to facilitate emancipatory knowledge that can be used to challenge existing power relations*.

The collegiality and solidarity offered by European Group conferences and the visions of social justice that they promote are undoubtedly even more important under neoliberal capitalism and its collateral consequences. Active participation in the European Group is perhaps higher today than at any other time in its history and with the development of new social media — YouTube, Facebook, Twitter, and so on — the reach and presence of the European Group in the lives of academics, students and activists can now be a daily experience.[2] The European Group's coordinator and secretary also compile a detailed monthly newsletter delivered to over 1,000 subscribers, which includes updates on activism and articles from members.

There are, then, key continuities in the history of the European Group: its independence, both politically and financially, from State agencies; its willingness to answer clearly the question of whose side it is on, consistently aligning itself with the weak and the oppressed; a clear understanding of the relationship between theory and practice/action; and a commitment to resisting hierarchies and elitism. Despite a

---

[2] See, for example, the European Group Facebook page:
https://www.facebook.com/groups/105017501664/

proliferation of international conferences on the topics of 'crime, deviance and social control', most notably the now well-established meetings organised by the *European Society of Criminology*, the distinctly radical and emancipatory values and message of the Europe Group is today reaching an ever-widening audience.

Visions of the future

In the late 1980s, Stan Cohen identified three neglected areas in critical criminologies: white-collar/corporate crime, social control, and comparative criminology (McMahon and Kellough, 2013). Cohen's call for a refocusing of attention away from "young male working-class property offenders" towards the "crimes of the powerful"[3] has been responded to by the European Group in both the agendas of its conferences and the scholarly outputs of its members. In particular, it is from the European Group that a fundamental critique of criminology and the sociology of deviancy — zemiology — has emerged. Cohen's selection of social control as his second neglected area is a little more surprising. However, his critique is directed specifically at the tendency of studies of social control to focus on "the State organized criminal justice system" and he argues for a broader exploration of social control that encompasses the whole range of social organisations that exert control, including "families, schools, the media, and consumer culture" (Ibid.).

This critique remains relevant. A possible challenge for the European Group in the coming years will be to broaden its focus on social control, punishment and the penal system to incorporate fully the mechanisms for regulating (or not) individuals, corporations and States. Drawing on a long tradition of engaging critically with the rationale of social control interventions, the European Group has consistently argued that 'sites of confinement' should be evaluated within wider moral and political contexts. It is the weakest and most vulnerable who are targeted by penal interventions which are carried out in institutions that fail to respect human dignity or adhere to the demands of social justice.

Cohen's final neglected area is comparative criminology, which he dismisses as "what happens when Western criminologists get on a plane and land in some place and come back and write about it" (Ibid: 50-51). The European Group has been in a unique position to address this defect,

---

[3] All quotations from Stan Cohen are from the interview in 1987 with Maeve McMahon and Gail Kellough, republished in Gilmore et al (2013) *Critique and Dissent*.

but whilst its conferences have often provided the opportunity to explore areas from different national perspectives, more could be done to develop work that is truly comparative. Rene van Swaaningen (2013: 83) has also highlighted the importance of a "more explicit international orientation" so that the European Group can allow for a genuinely comparative critical criminology to emerge. Whilst it is important to retain the European Group's commitment to social justice, this must be complemented by a far greater appreciation of diversity. For Swaaningen (2013), an international critical criminology cannot be based on "uniform paradigms and strategies which are supposed to be applicable in every country" but needs to able "to do justice to [the] diversities" of different countries' political, economic and legal structures. With (relatively) cheaper travel and more enhanced global networks, some of the problems of comparative critical research have diminished, but the call for scholarly and ethnographically rich comparative studies remains as important today as it did when Stan Cohen made his plea many years ago.

Throughout its history, the European Group has remained critical of many criminological enterprises, critiquing the way that criminology generates knowledge to serve the interests of the powerful. In turn, this has led to those operating at the centre of State-sponsored criminology to dismiss the European Group and its members' contributions as unimportant, idealistic and irrelevant. Phil Scraton (2013), though, has argued that the European Group is far from marginal, and suggests that if the European Group is indeed placed on the margins in comparison to mainstream and administrative criminologies and the priorities of government agencies, then this should be seen as a strength. This reflects the group's broader commitment to breaking away from dominant analytical frameworks for understanding deviancy and social control, and offering a genuinely critical and emancipatory politics and praxis.

References

Barton, A., Corteen, K., Scott, D. and Whyte, D. (2006) 'Developing a Criminological Imagination' pp 1–25 in Barton, A., Corteen, K., Scott, D. and Whyte, D. (eds) *Expanding the Criminological Imagination: Critical Readings on Criminology* Devon: Willan

Behr, C.B., Gipsen, D., Klien-Sconnefeld, S., Naffin, K. and Zillmer, H. (2013) 'The Use of Scientific Discoveries for the Maintenance and Extension of State Control — On the effect of legitimation and the utilization of science' in Gilmore, J., Moore, J.M. and Scott, D. (eds) (2013) *Critique and Dissent* Red Quill Press

Bell, E. (2013) 'Neo-liberal Crime Policy: Who profits?' in Gilmore, J., Moore, J.M. and Scott, D. (eds) (2013) *Critique and Dissent* Red Quill Press

Ciacci, M. and Simondi, M. (2013) 'A New Trend in Criminological Knowledge: The experience of the European Group for the Study of Deviance and Social Control' in Gilmore, J., Moore, J.M. and Scott, D. (eds) (2013) *Critique and Dissent* Red Quill Press

Cohen, S. (1985) *Visions of Social Control* Cambridge: Polity

Cohen, S. (2010) *Personal correspondence with David Scott*, 20 September 2010

Gilmore, J., Moore, J.M. and Scott, D. (eds) (2013) *Critique and Dissent* Red Quill Press

Hillyard, P. (2013) 'Zemiology' in Gilmore, J., Moore, J.M. and Scott, D. (eds) (2013) *Critique and Dissent* Red Quill Press

Hillyard, P. and Tombs, S. (2004) 'Beyond Criminology?' in Hillyard, P., Pantazis, C., Tombs, S. and Gordon, D. *Beyond Criminology: Taking Harm Seriously* London: Pluto Press

McMahon, M. and Kellough, G. (2013) 'Interview with Stan Cohen' in Gilmore, J., Moore, J.M. and Scott, D. (eds) (2013) *Critique and Dissent* Red Quill Press

Scheerer, S. (2013) 'Law-making in a State of Siege: Some regularities in the legislative response to political violence' in Gilmore, J., Moore, J.M. and Scott, D. (eds) (2013) *Critique and Dissent* Red Quill Press

Schumann (2013) 'On Proper and Deviant Criminology — Varieties in the production of legitimation for penal law' in Gilmore, J., Moore, J.M. and Scott, D. (eds) (2013) *Critique and Dissent* Red Quill Press

Scott, D. (2102) *Opening Address of the 40th Annual European Group Conference September* http://www.youtube.com/watch?v=YOBsQjQ5xus

Scraton, P. (2013) *Personal correspondence with the authors*, 18 June 2013

Scraton, P. and Chadwick, K. (1991) 'Challenging New Orthodoxies: The theoretical and political priorities of critical criminology' in Stenson, K. and Cowell, D. (eds) *The Politics of Crime* Control London: Sage

Sim, J., Scraton, P. and Gordon, P. (1987) 'Crime, the State and Critical Analysis' in Scraton, P. (ed) *Law, Order and the Authoritarian State: Readings in Critical Criminology* Milton Keynes: Open University Press

Stalstrom, O. (2013) 'Profiles in Courage: Problems of action of the Finnish gay movement in crisis' in Gilmore, J., Moore, J.M. and Scott, D. (eds) (2013) *Critique and Dissent* Red Quill press

Swaaningen, R. van (1997) *Critical Criminology: Visions from Europe* London: Sage

Swaaningen, R. van (2013) 'The European Group for the Study of Deviance and Social control: inspirations and aspirations of a critical criminology' in Gilmore, J., Moore, J.M. and Scott, D. (eds) (2013) *Critique and Dissent* Red Quill Press

Wright, E.O. (2010) *Envisioning a Real Utopia* London: Verso

3.

Reawakening our Radical Imaginations: Thinking realistically about utopias, dystopias and the non-penal

This chapter is an edited and revised version of an article that was published in the European Group Journal Justice, Power and Resistance *in September 2016. The chapter is co-written with Emma Bell.*

Since the publication of Thomas More's *Utopia* (1516) some 500 years ago, the concept of utopia has been applied in widely different ways. The word has taken on both negative and positive meanings (Malloch and Munro, 2013). When used negatively, it is as an insult: it is a way of ridiculing an idea as unrealistic, impractical and hopelessly idealistic. This dismissive use of the term draws upon the original Latin meaning of 'utopia' as 'nowhere'. It regards utopia as the impossible dream, something/somewhere which does not exist. This view was particularly marked with the advent of the neoliberal consensus politics that followed the failure of utopian experiments across the world in the post-war period. This led to a 'crisis of utopias' (Duménil, 2016) and the assertion of TINA politics[1] advancing neoliberalism as the only possible programme adapted to the new realities of globalised capitalism.

There is, however, an equally strong tradition of using the term 'utopia' in a positive sense. In this tradition, which unites thinkers from a broad range of perspectives such as Feminism, Anarchism, and Socialism, and religious beliefs such as Christianity, the word 'utopia' is defined as 'a good place', as an ideal and desirable potential alternative to the present. The French economist, Gérard Duménil, describes utopias as follows:

> Highly optimistic projections towards a future of emancipation and humanity. Only utopias are capable of mobilising activist energies beyond societies based on class distinctions and neoliberal

---

[1] The term 'TINA' is a commonly used acronym for the idea that 'There Is No Alternative'. It was first used by the leader of the UK's House of Commons, Norman St John Stevas (1979–1981), to refer to Margaret Thatcher and her dogmatism.

desperation, whilst recognising that the process will be long and that perfection does not exist. From the Enlightenment and the French Revolution through to the formation of the workers' movement, a tremendous wave of hope rose up — only to turn to tragedy in countries which called themselves socialist. We need to start from scratch after having understood the reasons for this failure. (Duménil, 2014)[2]

So, although utopia is seen as a positive, emancipatory alternative to current injustices, it must also be realistic. Those proposing utopian visions must be aware of their potential pitfalls and be capable of critique, not just of the present, but also of past utopian experiments, in order to provide concrete, realistic utopian futures (Wright, 2010).

The word 'dystopia' — which literally means 'bad place' — was introduced into the modern lexicon in 1747 by Henry Lewis Younge. Dystopia is often presented as a vision that is in direct opposition to utopia; however, there is no neat separation between utopias and dystopias. For Terry Eagleton (1999: 31), "all utopia is thus at the same time dystopia" because both the positive and negative possibilities stretching into possible futures inevitably remind us that our current 'bondage' is historically contingent and that we must somehow break from the constraints of our historic conjuncture. Dystopias can also, of course, justify the present penal state by conjuring an image of an even worse future. They can frighten us into 'no change' and make people look backwards rather than forwards for visions of human communities. But the critical use of dystopia may also facilitate radical change, for it can also be seen as a warning of what will happen if we continue to follow current trends and practices. In pointing us towards the worst possible scenario, dystopias provide a warning from the future in our present. They give us new eyes to look at how current developments may evolve. Dystopias then also give us new ways of seeing and critiquing power, domination and exploitation:

---

[2] Translated from French by the authors: *"Par « utopies », j'entends des projections très optimistes vers un futur d'émancipation de l'humanité. Elles sont seules capables de mobiliser les énergies militantes au-delà de l'horizon des sociétés de classe et de la désespérance néolibérale, sachant que ce sera long et que la perfection n'est pas de ce monde. Des lumières et de la révolution française jusqu'à la formation du mouvement ouvrier, une vague prodigieuse d'espoir s'était levée - qui a tourné à la tragédie dans les pays qui se réclamèrent du socialisme. Tout est à refaire, en prenant d'abord conscience des causes de cet échec".*

> Whereas utopia takes us into a future and serves to indict the present, dystopia places us directly in the dark and depressing reality, conjuring up a terrifying future if we do not recognise and treat its symptoms here and now. Thus the dialectic between the two imaginaries, the dream and the nightmare, also beg for inclusion *together*. (Gordon et al., 2010: 2, emphasis in original)

Dystopic analysis then damns contemporary penal realities by projecting the critic's worst fears onto current penal realities — something which has in recent times been especially associated with the work of Loic Wacquant (2013) and his critique of the penal state, which provides a nightmare vision of a future of less freedom and more penalisation and social control unless we act urgently to stop current punitive developments. In other words, whereas "utopias seek to emancipate by envisioning a world based on new, neglected, or spurned ideas; dystopias seek to frighten by accentuating contemporary trends that threaten freedom" (Jacoby, 2005: 12).

As Stan Cohen (1988) has highlighted, dystopia and utopia are both part of the tradition of critical criminology, with its focus on both the 'dark side' of human interactions — such as social controls, state repression, dehumanising institutional practices — and on the 'light side' of these same interactions — such as the principles of libertarian socialism and visions of a more free society grounded in our cherished "values and preferences" (Cohen, 1985: 248). The utopia-dystopia coupling is evident in the work of Cohen himself, and especially his magnum opus *Visions of Social Control*. In this text, Cohen (1985) drew extensively upon the dystopian vision of George Orwell's *1984* to provide a vocabulary and imagery of contemporary "social control talk" in the "punitive city". Whilst dystopias such as Orwell's may well breed feelings of despair and sadness, they have also brought with them an imagery and vocabulary that can help us understand the present — Orwell's (1949) descriptions of 'Big Brother' and 'Room 101', as well as many of the other euphemisms that permeate his classic text, are now all part of modern-day understandings of state repression and a shorthand way of critiquing current policies and practices. Yet, in *Visions of Social Control*, Cohen also takes care to remind us of the importance of utopian visions. Although highlighting his concerns about "sentimental anarchism" (Cohen, 1985: 35) and the "flaws in beautiful theory" (Ibid.: 268), he tells us that much can still be done. Indeed, his "preference is to be pragmatic about short-term possibilities but to be genuinely utopian about constructing long-term alternatives" (Ibid.: 252). Despite his often dystopian tone, Cohen never loses his desire for building a new, more 'utopian' society on the principles of mutual aid, fraternity and good-neighbourliness (Ibid.: 267). As Joe Sim (2009), a long-standing member of the European Group, has argued, we must learn to cultivate a more utopian and idealistic approach to thinking about 'crime' and social control. We can find a basis for such thinking in the late 1960s and early 1970s with the politics of the 'New Left' and emergence of the 'New Criminology'.

The 'New Criminology' and the 'New Left'

The 'critical' criminology that emerged from the 1960s was very much a product of its time. Like the new social movements that were developing, it set itself against the prevailing norms of patriarchal, authoritarian and capitalist society, questioning the status quo and promoting radical democratic alternatives to existing repressive practices. It was highly critical of institutionalised criminological endeavours which reinforced existing power structures by accepting state-defined definitions of 'crime' and deviance. Rather than seeing 'crime' as a phenomenon just waiting to be discovered, it argued that it is political in nature, defined and responded to by those in power (Becker, 1963).

Feeding off the new deviancy theorists of the 1960s, notably in America, which aimed to understand deviancy from below by working closely with the so-called deviants in an attempt to understand their behaviour from within, critical scholars followed Howard Becker (1967) in deliberately choosing sides. Rather than lining up with the rule-enforcers, whose viewpoint tends to be disproportionately represented on account of the fact that they sit at the apex of what Becker described as the "hierarchy of credibility", the new deviancy theorists attempted to give a voice to the subjects of the rule-enforcers in order to discover new social worlds, or at least to develop a new understanding of those we previously thought we were familiar with (Becker, 1967: 105). The new deviancy theorists explored lived realities and experiences, engaging directly with people to understand their worldview, thus contributing to an entirely new conception of deviancy. Their new studies of deviancy adopted an interactionist approach to the analysis of deviant behaviour, displacing the emphasis on individual pathologies towards the wider social and structural context in which the deviant acts occurred. This labelling perspective offered "replacement discourses" of deviancy, rule breaking and norm infraction, and shifted attention away from causal analysis and towards the interpretation of and social reaction towards such behaviour (Swaaningen, 1997).

The critical approach adopted by new deviancy theory was largely a reaction against positivism, notably its claims to scientific neutrality or what Bourdieu described as "the falsely rigorous observations of positivism" (Bourdieu and de Saint Martin, cited in Bourdieu and Wacquant, 1992: 27–8). Taylor, Walton and Young (2003 [1973]: 32), the inheritors of "new deviancy theory" and radical proponents of what they called the "new criminology" explained:

> The evocation of natural science presents the positivist with a powerful mode of argument. For the system of thought which produces miracles of technology and medicine is a prestigious banner under which to fight. It grants the positivist the gift of 'objectivity'; it bestows on his pronouncements the mantle of 'truth'; it endows his suggestions of therapy, however threatening, to individual rights and dignity, with the air of the inevitable.

The positivist approach which had dominated criminology since at least the end of the nineteenth century was, in many ways, more akin to a religion than a science (Gouldner, 1968: 116) — to the extent that it tended to reify empirical data thought capable of revealing the truth and moral laws of society. It ignored the fact that data are often detached from reality since they ignore the cultural and ideological contexts in which they are collected, leading to 'abstracted empiricism' (Mills, 2000 [1959]).

The new criminology specifically reacted against abstracted empiricism, attempting to place social problems in their political context. For David Matza, the study of 'crime' and deviance necessarily had to be linked to the study of the State, given that it is the State alone that has the power to criminalise and construct 'deviance' (1964; 1969). It was necessary to situate individual acts in their historical and structural context in order to develop a political economy of 'crime' (Taylor et al., 1973) capable of recognising that criminalisation is not a simple response to 'crime' but rather a means of exercising social control and neutralising resistance. For Taylor et al. (1973: 270), "the wider origins of the deviant act could only be understood [...] in terms of the rapidly changing economic and political contingencies of advanced industrial society".

Consequently, the new criminology did not limit its focus to the marginalised and 'deviant'. It also directed its critical gaze upwards in an attempt to understand the political need to control deviance. In *Policing the Crisis*, Stuart Hall et al. (2013 [1978]) argued that state reactions to 'crime' could only be understood in the context of the social and political crisis of the 1970s — namely, the "crisis of hegemony" that was in the process of undermining the political legitimacy of the State and its agents. 'Policing the crisis' meant attempting to stem the tide of unrest and to seek political legitimacy by scapegoating 'deviants' — often young black men — for contemporary social problems. Such work, often considered prophetic in its dystopian vision of the rise of "iron times" and authoritarian populist policies retrenching the welfare state, was taken forward by the long-time European Group member Phil Scraton and other collaborators in the important edited text *Law, Order and the Authoritarian State* (1987), which furthered understanding of the discriminatory and often brutal practices of the criminal justice system by placing them in the context of the Thatcher governments' need to strengthen the power of the State as a means of containing the unrest resulting from their social and economic policies. This entailed a significant reframing of the terms of the debate about 'crime' by situating 'crime' control in the wider context of political crisis and social divisions (Sim et al., 1987).

Crucially, the study of 'crime' and deviancy entailed the study of power relations. As such, critical criminology became political. The criminologists seeking to understand the power relations which underpinned social control practices could not be "bureaucratic intellectuals" (Merton, 1945), "servants to power" (Christie, 2016) or "social engineers" (Bourdieu, 2000) working to please state institutions, and serving simply to "rationalise the practical or pseudo-scientific knowledge that the powerful have of the social world" (Ibid.)[3], providing ideological programmes with scientific legitimacy (Chomsky, 2008 [1966]: 55) and masking state repression.

The new criminologists were politically engaged and their studies inextricably linked to the politics of the New Left and its project to link the personal and the political, and to formulate a political programme capable of challenging existing power structures. They did not just promote radical social change in the criminal justice system but also in broader power

---

[3] Translated from the French by the authors: *"une rationalisation de la connaissance pratique ou demi-savante que les membres de la classe dominante ont du monde social"*.

relations, engaging in a socialist critique of harms, power and repression that demands the organisation of society along the lines of solidarity, equality and mutuality (Tifft and Sullivan, 1980). The new criminologists adopted an explicitly normative position entailing the abolition of inequalities of wealth and power in order "to create the kind of society in which the facts of human diversity [...] are not subject to the power to criminalise" (Taylor, Walton and Young, 1973: 282). This entailed joining with other social movements in order to bring the 'outsiders' in, thus promoting social, racial and gender justice.

Bringing the 'outsiders' in

Feeding off the civil rights movement of the 1960s, the new criminology was especially concerned with 'race' issues. Stuart Hall and his colleagues highlighted the racialisation of street 'crime', notably mugging, demonstrating how the demonisation of black youths by the institutions of the State and the media created an authoritarian consensus around repressive state power (Hall et al., 1978). *Policing the Crisis* effectively demonstrated how 'race' issues were tightly bound together with questions of power and legitimacy. Along with other seminal texts, such as Paul Gordon's *White Law* (1983), the book helped to highlight the institutionalised racism endemic in the postcolonial British state long before the publication of the Macpherson Report (Macpherson, 1999).[4] The work of Hall et al. helped to spark a whole range of studies into the disproportionate criminalisation of people of colour, which highlighted the racialised bias inherent in official state definitions of 'crime'. Paul Gilroy (1987), in particular, investigated the myth of Black criminality which has been used to justify the over-representation of Black and Minority Ethnic (BME) communities in detention and in police stop and search statistics (see, for example, Equality and Human Rights Commission, 2015). Picking up on the earlier work of Paddy Hillyard on the Irish (1993), Pantazis and Pemberton (2009) have drawn attention to the existence of Muslims as new 'suspect communities' in the UK, considered as an 'enemy within' and specifically targeted by state

---

[4] The Macpherson Report published the findings of an official inquiry into the police investigation of the racist murder of black London teenager Stephen Lawrence in 1993. It noted that racism was "institutionalised", pervading "processes, attitudes and behaviour" throughout the English police service.

surveillance on account of their ethnic appearance rather than on the grounds of their behaviour.

Carol Smart's ground-breaking *Women, Crime and Criminology* (1976) helped to bring feminist issues to the forefront of critical criminology. The text highlighted the limitations of 'malestream' criminological and penological thought, and noted that criminological analysis had, in the main, been 'written about men, for men and by men'. The ontological and epistemological assumptions of 'malestream criminology' could not just 'add in women' to address its defects. Rather, there needed to be a new feminist epistemology, asking very different questions and grounded in sometimes very different values and principles. Feminist thought opened the pathway for thinking more critically about gender and sexuality — it opened up neglected dimensions not only about the experience of women but also started to ask questions about what it meant to be a man (Heidensohn, 1985; Collier, 1998). By placing new emphases on both concerns about the role of law, societal expectations and power relations regarding both masculinities and femininities, the feminist critique led to a new openness and creativity when thinking about knowledge production and mechanisms of social control.

Critical criminology has continued its connection with feminisms and broader social movements fighting against various forms of injustice and discrimination. Most recently, for example, the specific issues affecting LGBTIQ[5] groups, notably the use of the law to reinforce normative gender roles, have been highlighted by queer criminology (Dwyer, Ball and Crofts, 2015). Following on from the *National Deviancy Conferences*[6] of the late 1960s and early 1970s, the European Group has been particularly concerned to connect to contemporary social movements, linking concerns about the repressive apparatuses of the state with wider issues of social justice and equality.

The utopian imagination in critical criminology

Although critical criminology, since it emerged in opposition to mainstream criminology and the broader injustces it helped perpetuate,

---

[5] Lesbian, gay, bisexual, transgender, intersex and queer.
[6] The first *National Deviancy Conference* was first held in York, England, as a dissident group in opposition to the mainstream criminology promoted by the Institute of Criminology at the University of Cambridge. For discussion of the connections to radical social movements, see Sim et al. (1987), Cohen (1988) and Gilmore et al. (2013).

initially focused on the critique of existing institutions and power structures, it soon began to propose radical and utopian alternatives to hegemonic visions of justice. This became increasingly necessary as dystopian visions of justice began to gain ground as the post-war welfarist consensus collapsed, only to be replaced by a neoliberal consensus predicated on the logic of exclusion and rising social inequalities. Central to such a radical and utopian imagination in critical criminology has been a desire to promote justice, dignity, ethical responsibilities and mutuality (Tifft and Sullivan, 1980). Importantly, this entails finding new ways of framing issues and expanding our imagination regarding what is possible in the here and now. Below, we discuss two examples of what we mean by the radical and utopian imagination in critical criminology: penal abolitionism and zemiology.

Penal abolitionism and the utopian imagination
Penal abolitionists recognise that prisons are inherently problematic institutions — they are places of interpersonal and institutional violence and legal, social and corporeal death — and these terrible outcomes are structured within the very fabric of penal institutions (Scott and Codd, 2010; Scott, 2013a, 2015). It is possible that prisons can offer a place of reflection and refuge for a few people when all other options have failed but, given the deprivations, pains and iatrogenic harms that underscore daily prison regimes, these cases are the exceptions that prove the rule. Abolitionists, in common with libertarian socialist thinkers such as Peter Kropotkin (1976), highlight the impossibility of reforming such dehumanising institutions: "A prison cannot be improved [...] there is absolutely nothing to do but demolish it" (Kropotkin, 1976: 45). It is indeed entirely illogical to hope to be able to respond to harms by coercion and violence, which do nothing to address the problems that may have led to such harms in the first place, merely exacerbating them. As Rene van Swaaningen has argued:

> At its core, criminal law [...] is based on [...] repressive assumptions [...] From the beginning it has been seen to create problems instead of solving them. A penal reaction after the fact is not preventive but de-socialises an ever-increasing number of people. Therefore it would be better to abolish penal means of coercion, and to replace them by more reparative means. This briefly is the abolitionist message. (1986: 9)

Similarly, Louk Hulsman (1986) argues that the criminal justice system has an extraordinarily narrow focus, based as it is on limited state-defined notions of 'crime', that ignore the broader reality in which harmful behaviour may occur. He thus recommends studying strategies for abolishing criminal justice, namely "how to liberate organizations like the police and the courts [from] a system of reference that turns them away [from] the variety of life and the needs of those directly involved" (Hulsman, 1986: 80) This 'liberation' may only occur, however, once we move outside that frame of reference. It is therefore necessary to empower ordinary people — be they victims or offenders — involved in conflict to ensure that they may help to construct new frames of reference, ensuring that the authorities do not "have a monopoly on how to define what goes on in the relevant life world" (Mathiesen, 2008: 61). It is thus imperative to challenge the very definition of 'crime'.

For abolitionists, there is no clear structure connecting the wide range of situations brought together under the term 'crime'. Crime is a sociological and historical construction, and its definition has no temporal or spatial stability (Christie, 1986). It is difficult to find similarities and direct connections between all of the different behaviours that are defined under the criminal law as 'criminal'. They do not appear to have a common nature. In other words, this means "that there is no *ontological reality* of crime" (Hulsman, 1986: 28, emphasis in original). Further, the 'outsider' does not naturally exist; rather, he or she is created. These criminalised "suitable enemies" (Christie, 1986: 42) are not exceptional and do not in reality form a special category of a radically different people. Many abolitionists have questioned whether the concept of 'crime' is a viable starting point for responding appropriately to conflicts and social problems. Criminalisation reflects a particular definition and interpretive framework which is grounded in an individualising and punitive manner. Once followed, this path paralyses many possible creative solutions for dealing with social problems and we are driven down a punitive tunnel, inevitably dehumanising offenders and creating further social problems. This interpretation of certain behaviours leads to the reification and theft of human conflict, culminating in the application of a specialised form of social control: punishment (Hulsman, 1986: 63).

This is debate is significant because, as Hillyard and Tombs (2004) have pointed out, the very focus of the discipline of *criminology* (the study of 'crime') will inevitably legitimate the concept of '*crime*' itself. One of the main arguments for retaining the concept of 'crime' and the continued application of the criminal law is that it provides a symbolic means of denouncing harms and wrongdoing. In this sense, the criminal law is conceived as a progressive agent that can be used to symbolically condemn the wrongdoings of the powerful that might be culturally embedded, such as racial and sexual violence (Durkheim, 1895; Swaaningen, 1997). Yet punishment as a moral message is not necessarily any more effective than moral education. Then there is the problem that most 'serious wrongdoing and harms' are never embroiled in the criminal justice system in the first place. In this sense, we are not taking these harms seriously at the moment but simply scapegoating those few people who are caught (Mathiesen, 1990; Hudson, 2003; Scott, 2009).[7]

Further, whilst the law and its enforcement can, and sometimes does, protect the general population, the criminal process at the same time plays a decisive role in maintaining structural divisions in society. Mike Fitzgerald and Joe Sim (1982: 24) argued more than thirty years ago that:

> the sanction of imprisonment is invoked consistently against marginal, lower-class offenders. In so doing, imprisonment serves a class based legal system, which first defines the types of social harm which are singled out for punishment, and second, invokes different types of sanctions for different categories of social harm.

The central premise of Fitzgerald and Sim (1982) still pertains today. The almost exclusive focus by law enforcement agencies on the criminality and subsequent punishment of what have been described variously as the 'sub-proletariat' (Hall et al., 1978), the non-productive labour force and the un- or underemployed, has reinforced the social marginalisation of the most structurally vulnerable. Unsurprisingly, then, there has been considerable focus by penal abolitionists on the manner in which 'crime and punishment' have been manipulated as a means of legitimating state governance (Hall et al., 1978; Scott, 2013b). The Capitalist State, which is a configuration of alliances in a given historical conjuncture that mediates

---

[7] There is one further significant argument in terms of keeping a disciplinary focus on 'crime' and criminal 'justice'. This regards the specific nature and generation of penal harms through state punishment. Without a critical examination of the criminal process, the concern is that focus on the specific lived experience of prisoners and other people who have been criminalised may be lost. This is certainly the case when considering the significance of contemporary critical criminological perspectives such as 'convict criminology'.

power relations, is a site of constant struggle and negotiation (Gramsci, 1971; Poulantzas, 1978; Jessop, 1990). When consensus (the velvet glove) falters, the Capitalist State will fall back upon its repressive apparatus (the iron fist) to maintain control.

For penal abolitionists, it is important that we question the very nature of state punishment: the intentional infliction of harm, pain and suffering (Christie, 1986; de Haan, 1991). Undoubtedly, one pain cannot be compensated by another, and for abolitionists it seems to make sense that the aim of interventions following the incursion of harmful behaviour should be to reduce future harms. It can never be moral to perform deliberate acts of pain infliction on another human. This position by default questions the moral legitimacy of the criminal process. This has led to arguments that the new disciplinary focus around social harm could have greater transformative potential to change negative social realities and the ability to *challenge inequitable power relations*.

Zemiology and the utopian imagination
Critical criminology has constantly challenged traditional state-defined notions of 'crime' and criminology which tend to ignore the existence of a considerable number of harms such as those perpetrated by the State itself, notably, environmental, economic and social harms. The European Group, from its inception, has been involved in this task. Following on from the work of Tifft and Sullivan (1980) in the US, who sensitised us to the importance of thinking about how *harms* (not just formally defined *crimes*) prevent people from being fully human, researchers closely involved with the European Group — namely, Paddy Hillyard, Steve Tombs, Christina Pantazis and Simon Pemberton — explored the alternative conception of 'social harm' (Hillyard et al., 2004).

Asking "what is the theoretical rationale and political utility of retaining a commitment to the analysis of crime, (criminal) law and the criminal justice system?", Hillyard et al., (2004: 1) argue there should be a new focus examining all "the different types of harm, which people experience from the cradle to the grave". Hillyard et al. (2004) maintain that the separating out of harms defined as criminal from other kinds of social harms that are also socially, economically or psychologically damaging makes little sense. Rather, it would be more constructive to analyse all these different harms together, rather than bracketing off and focusing exclusively on criminal harms. This is not intended to downplay criminalised harms, but rather to expand our focus to encapsulate these and *other* harms. It means taking both criminal harms and non-criminal harms seriously.

The concept of harm reflects upon the "vicissitudes of life", analysing all the different factors which impact upon people during their life cycles (Hillyard and Tombs, 2004: 21). The focus on social harms thus allows for consideration of social *policy responses* and welfare interventions in reducing the amount of harm in society. Consequently, the call is for the development of a new and coherent discipline of *zemiology*, focused around the notion of social harm and rooted in the principles, politics and enhancement of social justice.

Hillyard and Tombs (2004: 19) provide a detailed definition of what the social harm perspective entails. First, a social harm perspective encompasses *physical* harms such as "premature death or serious injury through clinical iatrogenesis, violence such as car 'accidents', some activities at work (whether paid or unpaid), exposures to various environmental pollutants, assaults, illness and disease, lack of adequate food or shelter, or death, torture and brutality by state officials". Second, a social harm perspective considers *financial* and *economic* harms, including poverty, theft of property and "taking cognisance of the personal and social effects" (Ibid.: 20) of the social exclusion created through unemployment. It would also engender a commitment to social justice through the redistribution of wealth and income through the taxation of the wealthy and increased welfare provision for the poorer sections of the community. Third, the social harm perspective encompasses *emotional* and *psychological* harms. This can include the trauma, stresses and suffering created through the social harm. Finally, this perspective advocates *cultural safety*, which includes commitments to personal development through access to cultural and intellectual resources, and the protection of individual autonomy. What unites this focus on social harm with penal abolitionism is the joint recognition of the problem of *iatrogenic penal harms* — that is, the inevitable generation of harm, injury and death in the prison place.

Critical criminology and the 'crisis of utopias': from left realism to real utopias

Neither of these two examples of the radical 'utopian' imagination necessarily offer concrete alternatives to existing penal solutions but they do contribute to opening up utopian spaces in which new visions may be presented and enacted. They follow Mathiesen's exhortation to sketch out alternative visions rather than providing elaborate blueprints for change (Mathiesen, 1974). They may both be considered 'utopian' in the sense that they provide visions of a 'better place' (Malloch and Munro, 2013). For penal abolitionism, this good place is where there is an end to penal harms; for zemiology it is when harms — whether they be harms of (state or corporate) power directed against people, the ecological system, or non-sentient beings — have been curtailed (Walters et al., 2013). Yet, whilst utopianism and the radical imagination may be considered as some of the strengths of critical criminology, allowing it to go beyond the limited analyses of mainstream criminology, it has also been a source of tensions.

In the 1980s, critical criminology underwent its own crisis of utopias as some of its more utopian aspects were criticised by the 'left realists' (Lea and Young, 1984; Young and Matthews, 1986; Matthews, 2014). In some critical criminological writings, there was a certain utopian idealisation of those who broke the law.[8] In rejecting deterministic and pathological explanations for 'crime', Taylor et al. regarded criminality as a form of resistance to the dominant capitalist order:

> So long as authority takes the form of domination, [...] authority will always be problematic, and [...] any acts of deviance or dissent must be taken to be acts of resistance (however inarticulately expressed or formulated). (Taylor et al., 2003 [1973]: 252)

In this, there appeared to be a return to the classical criminological view of the criminal as a perfectly rational actor with the important distinction being that s/he does not choose 'crime' but resistance. S/he was even considered as a sort of working-class hero or Robin Hood (Cohen, 1996: 4). The real problem was not considered to be that of 'crime' or the harm it caused, but of criminalisation.

The left realists argued that this focus on the social harm caused by criminalisation, whilst important, tended to deflect attention from the harm caused by criminal acts. Jock Young, one of the original authors of the New Criminology (1973), together with John Lea, argued that 'crime' must be taken seriously, especially by the Left since it is a problem that disproportionately affects poor communities. Instead of presenting the fear of 'crime' as an ideological construction without ontological reality,

---

[8] Sources evidencing this claim are actually difficult to find, but there are indications of this 'utopian idealisation' in the New Criminology (Taylor et al., 1973), which was co-authored by two leading figures of left realism some years later — Jock Young and Ian Taylor.

they aimed to measure the real extent of the problem through victim surveys. This was thought to be a way of making critical criminology policy-relevant and ensuring that law enforcement attended to social inequalities and was democratically accountable.

The idea that the 'crime' problem should not 'belong' to the Right was taken up in Britain by Tony Blair in 1996 when he declared: "Law and order is a Labour issue. We all suffer from 'crime', the poorest and vulnerable most of all" (Blair, 1996: 68). Yet, New Labour appeared to be more influenced by 'right realism' when it came to discussing the causes of 'crime'. Following the conservative American sociologist Charles Murray (1996), it considered offenders as an 'underclass' that was culturally isolated from the mythological 'law-abiding' majority (Bell, 2011: 94–5). This image of the offender was radically opposed to that of the 'left idealists' (Young, 1979) but it was also very different from that originally proposed by the 'left realists'. Indeed, in focusing on pathological causes of 'crime', New Labour ignored one of the key principles of 'left realism': namely, the idea that capitalism itself can be criminogenic on account of its tendency to engender economic inequalities which feed feelings of relative deprivation.

That the structural causes of 'crime' should be ignored by politicians claiming to be inspired by left realism was no surprise to those who criticised the theory. Hillyard et al. (2004) have argued that the left realists' disproportionate focus on street 'crime' meant that other forms of harm were neglected. Indeed, zemiology, at least in part, emerged as a reaction against this focus on the most visible forms of 'crime'. Contrary to what left realism seemed to suggest, Hillyard et al. argue that critical criminologists did not want to play down the 'crime' problem, above all for the poor, but they aimed to show that white-collar 'crime' and harms perpetrated by the State and private corporations could be just as harmful as street 'crime' (Hillyard et al., 2004). Zemiology and penal abolitionism do not ignore the victims of 'crime'. On the contrary, the proponents of both critical approaches argue that taking harm seriously means that the notion of 'victimhood' must be understood in a much broader sense to include victims of social injustice, including victims of state violence.

The turn towards realism was perhaps understandable in a dystopian political context, but it lost too much of its radical 'utopian' imagination and ended up being co-opted by mainstream politicians in the 1990s who used it to justify penal repression. Today, the 'criminological imagination' is threatened by a revival of positivism and a 'realist' agenda promoting more evaluative research defined by the interests of policymakers and government (Young, 2011), and thus placing a 'straightjacket' on critical and independent thought (Barton et al., 2006). The recent move towards taking *harm* seriously is not radically opposed to the left realists' exhortation to take *crime* seriously, but by reframing the terms of the debate, it permits a much broader focus on all forms of injustice. It also allows us to go beyond the somewhat idealistic notion of criminals as political actors by showing that those who cause harm are equally likely to be situated at the top or the bottom of the social hierarchy. It is the social-harm approach, broadly conceived to encompass penal harms, that lays the groundwork for a reawakening of a critical criminological imagination (Barton et al., 2006; Copson, 2013), one which may be capable of moving towards a new form of realism: *the real utopia*.

For Erik Olin Wright, '*real* utopias' are:

> utopian ideals that are grounded in the real potentials of humanity, utopian destinations that have accessible waystations, utopian designs of institutions that can inform our practical tasks of navigating a world of imperfect conditions for social change. (Wright, 2010: 4)

A real utopia is something which already exists. Yet, whilst it is part of the present landscape, it is grounded in principles and values that can be considered as going against the countervailing norms of our advanced capitalist, neocolonial and patriarchal society. This concrete and already existing real utopia can help feed our imagination and inspire us to formulate radical alternatives to society and its institutions. In this sense, the real utopia can help us visualise new possibilities and foster a dramatic break with the present. It can provide a conduit in which we can transform everyday life and promote emancipatory change (Levitas, 1990). Like the 'good place' of the utopian imaginary, a real utopia provides us with a vision of an alternative, but this alternative is not simply in the mind — it is one which is rooted in concrete realities. The realism of this utopian vision adds plausibility and feasibility to its promotion. It indicates that the proposed alternative is possible within our given historical conjuncture: the alternative is historically immanent and potentially ripe for further development or expansion (Wright, 2010).

Thus, and in a hugely significant way, the real existence of the utopian practice can disrupt the ideological closure of the dominant institutions and practices of the present. It highlights how we can influence the present and realise a new 'good place' (Levitas, 1990). A currently existing utopian practice can provide a firm basis for critique and illuminate a pathway to radical change. Significantly, focusing on such a 'good place' — a real utopia — also provides an opportunity for critics of the existing society to define themselves positively in terms of something that they are for, rather than just what they are against — the 'bad place'. This understanding is underscored by an 'abolitionist real utopia' which envisages non-penal alternatives that are present in the here and now that can be drawn upon as a means of facilitating radical transformations, of handling conflicts and responding to problematic and troublesome behaviours. Such a position is abolitionist because it is based upon a clear set of normative principles and values; it uses this normative framework to assess, evaluate and critique the legitimacy of existing institutional practices and social structures, and, where appropriate, call for change; it has a strategy for transformation grounded in emancipatory politics and praxis; and, finally, it has a vision of non-penal 'real utopian' alternatives that are consistent with its normative framework (Scott, 2013a).

Reawakening our radical imagination

There is a pressing need to develop non-penal real utopias to provide a new cultural script and resources for a radical imagination to inspire transformative justice and an emancipatory politics and praxis capable of moving beyond repressive penal dystopia. Inspired by abolitionism and the social-harm approach, a non-penal real utopia should promote visions of radical alternatives. What is required is an alternative space designated to the fostering of *self-empowerment*, which utilises a holistic approach based upon principles of self-help and mutual aid. Non-penal interventions should help troubled individuals understand and, as far as possible, lessen or overcome their psychological, social and/or emotional issues and difficulties. It requires a *democratic* impulse aiming to foster a balanced and *supportive dialogue* between clients and staff where agreement and a consensus can be reached. Radical alternatives can aspire to engender respect for the self, the environment and other people, and develop new skills for interpersonal communication and action.

By promoting values and principles, such as empowerment, participatory democracy and mutual aid, we can also point to the defects of the existing operation of the criminal law and to social injustice.

Working backwards, so to speak, the non-penal real utopia can be a way of proposing ideas and principles upon which the penal apparatus of the Capitalist State can be judged. The daily workings of the intervention can help inform a normative framework challenging the pain, suffering, iatrogenic harms and death characterising the prison place. It thus gives us a solid and principled moral platform from which we can critique the failures of the penal law. Furthermore, non-penal real utopias should not be considered in isolation. Since the social harm that they seek to address is bound up with a whole range of other contextual issues, they need to be thought of as just one part of a project helping to inform a broader vision of social justice. They may do this by giving people the opportunity to see the world differently and encouraging them to understand the Other.

At a time when social and economic insecurities are encouraging scapegoating, it is ever more important to foster a more reflective understanding of the causes of social problems. Indeed, the darker the times, the greater the need for enlightened thinking. The reflection upon the principles and practices of non-penal real utopias present us with a clear ability to reflect upon social injustice in contemporary society. It offers us a template of the 'good life', a space in which we not only challenge but can imagine new radical alternatives. It therefore has *emancipatory* potential, encouraging us to think more broadly about how the principles and values of social justice can work in practice. A non-penal real utopia may help us to see beyond the constraints of the present neoliberal society that privileges the market above everything else, especially human need.

Thinking about non-penal real utopias must also be a collective endeavour if we are to hope to develop alternatives to current top-down, state-controlled penal practices. It is hoped that this collective exercise in imagination may help to foster visions of a society grounded in mutual aid and respect; democratic participation; communal living and equitable distribution of resources; and where people have a voice that is both heard and listened to. Thus, the radical alternative can provide us with a set of alternative values to neoliberal capitalism and can inform constructive criticism of the present. The very act of awakening the utopian imagination may be constitutive of wide-ranging change. It is to be hoped that the (re)awakening the critical criminological imagination in a real utopian direction will provide the basis of an ongoing debate which may lead to transformative, emancipatory change, thus offering a way out of the 'crisis of utopias'. The task of critical criminology, together with progressive thinkers and activists, could not be more pressing.

References

Barton, A., Corteen, K., Scott, D. and Whyte, D. (eds) (2006) *Expanding the Criminological Imagination* London: Routledge

Becker, H. (1963) *Outsiders* New York: Free Press

Becker, H. (1967) 'Whose Side are We On?' in *Social Problems* Volume 14, No. 3 pp 239–247

Bell, E. (2011) *Criminal Justice and Neoliberalism* Basingstoke: Palgrave Macmillan

Blair, T. (1996) *New Britain: My vision of a young country* London: Fourth Estate

Bourdieu, P. (2000 [1972]) *Esquisse d'une théorie de la pratique* Paris: Seuil

Bourdieu, P. and Wacquant, L. (1992) *An Introduction to Reflexive Sociology* Cambridge: Polity Press

Chomsky, N. (2008 [1966]) 'The Responsibility of Intellectuals' in Arnove, A. (ed), *The Essential Chomsky* London: The Bodley Head

Christie, N. (1977) 'Conflict as Property' in *British Journal of Criminology* Volume 17, January 1977 No. 1 pp 1–15

Christie, N. (1981) *Limits to Pain* Oslo: Oslo University Press

Christie, N. (1986) 'Suitable Enemies' in Bianchi, H. and van Swaaningen, R. (eds) (1986) *Abolitionism: Toward a Non-Repressive Approach to Crime* Amsterdam: Free Press

Christie, N. (2016) 'Apartheid modernity' in *Justice, Power and Resistance*, Foundation Volume, September 2016

Cohen, S. (1985) *Visions of Social Control* Cambridge: Polity Press

Cohen, S. (1988) *Against Criminology* Cambridge: Polity Press

Cohen, S. (1996) 'Crime and Politics: Spot the difference' in *British Journal of Sociology* Volume 47, No. 1 pp 1–21

Cohen, S. (2010) *Personal correspondence with David Scott*, 20 September 2010

Collier, R. (1998) *Masculinities, Crime and Criminology* London: Sage

Copson, L. (2013) 'Towards a Utopian Criminology' in Malloch, M. and Munro, B. (eds) (2013) *Crime, Critique and Utopia* London: Palgrave de Haan, W. (1991), 'Abolitionism' in Stenson, K. and Cowell, D. (eds) (1991) *The Politics of Crime Control* London: Sage

Duménil, G. (2014) 'Les utopies peuvent mobiliser les énergies', *La Marseillaise*, 9 December

Duménil, G. (2016), Seminar delivered to 'Les amis de Veblen', Lyon, 2 March

Durkheim, E. (1970 [1895]) *The Division of Labour* London: Macmillan

Dwyer, A., Ball, M. and Crofts, T. (2015) *Queering Criminology* Basingstoke: Palgrave Macmillan

Eagleton, T. (1999) 'Utopia and its Opposites' pp 31–41 in Panitch, L. and Leys, C. (eds) (1999) *Necessary and Unnecessary Utopias: Socialist Register 2000* Rendlesham: Merlin

Equality and Human Rights Commission (2015) *Stop and Think: A Critical Review of the Use of Stop and Search Powers in England and Wales*, http://www.equalityhumanrights.com/sites/default/files/documents/raceinbritain/ehrc_stop_and_search_report.pdf

Fitzgerald, M. and Sim, J. (1982) *British Prisons* Oxford: Blackwell's

Gilmore, J., Moore, J.M. and Scott, D. (eds) (2013) *Critique and Dissent* Ottawa: Red Quill Books

Gilroy, P. (1987) 'The Myth of Black Criminality' in Scraton, P. (1987) *Law, Order and the Authoritarian State* Milton Keynes: Open University

Gordon, M.D., Tilley, H. and Prakash, G. (2010) 'Utopia and dystopia beyond space and time' pp 1–20 in Gordon, M.D., Tilley, H. and Prakash, G. (eds) (2010) *Utopia/Dystopia: Conditions of Historical Possibility* Oxford: Princeton University Press

Gordon, P. (1983) *White Law: Racism in the Police, Courts and Prisons* London: Pluto Press

Gouldner, A. (1968) 'The Sociologist as Partisan: Sociology and the welfare state' in *The American Sociologist* Volume 3, No. 2 pp 103–116

Gramsci, A. (1971) *Selections from the Prison Notebooks* London: Lawrence and Wishart

Hall, S., Critcher, C., Jefferson, T., Clarke, J., Roberts, B. (2013 [1978]) *Policing the Crisis: Mugging, the State and Law and Order* London: Macmillan

Heidensohn, F. (1985) *Women and Crime* London: Macmillan

Hillyard, P. (1993) *Suspect Community* London: Pluto Press

Hillyard, P. and Tombs, S. (2004) 'Beyond criminology?' in Hillyard. P., Tombs, S., Pantazis. C. and Gordon, D. (eds) (2004) *Beyond Criminology: Taking Harm Seriously* London: Pluto

Hillyard, P., Tombs, S., Pantazis, C. and Gordon, D. (2004), 'Introduction' in Hillyard, P., Tombs, S., Pantazis, C. and Gordon, D. (eds) (2004) *Beyond Criminology: Taking Harm Seriously* London: Pluto

Hudson, B. (2003) *Understanding Justice* Buckingham: Open University Press

Hulsman, L. (1986) 'Critical Criminology and the Concept of 'Crime'' in *Contemporary Crises* Volume 10, No. 1 pp 63–80

Jacoby, R. (2005) *Picture Imperfect: Utopian Thought for an Anti-Utopian Age* New York: Columbia University Press

Jessop, B. (1990) *State Theory* Cambridge: Polity Press

Kropotkin, P. (1976) *The Essential Kropotkin* London: Macmillan

Lea, J. and Young, J. (1984) *What is to be Done About Law and Order?* Harmondsworth: Penguin

Levitas, R. (1990) *The Concept of Utopia* Oxford: Peter Lang

Macpherson, W. (1999) *The Stephen Lawrence Inquiry*, Cm 4262-I London: Home Office

Malloch, M. and Munro, B. (eds) (2013) *Crime, Critique and Utopia* London: Palgrave

Matthews, R. (2014) *Realist Criminology* Basingstoke: Palgrave Macmillan

Mathiesen, T. (1974) *The Politics of Abolition* Oxford: Martin Robertson

Mathiesen, T. (1990) *Prisons on Trial* London: Sage

Mathiesen T. (2008) 'The Abolitionist Stance' in *Journal of Prisoners on Prisons* Volume 17, No. 2 pp 58–63

Matza, D. (1964) *Delinquency and Drift* New Brunswick: Transaction

Matza, D. (1969) *Becoming Deviant* New Jersey: Prentice Hall

Merton, R. (1945) 'The Role of the Intellectual in Public Bureaucracy' in *Social Forces* Volume 23, No. 4 pp 405–415

Mills, C.W. (1959) *The Sociological Imagination* Oxford: Oxford University Press

Moore, J.M., Rolston, W., Scott, D. and Tomlinson, M. (eds) (2014) *Beyond Criminal Justice* Bristol: EG Press

More, T. (1990 [1516]) *Utopia* Harmondsworth: Penguin

Orwell, G. (1949) *1984* Harmondsworth: Penguin

Pantazis, C. and Pemberton, S. (2009) 'From the "old" to the"new" Suspect Community' in *British Journal of Criminology* Volume 49, No. 5 pp 646–666

Poulantzas, N. (1978) *State, Power, Socialism* London: Verso

Rusche, G. and Kirchhiemer, O. (2003) *Punishment and Social Structure* London: Transaction Press

Scott, D. (2006) *Ghosts Beyond Our Realm: A Neo-Abolitionist Analysis of Prisoner Human Rights and Prison Officer Occupational Culture* Preston: VDM

Scott, D. (2009) 'Punishment' in Hucklesby, A. and Wahidin, A. (eds) (2009) *Criminal Justice* Oxford: Oxford University Press

Scott, D. (2013a) 'Visualising an Abolitionist Real Utopia: Principles, policy and praxis' in Malloch, M. and Munro, B. (eds) (2013) *Crime, Critique and Utopia* London: Palgrave

Scott, D. (2013b) 'Unequalled in pain' in Scott, D. (ed) (2013) *Why Prison?* Cambridge: Cambridge University Press

Scott, D. (2015) 'Eating your Insides Out: Interpersonal, cultural and institutionally-structured violence in the prison place' in *Prison Service Journal* No. 201 pp 68-72

Scott, D. and Codd, H. (2010) *Controversial Issues in Prison* Maidenhead: Open University Press

Scraton, P. (ed.) (1987) *Law, Order and the Authoritarian State* Milton Keynes: Open University

Sim, J. (2009) *Punishment and Prisons* London: Sage

Sim. J., Scraton, P. and Gordon, P. (1987) 'Introduction' in Scraton, P. (ed) (1987) *Law, Order and the Authoritarian State* Milton Keynes: Open University

Smart, C. (1976) *Women, Crime and Criminology* London: Routledge and Kegan Paul

Smart, C. (1989) *Feminism and the Power of the Law* London: Sage

Swaaningen, R. Van (1986) 'Abolitionism' in Bianchi H. and Swaaningen R. Van (1986) *Abolitionism: Towards a Non-Repressive Approach to 'Crime'* Amsterdam: Free University Press

Swaaningen, R. Van (1997) *Critical Criminology: Visions from Europe* London: Sage

Taylor, I., Walton, P. and Young, J. (2003 [1973]) *The New Criminology: For a Social Theory of Deviance* London: Routledge and Kegan Paul

Tifft, L. and Sullivan, L. (1980) *The Struggle to be Human: Crime, Criminology and Anarchism* Orkney: Cienfuegos Press

Wacquant, L. (2013) 'Crafting the Neoliberal State: Workfare, prisonfare and social insecurity', in Scott, D. (ed) (2013) *Why Prison?* Cambridge: Cambridge University Press

Walters, R., Westerhuis, D.S. and Wyatt, T. (eds) (2013) *Emerging Issues in Green Criminology* London: Palgrave

Wright, E.O. (2010) *Envisioning a Real Utopia* Cambridge: Polity Press

Young, J. (1979) 'Left idealism, Reformism and Beyond: From new criminology to Marxism' in Fine, B. et al. (eds) *Capitalism and the Rule of Law: From Deviancy Theory to Marxism* London: Hutchinson

Young, J. (1999) *The Exclusive Society* London: Sage

Young, J. (2011) *The Criminological Imagination* Cambridge: Polity Press

Young, J. and Matthews, R. (eds) (1986) *Realist Criminology* Sage: London

4.

A Disobedient Visionary with an Enquiring Mind: An essay on the contribution of Stan Cohen

This chapter was originally published in the European Group Newsletter *in September 2013.*

Stan Cohen died on 7 January 2013. He was a sociologist and moralist whose work epitomised the 'sociological imagination' (Mills, 1959). Ultimately, his writings were characterised by political commitments to social and transformative justice. His work was relevant, interventionist and filled with theoretical insights. Five of his most important works over the last four decades are *Folk Devils and Moral Panics* (1972), *Psychological Survival* (with Laurie Taylor, 1973), *Visions of Social Control* (1985), *Against Criminology* (1988) and *States of Denial* (2000). In reading these books, we are, in effect, reading the history and contemporary scope of criminology in the UK and elsewhere, for many of the axiomatic assumptions, research questions, concepts and problematisations in the discipline of criminology today originate from these texts or in the papers which they bring together.

Stan Cohen was a *founder* rather than a *follower*. The sociology of deviance and criminology has walked in his 'footsteps in the sand'. To talk about criminology today without reference to Stan Cohen is like talking about ethics without reference to Kant. He had the rarest of skills — which have been rightly compared to those of the great socialist thinkers Noam Chomsky and George Orwell — to write for a number of different audiences at the same time and yet deliver a multilayered analysis carrying the greatest of insights that could be appreciated by all.

In some way, it is hard to describe his contribution to criminology because, quite frankly, it is so enormous — his work is of such significance that, perhaps more than any other thinker in the last four decades, it has come to shape and define the discipline of criminology itself. This is quite a remarkable achievement, not least because he was an *anti-criminologist* — that is, it was his explicit aim to challenge the 'positivist' or scientific study of crime which dominated the subject in the UK when he started his career. And yet it would be wrong to say that his contribution or influence is restricted merely to 'critical criminologies' — teachers and researchers from various criminological perspectives and indeed academics, practitioners and activists outside criminology entirely, have found his work valuable and important. Alongside his friends and colleagues at the *New Deviancy Conferences* in the late 1960s, Stan Cohen challenged the dominant administrative criminology, which closely followed government agendas and rooted its analysis largely in quantitative data, and firmly embedded in the academy a more sophisticated, theoretical and sociologically informed approach to the study of 'crime', deviance and social control. What is taught on undergraduate and postgraduate 'criminology' degrees today would be very different had not Stan Cohen, alongside Jock Young and others, so influentially introduced the sociology of deviancy to the UK.

Though criminology and its key themes have evolved in the last four decades, the writings of Stan Cohen have remained as relevant and inspirational as ever. His work not only profoundly influenced his peers but has also had an impact on every generation and cohort of criminologists that have emerged since the 1960s. As academic criminology developed in the 1970s, his writings on moral panic and the sociology of deviance shaped not only the criminology curriculum in universities but also the key questions posed and addressed in the criminological literature. In *Folk Devils and Moral Panics*, Stan Cohen developed the concept of 'moral panic' to explore how certain people, because of certain characteristics, behaviours or social backgrounds, were first defined as a threat to society and then presented as such to the rest of society by the mass media. Drawing upon the insights of Emile Durkheim and Howard Becker, and using the case study of 'Mods and Rockers', he revealed how moral entrepreneurs subsequently diagnosed and offered crime-control solutions that could contain this new apparent threat. An exercise in setting moral boundaries and articulating social anxieties about youth and affluence, for Stan Cohen (1972: 57) "the devil has to be given a particular shape to know which virtue is being asserted". The focus on moral panics set forth two key ideas that were to run through his many writings in the coming years — first, *why in some places at particular times are certain actions either underplayed or overplayed by the media?* and second, *what is the role of the media in shaping the reactions of the social audience?* Both of these questions were to be revisited at length in his book *States of Denial* (2001).

In his broader application of the sociology of deviance, Stan Cohen raised consciousness regarding the problems of radical differentiation and the classification of deviants. Rather than classify or differentiate, which could result in the construction of false hierarchies, he was firmly committed to acknowledging our 'common humanity', albeit with its vast and wonderful diversity. Once again, classification and differentiation would be issues that would be reflected in his research agenda for the next four decades, most notably in *Visions of Social Control*. He wanted to know what were the processes involved in the definitions of deviance and what, perhaps even more significantly, were their consequences. His concern — like that of his American sociology of deviancy counterparts, Howard Becker and Edwin Lemert, and the enigmatic French social theorist Michel Foucault — was how social control could play a part in *creating deviancy*. This insight instilled within him a strong intellectual scepticism towards both formal and informal mechanisms of social control and its net-widening capacities. His interest in the workings of social control, and especially those organised responses to deviance that are conceived and defined as 'social controls' by those who deploy them, was only to increase as the dark clouds of Thatcherism and neoliberalism cast their deadly shade across the land.

As the criminology curriculum developed in the 1980s to encapsulate both criminology and criminal justice, his Orwellian-inspired book *Visions of Social Control*, which many today consider his *magnum opus*, once again shaped the discipline. Drawing upon a wide range of theorists — Michel Foucault, Colin Ward, Emile Durkheim, David Rothman and Marxist political economists, Stan Cohen delivered his majestic overview of formal and informal control apparatuses in the later stages of the twentieth century. Cohen perceptively warned us that those with the best of intentions could end up promoting policies that had the worst of consequences — and this was a message not just for politicians and practitioners, but also a stark lesson to be heeded by criminologists of all persuasions, especially critical theorists and abolitionists. Yet, despite such scepticism, a clear message of hope is retained in his vision — radical activists could also explore the contradictions, unintended consequences and inconsistencies of State practices and policies. Whatever the difficulties and complexities of real life, we must continue to try and "do-good" when and where we possibly can. This once again was a theme that characterised his perspective.

Visions of Social Control is a thoughtful book raising crucial questions regarding contemporary developments in criminal processes and informal interventions devised to address problematic behaviour. Wide ranging in scope, there is little doubt that one of the primary intentions of the book was to question the moral legitimacy of the current workings of the penal machine. Stan Cohen identified how developments in the 1980s saw a deepening in the intensity of the control mechanisms of the Capitalist State — his warnings about privatisation and the role of volunteers as State agents proving to be particularly prophetic. In moving debates in criminal justice, avoiding a dry and legalistic analysis, *Visions of Social Control* inspired a generation. Drawing upon and synthesising complex and abstract theory, the book delivered an understandable and straightforward analysis and yet, at the same, was so deeply insightful that it set the agenda for the study of social control for the next twenty and more years. Paradoxically, for the man who so importantly and successfully critiqued classification in criminal process, one of his most important contributions was his ability to classify complex arguments and to draw out their hidden connections. As a critical thinker, he would also use such skills to make clear the problems and contradictions of the penal apparatus of the Capitalist State. *Visions of Social Control* identified the early impact of risk assessments and the possible dangers of community interventions, issues that were to dominate the penological literature throughout the 1990s. He foretold the shift in bureaucratic interests of universities away from scholarship, and revealed the growing strength of an 'evaluation' culture that had supplanted the search for the 'cause' of 'crime' and was strangling humane and socially just responses to individual and social problems.

Throughout his career, Stan Cohen engaged with one of the most profound tensions within criminology — the relationship between idealism and realism/utopia and immediate humanitarian reforms. One of the most powerful metaphors that Stan Cohen drew upon to explore this tension is the 'tale of the fisherman' by Saul Alinsky in *Visions of Social Control*:

> A man is walking by the riverside when he notices a body floating downstream. A fisherman leaps into the river, pulls the body ashore, gives mouth-to-mouth resuscitation, saving the man's life. A few minutes later the same thing happens, then again, and again. Eventually yet another body floats by. This time the fisherman completely ignores the drowning man and starts running upstream along the bank. The observer asks the fisherman what on earth is he doing? Why is he not trying to rescue this drowning body? 'This time', replies the fisherman, 'I'm going up stream to see who is

pushing these poor folk into the water' [...] but Alinsky had a twist to his story — while the fisherman was so busy running along the bank to find the ultimate source of the problem, who was going to help those poor wretches who continued to float down the river? (Cohen, 1985: 236–7)

In *Visions of Social Control*, he highlights the centrality of idealist utopias and romantic/sentimentalist anarchist literature in providing the vision we need to create radical and libertarian socialist transformations of society. His interests in anarchism, idealism, new deviancy theory and anti-criminology drew him towards 'penal abolitionism' — an ethical perspective which challenges the moral legitimacy of punishment. Most penal abolitionists are not 'absolutists' that argue that we should never punish anyone under any possible circumstance, but rather that we should, as Nils Christie puts it, punish with great sadness, regret and a sense of mourning. Rather than feel good about punishment we should punish as little as possible and with a bad conscience, because punishment has no moral legitimacy. Stan Cohen wrote extensively about abolitionism in his book *Against Criminology*, edited a special edition of *Contemporary Crises* in 1986 on abolitionism, attended the *International Conference of Penal Abolition* (ICOPA) in the mid-1980s and was a leading member of the abolitionist pressure group *Radical Alternatives to Prison* in the 1970s, with which he published the important pamphlets *Prison Secrets* in 1977 (with Laurie Taylor) and *Crime and Punishment* in 1979.

But Stan Cohen (1985) was always the 'cautious abolitionist' and though he found the penal abolitionist arguments very persuasive, he worried about their problems regarding blame allocation and moral responsibility. Consequently, he committed to only a guarded and careful appraisal of the position. At the same time, he never forgot his social-work roots and reminded us of the desperate need for humanitarian interventions in the here and now. I think that this tension between trying to change the world so that it is more socially just but at the same time helping those most in need right now runs through nearly all of his work, and indeed perhaps defines it. For Stan Cohen (1990), penal abolitionists must be prepared to honestly answer the question *what can we do right now* to mitigate the humanitarian crises confronting contemporary penal practices, without abandoning the broader obligation to promote radically alternative responses to troublesome human conduct. Stan Cohen (1995) clearly favoured the language of human rights. For him, human rights could bridge the realism/idealism divide. Human rights, when codified as legal rights, could provide immediate aid and ease human suffering. They could act as a 'shield' in times of regressive civilisation. But they could also act as a 'sword' — human rights could be bearers of latent utopian ideals and carry with them the ideals of social justice.

Stan Cohen was also concerned about how 'alternatives to punishment' could become even more insidious than the prison. This critique, now one his most famous, has been popularised in his phrase 'net widening', a term he first used in *Folk Devils and Moral Panics*. In *Visions of Social Control*, he used the metaphor of 'fishing nets' to explain how more and more people, who have generally committed petty offences, were being sucked into the criminal 'justice' system. As ever, the work of Stan Cohen captivated a number of different audiences. The book connected with radicals working within the State machine, social workers and radical activists, and so once again his influence stretched well beyond the walls of the academy.

As criminology evolved to take a more detailed and analytical approach to 'crimes' of power and State crime, his final single-authored book, *States of Denial: Knowing About Suffering and Atrocities*, once more led the way. Stan Cohen never lost sight of the importance of drawing our attention to "unwelcome knowledges" such as human rights abuses and atrocities. In *States of Denial*, he asked us some of the most profound questions of the day: *why is there so much suffering yet such little effort to alleviate it? how do people respond to knowledge about the suffering of other humans?* and, *why do some people help?* By asking his reader these questions, Stan Cohen highlighted both the general and the particular. In general, the book leads the reader to recognise that 'denial' is something that characterises human life, and in certain personal circumstances may even have a positive impact. In particular, the book is so profound and is written in such an open and honest manner that inevitably the reader will recognise the use of 'techniques of denial' in their own daily lives. His main focus was upon political denial and the failure to act when we have knowledge, whether in terms of personal experiences or via other media. The book was therefore not only a brilliant intellectual overview but also a direct intervention attempting to breach denials. His final book, then, is one great courage, honest reflections of the problems and possibilities of our times, and more than anything else a great endorsement of humanity despite its limitations — for I think he grasped better than most its frailty, beauty and diversity. There was a difference between passivity and moral indifference. We may, as he put it, care intensely and yet still fail to act. It is this insight into the human condition which I think made him such a unique and important contributor to criminology and the social sciences more broadly. It will be this insight which ensures that his work will be of continued benefit to the coming generation of scholars in criminology and related fields.

Indeed, every new generation of academics and students in criminology over the last few decades has engaged with the work of Stan Cohen and the issues he brought to prominence. Not only has he set the criminological curriculum, raised the most pertinent questions, made the most complex of issues understandable through his scholarship, but he also provided the theoretical vocabulary by which the discipline of criminology today engages with its subject matter. Criminology uses his language to explore the problems of today and, I think, also of tomorrow. Where would criminology be today without the common language of 'social control talk', 'net widening', 'denial and acknowledgement', and so on and so forth?

Despite his enormous influence, I think there is still much that criminology (and related disciplines in which his work is of considerable influence) can learn from Stan Cohen. He was never a dedicated follower of academic fashion. We must remember that criminology is a discipline that draws upon a number of different subjects. Stan Cohen was both a sociologist and a moralist, and both should be central to the future of criminology, critical or otherwise. His focus on the 'moral' was not just restricted to 'moral panics'. His moralism, which he referred to as 'moral pragmatism', is outlined in his book *Visions of Social Control*. In this text, he wrote about the importance of clarifying our cherished moral values — in other words, what we think is most important, what it is in life that we must protect, and what our key priorities are. Among these cherished values for him were social justice and human rights. It is absolutely crucial that criminology continues to focus upon justice, both in its formulation and breach, rather than become obsessed once again with the government-set agenda reflecting the interests of the powerful, evaluation studies or securing State funding (Cohen, 1985). But his moralism also goes to the very heart of what it is *to be a criminologist* as a member of a professional vocation today. Stan Cohen recognised that your academic life and *who you are* as a human being are indistinguishable. In other words, the criminologist's biography is important — what you write and talk about should be reflected in who you are. Given his writings, then, it should come as no surprise that the man Stan Cohen was widely recognised as being gentle, kind and understanding.

He also led the way with his scholarship — he would have read literally everything written on the topic that was available and then carefully presented this to the reader. How often in his books do we see the phrase 'I have read thirty books on this topic and they all pretty much say this...'. No stone was left unturned and, as a result, his research was exemplary. The message for criminologists is that we ensure that our research and theoretical models are accessible and relevant — the value to cherish is that we should keep our writing styles simple — as he put it, 'it is always better to adopt the simplest approach'. Further, and at least as equally important, if not more so, we should continue to be critical and raise those questions that need to be answered by those in power. Stan Cohen was a disobedient visionary with an enquiring mind. He told truth to power, and more. He also told truth to the powerless. He did more than most in supporting a view from below. Perhaps here, also inspired by Michel Foucault, he encouraged Walter Probyn, a prisoner he had befriended whilst doing the Durham E Wing research for *Psychological Survival*, to write his autobiography *Angel Face*. He wrote the introduction and a commentary/postscript for the book (see Cohen, 1977a, 1977b).

For Stan Cohen, criminologists should explore human suffering in its very many manifestations, which have been denied or where there is only limited political action aiming to address such personal troubles. Academics should intervene. They should make their voices heard. In *States of Denial*, Stan Cohen makes the case very strongly, and correctly, that academic indifference or silence is not acceptable:

> Intellectuals who keep silent about what they know, who ignore the crimes that matter by moral standards, are even more morally culpable when their society is free and open. They can speak freely, but choose not to. (Cohen, 2000: 286)

We live and work in different social and economic times to when Stan Cohen started his academic career. Many universities today, at least in the UK, are run like businesses looking to deliver employability skills rather than focus on education as an end in itself. Outside of the academy, the same government-orientated agendas that Stan Cohen objected to in the 1960s continue to offer the promise of prestigious careers to ambitious academics, whilst within the academy, research careers are increasingly made or broken depending upon the individual's willingness to adhere to the new 'rules of the game' and meet the demands of income generation above all other considerations. Stan

Cohen's work has helped us understand the profound changes that have taken place since the late 1960s, but the values he cherished then should also be the values cherished by criminologists today. Holding such an approach in academia today can, in the end, mean 'not playing the game': at a time when the economic rational trumps those moral and political commitments, criminologists should bear in mind that it is not the research grant which is important, but the scholarship and quality of the research undertaken. Scholarship for Stan Cohen was a *cherished value* and the credibility of criminology as a discipline in the future will ultimately depend on how closely it continues to adhere to this value.

References

Cohen, S. (1972) *Folk Devils and Moral Panics* London: Routledge

Cohen, S. (1977a) 'Introduction' in Probyn, W. (1977) *Angel Face* London: George Allen and Unwin

Cohen, S. (1977b) 'Commentary (by Stan Cohen): Notes on the reformation of a criminal' in Probyn, W. (1977) *Angel Face* London: George Allen and Unwin

Cohen, S. (1979) *Crime and Punishment* London: Radical Alternatives to Prison

Cohen, S. (1980) 'Introduction' in Dronfield, L. (1980) *Outside Chance* London: Newham Project

Cohen, S. (1981) 'Footprints in the Sand' in Fitzgerald, M., McLennan, G. and Pawson, J. (1981) *Crime and Society: Readings in History and Theory* Milton Keynes: Open University Press

Cohen, S. (1985) *Visions of Social Control: Crime, Punishment and Classification* Cambridge: Polity Press

Cohen, S. (1986) 'Abolitionism' in *Contemporary Crises* (special edition on penal abolitionism edited by Cohen, S.) Volume 10, No 1 pp 1-3

Cohen (1988) *Against Criminology* Cambridge: Polity Press

Cohen, S. (1990) 'Intellectual Scepticism and Political Commitment: The case of radical criminology' pp 98–129 in Walton, P. and Young, J. (eds) (1998) *The New Criminology Revisited* London: MacMillan

Cohen, S. (1995) 'Social control and the Politics of Reconstruction' in Nelken, D. (ed) (1995) *The Future of Crime Control* London: Sage

Cohen, S. (2000) *States of Denial: Knowing about Suffering and Atrocities* Cambridge: Polity Press

Cohen, S. and Taylor, L. (1981 [1972]) *Psychological Survival* Harmondsworth: Penguin

Cohen, S. and Taylor, L. (1977) *Prison Secrets* London: National Council for Civil Liberties and Radical Alternatives to Prison

Mills, C.W. (1959) *The Sociological Imagination* Oxford: Oxford University Press

Probyn, W. (1977) *Angel Face* London: George Allen and Unwin

5

Critical Criminology in the Corporate University: Results from a survey in England, Wales and the North of Ireland

This chapter was first published in the European Group Newsletter *in June 2014.*

> If you have flicked through the pages of 'Criminology' in the past
> ten years, then I'm sure you are aware of the monstrosity that
> mainstream 'high impact' journals have become — to me they are
> almost unreadable. (Respondent 11)

This chapter[1] draws upon research undertaken between 14 March – 12 May 2014 with critical criminologists currently working in universities in England, Wales and the North of Ireland. Overall, twenty-four academics from twenty different universities participated in the study.[2] The 'Critical Criminology Questionnaire',[3] from which both the quantitative and qualitative data are derived, is available on the *European Group for the Study of Deviance and Social Control* (European Group) website.[4] The European Group would welcome contributions to this survey from members of the European Group from all around the world. The following discussion explores how, despite the contemporary challenges to university life under neoliberal capitalism and other hierarchies of power, the values and principles of the European Group continue to have relevance for critical pedagogy[5] and critical analysis today.[6]

---

[1] Thanks to all those who attended my session on 'Critical Criminology Programmes in the UK: Expanding the Criminological Imagination?' at the University of Padova, 19 May 2014 and for the helpful and supportive comments on this paper. Thanks also to Francesca Vianello for inviting me to talk on this issue.

[2] See further details in Appendix 4 and Appendix 5.

[3] See Appendix 6. Many thanks to Alana Barton, Emma Bell, Victoria Canning and Joe Sim for very helpful comments on earlier drafts of the survey questionnaire.

[4] www.europeangroup.org

[5] Critical pedagogy is an educational philosophy which privileges reflective, independent and critical thinking. Teaching is conceived as a political intervention facilitating self-actualisation, personal development and life-long learning. Key is the emergence of an

1. The appeal of critical criminology

Evidence from the survey's findings suggests that the acknowledgement of social divisions and structural inequalities, and the 'holding of power to account' (Respondent 7), continue to be privileged in both critical criminological teaching and research.

> We try to approach criminology from a varied and critical perspective, placing issues such as gender, race, diversity and class at centre stage [alongside] those criminological theories which adequately consider these issues and challenge inequality and bias. (Respondent 2)

> The content of the programme has been designed around the key concerns of critical criminology — challenging legalistic definitions of 'crime', problematizing the limitations of 'crime' as a focus of analysis, focusing on notions of 'harm', structural inequalities, the politics of crime control and governance, and focusing on crimes of the powerful. (Respondent 8)

> With one or two exceptions we as a team seek to deconstruct the common-sense views of crime and to refocus students on other social harms. We seek to explore issues of state crime and human rights abuses and compare these with the caricatured and amplified harms which Criminal Justice concentrates upon. Thus we steer away from the CJS [Criminal Justice System], representing it as a failed 'system', and wish to address the social policy approaches to dealing with complex social problems and injustices. (Respondent 19)

---

emancipatory 'critical consciousness' empowering individuals and challenging social inequalities through the transformation of 'common sense' into 'good sense'. Drawing upon the student's experiences and/or conceptions of the world, old assumptions are problematised and new ways of interpreting the world formulated. Critical pedagogy connects theory, policy and praxis. The teacher is an 'organic' or 'transformative' intellectual — a conduit for change.

[6] For good overviews of 'critical criminology' and the critical analysis of 'crime', deviance and social control in the UK and elsewhere, see Taylor, I. et al. (eds) (1975) *Critical Criminology* London: Routledge; Scraton, P. (ed) (1987) *Law, Order and the Authoritarian State* Milton Keynes: Open University Press; Barton, A. et al. (eds) (2006) *Expanding the Criminological Imagination* Devon: Willan/Routledge; Gilmore, J. et al. (eds) (2013) *Critique and Dissent* Quebec: Red Quill Publishers.

> We have a culture that is sympathetic to providing education that questions the taken for granted, which asks students to look at 'what lies beneath' and generally learn the art of critique. (Respondent 1)

There is also evidence from the surveys that students, especially postgraduate and research students continue to be strongly attracted to critical criminology programmes. Though many respondents indicated that some students were unable to differentiate between critical and positivistic programmes, and that others would prefer the certainty of 'scientific' analysis, a good number noted that critical criminology continues to have a strong appeal.

> The responses of applicants to presentations on Open Days and Visit Days indicate they are generally interested in areas like inequalities, social construction of crime, crimes of the powerful etc. However, the impact of TV programmes is still felt — students still have a strange fascination with the 'serial killer' and still talk about wanting to 'get into the mind of the criminal' and so on. (Respondent 8)

> Honestly, I think some students have absolutely no idea about either one until they get to university. But, then, I firmly believe that if they are exposed to both [positivism and critical analysis] they will more often choose the critical courses because they're more interesting and thought provoking. I recently gave a guest lecture in a (unnamed) positivist department, where students mostly only get quantitative training and very little theoretical or critical engagement. They voraciously consumed the critical perspectives I offered, as if they were starving. So, I think, actually that what critical perspectives offer is more in line with what students imagine their University experience will be like (i.e., challenging and controversial and maybe a little infuriating, but endlessly interesting). (Respondent 1)

> I believe students do engage with critical criminology courses as is evidenced by our student recruitment and the growing recruitment of Masters and PhD students here. (Respondent 2)

> I think students are attracted to both approaches although quickly realise that positivist approaches are often exclusionary and esoteric whilst critical approaches are inclusive and empowering, hopefully. (Respondent 4)

It depends how they're sold [...] It isn't hard to "sell" if done properly and compared to the failure of traditional Criminal Justice and positivistic approaches which so evidently have failed and only manage and contain the conflicts endemic to advanced capitalist societies. (Respondent 19)

What the following summary of the findings of the survey explores, therefore, is how contemporary university policies and practices in the UK have impacted upon critical criminology teaching and research *and* how critical criminologists, individually and collectively, can best exploit or negate such developments for the furtherance of their key values, principles and political commitments.

2. The challenge: neoliberalism and the corporate university

Contributors to the survey demonstrated a sophisticated understanding of the neoliberal/corporate university and how it may pose a significant threat to the 'critical criminology imaginary' (Respondent 22).

A neoliberal university is characterised by internal cost-centred markets, which — externally facing — is desperate for funding of almost any kind, seeking new [national and international] markets relentlessly, with highly commodified relationships between staff, students, administrators. (Respondent 6)

The neoliberal university is run for a different purpose than that of education — it runs as a market-driven enterprise — it sees other universities as competitors whereas we see them as colleagues [...] The neoliberal university tries to maximise income by bringing in as many [national and international] students as possible — the students know that they are income-generators and feel a very different connection to the university as a result. (Respondent 7)

The neoliberal university is a corporation wherein knowledge is a cash commodity which we're encouraged to sell to students and prostitute our research to the highest bidders. (Respondent 19)

Neoliberalism turns universities into super markets, where students 'buy' degrees. (Respondent 3)

It is a hierarchical, macho, managerial style based on a business model of organisation where the free market dominates individual and strategic decision making. [...] It is the model of science, engineering and technology imposed on humanities and social science and it is not only pedagogically philistine but lacks any sense of democratic accountability. (Respondent 14)

It relates to trends towards corporatisation in the university, increasing emphasis on auditing and 'measuring performance' [of staff] and of seeing students as consumers, high tuition charges for students, pressure to enter into research relationships with industry, and an increasingly insecure, part-time workforce. (Respondent 1)

I see it as part of a system that reproduces and does little to contest the current situation of 'worker insecurity'. Students come to university knowing jobs are limited and they know they have to be competitive. Part of being competitive is keeping quiet. Not asking for higher wages, not asking for better conditions, not striking and so on. The university is now taking on this corporate business model and producing and reproducing these structures. (Respondent 21)

The logic of "academic capitalism" (Slaughter and Rhoades 2004) commodifies knowledge and transforms universities and educational praxis into spaces and modes of service-delivery. Power relations have shifted from professionals to management (Beckmann and Cooper 2004) and in this context managerial "information" and strategic-competitive rationalities come to supersede critical and reflexive forms of understanding [...] This shift is threatening existentially important possibilities of socio-political and cultural participation, innovation and vision that could and should be fostered in educational spaces. (Respondent 12)

The impact of neoliberalism on daily working practices appears to be felt far and wide by critical criminologists, and the survey highlighted a number of significant concerns, including:

i) Schools, departments and management

- Isolation of critical criminologists in some schools/departments
- Marginalisation of critical analysis as a 'sub-discipline' taught in a tokenistic way

- Critique by school management for delivering 'Marxist propaganda'
- The appointment of non-critical staff in a given department/school to dilute a critical criminology curriculum
- Top-down hierarchical management styles and centralisation of power
- Micro management
- Anti-democratic and authoritarian tendencies in university management

ii) Courses and workload pressure

- Combined curriculum with, for example (forensic) psychology or policing studies, and 'pick n' mix' degrees
- Greater emphasis on vocational courses
- Cost-saving activities, including large class sizes and library budget cuts
- Increases in student contact time at the expense of research time
- Increases in teaching and marking loads
- Increased links (both teaching and research) with the priorities of institutions of the criminal law and government-security agendas

iii) Activism, research and academic profession

- Less time for critical reflection, and undertaking independent and unfunded study
- Lack of recognition for activism and activities which enhance student learning/reflect the priorities of critical pedagogy
- Pressure to publish in a limited number of journals with high impact status
- Difficulties in generating funding for controversial topics/increased pressure to 'follow the money'
- Limitations of professional discretion and autonomy
- Further moves towards de-professionalisation/'degradation' (Braverman) through, for example, workload pressures, zero-hour contracts and the overuse of part-time and less qualified staff

iv) Wider educational policy

- A schooling system which infantalises, spoon-feeds and teaches people only to pass tests
- An emphasis on passing qualifications requiring only superficial rather than deep learning

- Government policies promoting competition between colleagues and universities
- Government priority/increasing focus on STEM subjects[7]
- University league tables emphasising performance and productivity

Alongside the above, issues were also raised in the survey around the following related areas:

> The decoupling of research from teaching is a form of McDonaldisation of the workplace. Teachers become, in effect, glorified disseminators of textbook knowledge — which is not to demean good pedagogy — while a small elite of researchers, research in elite institutions. As a result, the baseline for entering the classroom is much lower — they needn't have lived experience of the field, they just need to be able to convincingly relay textbook knowledge. And without the added plus of being a leading expert, academic workers can be pushed into longer hours and more mundane tasks. Yet what gives students' the most satisfaction is when they have someone on the cutting edge of their field, with lived experience of its empirical and theoretical fault lines, giving classes. It turns an abstract experience into a concrete one. (Respondent 10)

> What is insidious is the whole emphasis now on risk and ethics, now that is something which is having an impact on critical criminological work in a whole series of ways not least because university managers do not understand the theory, methodology and method that underpins critical criminological work and the fact that we are often researching institutions which are institutionally racist, sexist, violent, mendacious or whatever. The new university emphasis on ethics fails to see this never mind address it, a problem with criminology more generally as well. (Respondent 14)

> I think that the managerial priorities that are coupled with the neoliberal university manage to both prioritise and value the concept of 'realism'. The neoliberal university has arguably brought with it an institutionalised acceptance and indeed demand for research based on 'real world' or 'policy relevant' issues. (Respondent 22)

---

[7] STEM subjects include subjects in the fields of mathematics, engineering, chemistry, physics, computer and information technology science, and so on and so forth.

I think the main obstacles confronting researchers working in universities is lack of time and a REF-driven[8] research agenda, and particularly the emphasis on 'impact'. These problems are compounded for critical researchers. A lot of critical, campaigning research is long-term (take Scraton's Hillsborough work, for example, or the work of Tombs and Whyte around corporate crime) and is underpinned by far more important priorities and principles than 'impact statements' and REF scores. The REF is a divisive project and it does not enhance the quality of research or teaching. It may improve the number of publications individuals produce but the setting up of restrictive 'research themes' which 'force' staff into researching areas that fit with particular groups or 'units of assessment' negates against creative, critical work. The focus on numbers of outputs and the hierarchy of outputs also has the effect of potentially stifling critical criminological research. (Respondent 8)

For me the keenest pressure point is student marking, this seems rigged to an anodyne prescription; for instance our rubrics for marking cover 0–100, logically this would follow quartiles categorising achievement hinged at a mid-point, but no. In fact anything but. So what we have is 'exceptional' (90+), 'outstanding'(80+), 'excellent' (70+), 'very good'(60+), 'good'(50+), 'adequate'(40+) and 'poor' (>30+). There is no below 30, feedback must be positive and focused on how to improve. This is fine but there is pressure not to fail students, and not to give low end marks, furthermore the teaching staff have [been given] targets for how many students get particular grades (1st, 2:1 etc.), an obvious conflict of interest. (Respondent 18)

One respondent poetically summed up his position by claiming that neoliberalism was "turning academics into fund raisers, namely shopkeepers. Wasn't Napoleon right when he said that England is a country of shopkeepers?" (Respondent 3).

Three further issues central to the contemporary 'corporate university' were highlighted in the questionnaire: these were 'employability'; the construction of students as 'consumers'; and 'grant capture'. A number of respondents highlighted concerns with the 'employability' agenda, especially its implications in terms of criminal 'justice' training and its detrimental impact on deep learning.

---

[8] REF — Research Excellence Framework — which is the model used to evaluate academic research and give scores from 1–4 (with 4 being the highest).

Focus on 'employability' in a manner that devalues critical thinking and instead focuses on writing CVs and lots of talks from people in uniforms. (Respondent 5)

Employability is at the heart of the problem. Criminology will soon be criminal justice studies [...] The university is now a place to train students' for future employment, rather than a place of education. (Respondent 23)

Criminology, unfortunately, appears to be a training school for the police/probation — this I believe, is an inherent problem with criminology, further evidencing, as critics have argued, that criminology in its existence legitimises the state's CJS. (Respondent 17)

'Employability', which is nothing but a blatant intrusion of employer demands on the substantive educational processes, directly affects theoretical work and the familiarisation of students with the process of working with more abstract concepts. By nature, critical criminology depends on a theoretical critique of existing social structures and also on different modes of thinking about society. If this element is being marginalised or sacrificed in the name of labour market desirable skills and employability, then critical criminology will also be marginalised. (Respondent 11)

This emphasis on employability almost removes the academic soul from the discipline of criminology. (Respondent 22)

Do not even start... this is killing off any imagination, it forces people far too early to make life-changing choices and often only serves as a 'get a job' service instead of really finding out people's potential. (Respondent 12)

In addition, a number of colleagues raised concerns about the potential damage to working practices through the adoption of the language of consumerism.

In a climate in which the student has been encouraged to see themselves more and more as customers, and their degree classifications as 'the product', those courses perceived as more difficult or theoretically challenging may be viewed with trepidation and be less likely to be preferred. (Respondent 16)

The 'customer revolution' of higher education places a huge amount of responsibility upon university lecturers. 'The customer is always right'. (Respondent 22)

The pressure to 'give them what they want' is increasing rapidly and includes the expectation to provide massive amounts of 'support' and 'guidance' (which, in many cases, borders on 'doing it for them') [...] I have read that student complaints have risen in the last couple of years and whilst I obviously believe students have the right to take issue if they feel they are getting a raw deal and/or if they feel they have been treated unfairly, the idea that they are now 'paying for a degree' seems to be greatly exacerbating the problem of unreasonable or unfair complaints. (Respondent 8)

Most students do still respect the learner-teacher relationship just as they always have done — just an occasional few seem to believe our primary purpose is to provide a service of guaranteed grade delivery. But, I've certainly had to evolve far more rigorous boundaries and work harder to manage expectations on levels of support. (Respondent 16)

Some students will talk in these neoliberal terms but they are few and far between. The impact has been in how managers persistently use this discourse or something very similar, i.e., the 'student experience' to justify illogical, poorly conceived and indeed damaging policies. That is where the real problem lies. The interesting thing is that no matter how many times managers are told that the student experience is not homogenous and that many students want small class sizes, good teaching and serious engagement, managers still persist in reifying the 'customer/experience' model which is simplistic and out of touch. (Respondent 14)

Alas, intellectual labour cannot deliver the instant gratification that burgers, shoes, mobile phones and other gadgets can. (Respondent 11)

A third theme that was explored in depth in the survey was whether the current focus on income generation has curtailed or enhanced space for independent critical criminological research. A number of respondents were concerned about the possible negative implications of this trend.

I feel the steady focus of funding into certain areas of positivistic chronological research is damaging for critical criminology. (Respondent 2)

Projects likely to be funded are often (although not always) policy driven or evaluative projects which lack real criticality. (Respondent 8)

It has curtailed the space for serious theoretical work, regardless of the vantage point. Some of the most important scholarly work takes place over several years in the study, immersing oneself in complex ideas, and trying to develop new connections and combinations. But of course this does not bring in income and thus is demeaned. But when income generation is forced through using targets, and high pressure managerial tactics, it blunts all scholarship, regardless of its focus. (Respondent 10)

More important is relationships with commissioners, upsetting this apple cart threatens future bidding success, this is as sure as night follows day. One cannot be too critical of one's paymasters, be it in the policy evaluation field, or other research areas. This makes a lot of governmental research of rather limited value, I know this as I produce some of it — personally I wouldn't trust most of it, or at least read it very sceptically. (Respondent 18)

I am aware of pressure on researchers who have received funding from state organisations such as the police (e.g., through an ESRC CASE PhD studentship[9]) who have felt pressure from universities to 'sanitise' their research findings in order to make it more acceptable to partners and thus avoid threatening future funding collaborations. (Respondent 20)

The emphasis on income generation coincides with the dominant position of a criminological discipline fixed on 'problem solving' as opposed to Nils Christie's 'problem raising' approach to criminology. The discipline of criminology, within an income led era, has become embedded within the very structures that it ought to be critiquing [...] This embedded criminology operates more as a 'civil service criminology' which simply carries out particular functions for particular means. (Respondent 22)

---

[9] Economic and Social Research Council. For further details, see:
http://www.esrc.ac.uk/funding-and-guidance/postgraduates/prospective-students/

So does this all mean that the future of critical criminology is under significant threat? For some, but by no means all, of the respondents, the problems we face today are insurmountable.

> Criminology may be taught by police officers and prison governors in the near future. (Respondent 3)

> I think the 'sociology of deviancy' type criminology is reaching the end of its life and there will be a gradual move towards crime science and other more applied variations (e.g., policing degrees). (Respondent 5)

> Metaphorically speaking, [in ten years' time, critical criminology will be] probably stacking shelves in Tesco whilst mumbling something about structural inequality, hegemony and social harm. (Respondent 21)

Significantly, though, as Respondent 14 noted, "the problem is that I am not sure if [all the difficulties discussed above] are unique to critical criminologists". Further, there were also many voices of optimism and hope about the future of critical criminological teaching, networks and research in the UK.

> I personally think that critical criminology will grow in strength in the next 10 years. A number of centres are being set up across the country and there is cooperation between some of the academics involved. Our course will continue to grow and with the intake of PhD students will be able to influence developments in the future. (Respondent 2)

> Realistically, I think it will probably be slightly stronger than it is right now and holding its own. I don't imagine it 'taking over the world', but I think it will be continuing to fight a good fight. (Respondent 1)

> I hope we will have educated a new generation of critical scholars — given the critical discourses coming from students over the last few years there is space for optimism. (Respondent 7)

> I think we will resist — it is the one subject I have hope and faith in, so I see us carrying on, but with significant struggle. (Respondent 13)

> The European Group is in a more healthy state as far as I can see than the European Society of Criminology which has its yearly meeting and that's about it. I couldn't contemplate being involved in that kind of organisation/conference, I would rather watch paint dry, criminological or otherwise. (Respondent 14)

It is to these voices of hope and the possibilities of resistance and contestation against some the most problematic tendencies of the corporate university that this summary now turns.

3. The critical criminological imaginary: there is an alternative

> I think academics have a real tendency to moan a lot (myself included). In fact, the job is still a very good one in terms of pay and autonomy. Conditions of service are another story. So there is a process of degradation going on as described brilliantly by Braverman but I think it is still really important to keep this in context so while a relativistic perspective can only take one so far, nonetheless academics are not standing in food banks or working in factories with terrible death rates. This is not to underestimate the pains of academia that sometimes occur, which is central to a capitalist division of labour, but I am a bit sceptical of academics who cry that their professionalism is being undermined when their everyday practices leave a lot to be desired both professionally and personally. (Respondent 14)

Findings from the survey indicate that there are a number of ways forward that are immediately available to us, individually and collectively.

i) Acknowledging our strengths

It should be recognised that, despite the unwelcome changes brought about through the corporatisation of the university, much of the critical criminology curriculum has remained unchanged. Critical criminology in the UK is still in a considerable position of strength in terms of numbers of full-time academics, postgraduate students and the content of criminological programmes. Some schools/departments in universities are in stronger positions than others, but, at this time, we are definitely not witnessing the terminal decline of critical criminology.

> In terms of *what* we teach, there is virtually no interference; we are left to get on with what we want to do. It is interesting as we might

have thought that, given the neoliberal propensity to dominate and subjugate, as well as successive government changes to the education system, that the curriculum in HE [Higher Education] would have been affected. So far that has not happened although there are signs: for example, the endless demand that students learn and indeed pursue work-based programmes is a possible sign of things to come. (Respondent 14)

The university is mostly concerned with numbers of students rather than the educational content of their degrees. I think the latter matters very little to some senior managers and, in a perverse way, this has benefited us as they don't really care if the degree content is critical or not. (Respondent 8)

In some respects I think critical pedagogy can be preserved within this context, provided those who are writing the modules and programmes remain committed to a critical edge. Sometimes the demands of the 'bean counters' and those who are interested in 'marketing' within universities can be pacified with careful language and branding. On the other hand, I think certain disciplines/fields (like criminology) can marshal strong arguments for why a critical pedagogy is essential at this particular historical moment and within this 'neoliberal' context. (Respondent 1)

ii) Recognising continuities and drawing on past successes

We also need to very carefully consider just how different the problems in the 'corporate university' today are from the past. We need a sophisticated analysis of the socio-economic, political and policy dimensions shaping universities in our historical conjuncture, but we should be equally aware of continuities as well as discontinuities.

Well, look [...] I would say that things do not get harder nor easier necessarily — depending on what the comparison point is, new problems arise — while some are enduring (and others diminish). (Respondent 6)

Apart from the emphasis on work-based learning, and the micro management of our working lives, I don't think it is that different except we had more time in the past, especially during the summer period. The vanishing act around time has had a crucial impact. It is important not to idealise the past, critical criminologists are also agents in their own destiny, more so than many occupational groups, so I think it is really important not to valorise the problems we are experiencing at present. (Respondent 14)

Indeed, conditions may be different, but even in our troubled times this should not lead to overly pessimistic analysis. There are undoubtedly some signs pointing towards guarded optimism for the future.

> I think we may be at a moment when critical research is poised to get more attention. The current government's blatant disinterest in 'evidence' and their explicit emphasis on ideology and a particular political agenda means that criminological knowledges — of any description — are not particularly powerful at the moment, unless they fit exactly with government thinking (and not much research does). It seems that this is a good moment for critical researchers to engage more forcefully in what are now unambiguously *political* arguments about crime and criminal justice. (Respondent 1, emphasis in original)

> I think there is space for optimism, given the popularity of criminology. (Respondent 15)

> I think actually we are in a stronger position [than in the past] because a) critical criminology has withstood the test of time — it is still here and it's growing; b) administrative approaches REALLY haven't worked; and c) we are in a political moment when there is a potential opportunity to argue more forcefully against the 'mainstream'. (Respondent 1, emphasis in original)

Critical criminology must also continue its tradition of critiquing domination and oppression (including those forms that pertain to the university) and promoting the goals of liberation, emancipation and human freedom. We must adopt a holistic approach drawing upon critical theory to help us understand our own lived working realities.

iii) *We can make a difference: exploiting contradictions and subverting the logic of the corporate university*

It is possible to challenge the logic and practices of the corporate university. Whilst we must acknowledge that we are working with considerable constraints, we can still devise strategies within our own workplaces that can rearticulate policies to reflect the interests of critical analysis. There remain countervailing tendencies and opportunities for the greater enhancement and development of critical analysis. As Respondent 14 notes, within universities there remains contingencies, "contradictions and opportunities for contestation".

> Increasing pressure and homogenisation leads to cracks. Calls for social justice increase. Academics can still carve out spaces and the classroom is a privileged arena. (Respondent 4)

> I don't see new openings per se, but what I do see is critical researchers becoming more savvy. Taking on board Gramsci's advice and treating spaces within the university as contradictory, even spaces that were designed to side-line our work. Impact is one example, it was brought in to in effect give solace to policy-friendly, corporate-friendly research. But a lot of critical colleagues are learning how to evidence critical research that is producing far more meaningful change than a bit of policy advice. So all dimensions of our workplace are subvertable. (Respondent 10)

> [What is] crucial is recognising that history is not closed off: it is one of the most important things that Stuart Hall emphasized, it is full of possibilities, so it is easy to become melancholic and pessimistic but the academic workplace like everywhere else has its own problems around legitimacy, like the state more generally. So challenging, contesting and being involved at all sorts of levels was and remains the key to struggle. (Respondent 14)

A number of strategies were suggested that could help challenge neoliberal policies. Respondent 1 gives an example of arguments deployed to resist market pressures and management demands for combining curriculums.

> There is some pressure, of course (like everywhere), to cost cut. This priority has been recently manifesting in a certain amount of pressure on us to offer a combined curriculum with forensic psychology (which the market research shows is a popular student choice combined with criminology). This is being resisted by the criminology team because taking an 'individual pathology' approach to studying problems of crime and justice is in diametric contradiction to our approaches. Moreover, we are arguing that combining these areas lacks coherence from a student perspective and, in actual fact, we think making such combinations would negatively affect student retention. So far, we have been successful in making these arguments, despite the pressure. (Respondent 1)

The emphasis on employability can also be used as a means to strengthen the critical criminology curriculum.

> We have tried to delimit the harms of employability, we are pragmatic enough to understand our students will need and want to work and thus we have designed our programme to equip students for a wide range of employment opportunities. My favourite example is how many start our courses wanting to join the police compared to so few who finish the course still wanting to. They refocus their career aspirations into much more social and critical employment activities. (Respondent 19)

> We have, so far, been able to focus on skills that we feel are defensible, such as: constructing and representing robust arguments, presentation skills, critical thinking skills, effective time management, collaborating/cooperating with others. We have argued that the fields of crime and criminal justice are so changeable that we need to equip students, first and foremost, with independent thinking and learning skills, rather than the 'nuts and bolts' of a (broken) and ever changing system. (Respondent 1)

> Arguably, for students who want to work within the fields of social or criminal justice etc., critical thinking and a deep understanding of power relations and structural inequalities are essential and, I would imagine, things like creative thinking, empathy, teamwork and the ability to be independent would be desirable qualities for employers. (Respondent 8)

> Some of our most successful candidates are students who have really embraced critical criminology; they have proven to be the left-field thinkers and the devotees of social justice, participating in volunteer projects. As a result they find jobs in research and NGOs after university. This probably is not given its dues by the professional development unit. (Respondent 10)

> The time it [employability] takes up for a start and its encroachment across all of the different years of the degree, I don't like that dimension to it. Like everything else though it is contradictory as a lot of students want to go into what might be termed social democratic jobs: probation, youth work, social work, rape crisis centres etc. So working for a couple of hours a week in these kinds of organisations can be terrific for them. I am not really

convinced that the universities are pushing people into being clones of the state, e.g., police officers: it is more complex as the universities, given they are so free market orientated, would not bother if all of our students became social workers, so long as the universities can point to healthy employment statistics. So as I say it is really complex and contradictory I think. (Respondent 14)

'Employability' can be a genuine opportunity for building greater links with radical community activists, pressure groups and NGOs, and work experience with such organisations can help facilitate emancipatory objectives. Further, there are opportunities for critical researchers to gain research grants and develop research profiles within the corporate university.

The focus on income generation can have positive effects, it depends how it is handled. When it is used to encourage fieldwork, rather than meet targets, it is a fantastic tool. Indeed, critical criminologists have demonstrated critical scholarship can win big research council grants, and as a result forge new spaces for critical inquiry and early career researchers. (Respondent 10)

Some alternative funders (e.g., Leverhulme[10] are particularly interested in funding 'alternative' types of projects. (Respondent 1)

I think that grants in terms of being bought out would make life easier. There is no doubt about that given the everyday demands of the job and the intense micromanagement that is intrinsic to everyday academic life. On the other hand, it is still possible to do critical work, without the benefit of a huge grant. It is certainly possible to do critical interventionist work without any grant, just show up at the organisation or place where you want to help out. In that sense I think sometimes critical criminology has lost its way and uses the emphasis on grants as an excuse (although maybe that's too strong a word) to almost imply that without grants interventions are not possible. I don't believe that. [...] Interestingly enough some of the most influential books in criminology as a discipline overall have been written by critical criminologists, e.g., Hall et al., Foucault, Brownmiller, Smart, yet received little by way of grants to write them, so there is a very interesting contradiction lying at the heart of what constitutes scholarship and research, and

---

[10] An independent body that makes funds available for education and research. See http://www.leverhulme.ac.uk/

the impact of both. Also what differentiates critical criminology clearly is that those who see themselves as critical criminologists are still very clear that they will not take grants to make the state function better. There is still some clear red water there between 'us' and 'them'. (Respondent 14)

There are also other university policies that may provide new space for critical engagement.

One thing I am proud of about the institution I work for is they support and encourage critical and reflective teaching and engagement with the wider community to enhance all the population's chances of access to higher education and to enable academics to make a real positive contribution to the community they service and the discipline in which they undertake research to influence policy. [...] The emphasis the university places on widening participation, recognizing many of our graduates will work in professions that can support and enhance the experiences of some of the marginalized and excluded groups within society. Also the faculty prides itself on the engagement of its academics in research that relates to the issues in the local area and tries to influence policy. This is supported by managers in terms of supporting seminars, conferences and other activities, which give back to the community and the students they service. (Respondent 2)

Diversity policy indirectly supports the development of critical criminological programmes. (Respondent 4)

Critical criminologists must continue to emphasise what critical analysis brings to the table — how it can assist students, making the right arguments, pointing to the importance of education as an end in itself rather than a means to an end (employability) and the personal rewards of a good education. Alongside this, critical criminologists must continue to perform the role of the 'transformative' or 'organic' intellectual looking to change common sense into good sense in the classroom and via their research.

iv) Fostering collegiality, mutual support, cooperation and solidarity

What is essential is that we identify the problems we face collectively in our given historical conjuncture, and share best practice and ways of challenging policies which hinder rather than enhance critical pedagogy and emancipatory politics.

> If we are strategic, and collaborative, our socialist ethos and communitarian practice could be our ace card. We need to work together, across institutions and across nations. We have to use these collaborations to build the foundations for major research grants which can create spaces for critical inquiry, and to support top quality publications. In addition, we need to share wisdom — for example, critical colleagues who have built 4* impact case studies need to share their success, and explain how it can be done. In short, solidarity rather than competition is a wonderful glue, how can we be strategic and employ this solidarity to play the REF game. Not just so we can 'win' the REF game, but so critical researchers obtain the space to do emancipatory scholarship, and become highly rated individuals within their own institutions. (Respondent 10)

> I think we should form alliances with others like us who want to keep on carrying out research on our terms — to work and publish together and develop a critical mass of academics who are resisting by making our own meaningful and fruitful connections. (Respondent 7)

> Collaboration and cross-fertilisation of ideas is always the best way to enhance research and teaching in my opinion. (Respondent 2)

A number of respondents indicated that European Group provided such a sense of solidarity and support.

> We share ideas, materials, experiences, we provide mutual support and at times it is a bit of a haven. Most of all I think we try to show through what we do and how we do it and indeed who we do it with that there are other ways of working and other kinds of work than that which dominates the discipline. (Respondent 6)

> To me the group and its members help me to recharge, to continue to believe in good people and a better world. (Respondent 12)

> The annual conference is inspirational. The existence of the group, its communications and of course the conference provides intellectual support and a sense of a community of critically like-minded scholars, which is invaluable. (Respondent 16)

We must resist individualisation and competition and continue to provide support to colleagues in 'competitor universities'. This is a choice academics can still make. We decide how much of the neoliberal logic we internalise. We must not lose our understanding of human agency and the importance of aspiring to critical values in our daily working lives.

Direct engagement with students is fundamental to the role of teacher/facilitator in higher education. Relations with students, and student engagement with the theoretical and political priorities of critical criminology, were also covered extensively in the survey. A number of respondents indicated how consumerism could be challenged 'on the ground'.

> [Consumerism] has made students a little more demanding and perhaps less forgiving. As they are paying for their education, they sometimes think that means they are 'purchasing a product'. But, there are ways of helping students to think differently about this and setting out a different way of thinking about their role in the learning process early on can really help set the tone on a module and get them more involved in their own learning. My favourite way to do this is to tell them that they can't just buy a gym membership and expect to get fit without going to the gym. They have to lift the weights and run on the treadmill. So it is with their education. They have to read the books and work hard at completing their assignments, etc... (Respondent 1)

> I sympathise greatly with students having to borrow tens of thousands of pounds to pay for their education and I oppose this strongly. I also understand that criminology students (and students of other social science or humanities subjects) might ask why they are paying exactly the same fees as students who study sport or drama or media (and who obviously have daily access to costly facilities). (Respondent 8)

To some, making alliances with students and presenting a united front against the realities of neoliberal policies in universities today may seem naive. It is almost taken for granted for students to be dismissed as disengaged and conservative. But are students less radical than in the past? And can students be re-engaged? The survey findings indicate that things are perhaps not as clear-cut as they first seem.

I am not sure [if students are less engaged]. It is hard to gauge. The 'massification' of HE means that we need to be careful about confusing absolute and relative numbers in any longitudinal comparisons. (Respondent 6)

Over the last 3 years students have appeared to be much more engaged with critical discourses I am glad to say — that is not surprising given the context in which they have grown up and the problems they are currently subjected to. (Respondent 7)

[Are students more or less engaged than in the past?] Difficult question as some of the most profound challenges to what has been happening in the last few years have come from student protests, the fall-out and collateral damage from these protests has been shamefully ignored by academics, I think, including critical criminologists. On the other hand, my overall feeling from my classroom experience is that there is a distinct lack of engagement in class. On the other hand, it is easy to idealise the past, seminars 40 years ago were also dull and the lecturers were always complaining at the lack of reading so the idea that everybody was sitting around reading and digesting Marx, Engels and the New Left is glamorising a past that never really existed either. It is a bit like rock music, everybody idealises the 1960s but Engelbert Humperdinck had the three best-selling singles in 1967 and in 1968, the year of the barricades, the best-selling single was 'What a Wonderful World' by Louis Armstrong followed by 'I Pretend' by Des O'Connor, the seventh best single was 'Little Arrows' by Leapy Lea and 'Hey Jude' by the Beatles was only number 10. The point I am making is that memory, including criminological memory, has to be treated with some respect and indeed scepticism. (Respondent 14)

I think students remain committed to political issues, rather it is contemporary political culture that is alienating to students. (Respondent 15)

Strategies were also suggested that could enhance student engagement through critical pedagogy.

[To overcome student disengagement] I think the best ways are through the pedagogic approach — good use of films, newspaper articles, controversial stories, narrative accounts — and getting them debating some of the issues. (Respondent 1)

I think our students have fewer opportunities to engage with contemporary political and socioeconomic issues because of the absence of any significant organisational levers locally. The student union is purely cosmetic in this respect, and local party and other activist organisations are disturbingly quiet. No matter how persistently we aim to bring these issues to the attention of students in the classroom, the wider environment is not really conducive to higher social and political awareness. (Respondent 11)

Like Leonard Cohen's song, I "have grown old and bitter" so I bang my drum, challenge their apathy, but I understand their status and location. I aspire merely to make them less ill-liberal and more humane and empathetic but for many that is a radical challenge as they're the generation who are most entrenched with the ideology that there is no alternative. The poor bastards — what a world we've bequeathed them! (Respondent 19)

Critical criminologists must continue to emphasise the need for research-informed teaching, deploy critical pedagogy and highlight the importance of making critical theory accessible and understandable in modules.

v) A voice that needs to be heard: disseminating emancipatory knowledge and challenging power

As highlighted above, critical analysis needs to continue to acknowledge current power relations and problems associated with the corporate university. The voice of the critical criminologist is important and needs to be heard. One way in which we can disseminate emancipatory knowledge is through engagement with the media.

It's important for European Group [EG] members to engage with the media in order to counter dominant narratives around crime and deviance. EG members should be encouraged to draft press releases to highlight critical findings (many universities are actually very good at offering assistance with this). (Respondent 20)

I suppose finding sympathetic journalists is one strategy. Another is joining *The Conversation* — which is a consortium of universities which cover the news from an academic perspective. There are seldom stories covered by *The Conversation* on crime and justice issues and it would be great for critical voices to become the ones most frequently heard on these topics. (Respondent 1)

Start blogging for something like *The Conversation* (http://theconversation.com/uk). You receive a wide audience and things do get picked up from there in the mainstream media. (Respondent 16)

There is space, but this has to be imaginative and not through the conventional channels (typically sound bites for the local press), but through engaging documentary film makers (for example). (Respondent 15)

Re strategies:

1. You need to have a newsworthy story, a hook, something that implicates a high profile figure, or exposes a sham within a government department [...] I have never had a journalist pick up a story because it was rigorous and important research. But when it implicated a high profile figure, it was game on.

2. You need to develop rapport with journalists in your area, often it begins with the odd interview, and before you know it you are sharing leads. But at the end of the day we have to be the gold mine. The more gold you offer a journalist, and the more regularly you do it, the more collateral you build with them. But one has to be astute, 95% of journalists are wastes of time, you need to give the gold to those who are serious about their work and its important power-challenging function.

3. You need to tie everything together and give it in a gift wrapped box to journalists.

4. Documentary filmmakers are great value, many have the method of a critical social scientist. My most enjoyable relationships with the media come from this angle.

(Respondent 10)

There is also the fact that that we *don't* need to get involved with the media, there are times when it is better not to engage with them, e.g., what use is a 10 second sound bite on a TV programme, will that change hearts and minds? — I doubt it. I think actually that critical criminologists need to work out their strategy for the media which I don't think they have. For a discipline that spends a lot of time critiquing the media, that critique seems to vanish a bit when it comes to media invites. Engagement should be approached with a seriously sceptical hat and head on, especially given that universities are desperate for any media appearances, which should make us extremely suspicious. (Respondent 14, emphasis in the original)

When dealing [with] the media you can often find yourselves engaging in or using the language of the state. So while media engagement may be beneficial in getting a certain message across (e.g., campaign against certain development), in doing so one may be encouraged or indeed coerced into sacrificing or shedding some of his/her true critical opinion [...] In short, good for getting your message across — bad for the soul of the critical criminologist! (Respondent 22)

Some medium of getting 'the message out' is essential but we must not become mere technicians of the state and the powerful, and must be aware of pitfalls.

vi) The European Group: promoting craftsmanship, confidence and support

The European Group has a tradition of promoting craftsmanship and could perhaps provide a role in ensuring that standards in teaching and scholarship are maintained. A number of respondents highlighted strategies that could be adopted by the European Group to help sustain critical analysis in universities in the UK.

- Mentoring of junior colleagues
- Research collaboration between junior and senior colleagues
- Treating students as learners and critical thinkers, not customers
- Brainstorming sessions and support groups on the best ways to gain funding and to develop ideas for research bids
- To be a professional body/society with accreditations to support isolated colleagues, and perhaps a membership fee
- Development of a critical pedagogy working group
- European Group publications (book series and journal)
- Work out our own alternative 'benchmark' for criminology programmes
- Steering group intervening publicly and expressing a critical criminology voice in current policy debates
- Sharing information, struggles and points of contestation

How the European Group should engage with other criminologists was unclear in the survey, with some suggesting it should have a less open and pluralistic approach, whilst others argued that it should engage more readily with more mainstream criminologies.

> Continuing to be a strong organising influence and place of support for critical scholarship and helping scholars to be uncompromising about insisting on [a] critical curriculum. (Respondent 1)

> The Group needs to organised along tighter lines, and perhaps sacrifice some of the pluralism in favour of actively fostering the intellectual lines that are more closely associated with the critical/radical tradition. (Respondent 11)

> I think the EG may also seek to 'cross the divide' with other 'less critical' criminologists. As someone educated at a critical criminological department and now working at a far less critical school — I think it would be worthwhile for the EG to try and reach out to 'realist' criminologists. (Respondent 22)

4. Facing the future with the philosophy of hope

What remains crucial is that we fully acknowledge the problems of our historical conjuncture, but that we go forward collectively with a sense of confidence and hope.

> Despite the extent of negative feeling within academia at present, we cannot forget the amount of brilliant critical work that is being carried out in the UK and abroad and the real impact that this work can have (the Hillsborough campaign being an obvious example). I also think critical criminology has managed to get a good foothold in British universities and whilst I think there will be real pressure to 'mainstream' or 'go forensic' in the forthcoming years, there are some really good new criminologists coming through and that is where the future of the discipline lies. So perhaps the future lies in good quality post-grad provision to ensure the next generation get a chance. (Respondent 8)

> I think the main thing is not to get overwhelmed with the idea that the state has unrelenting power that is simply running a neoliberal truck over us, things are bad, especially for the poor and the powerless but there are still some real spaces to engage in contestation. There is a real crisis of legitimacy with the police at

the minute and critical criminology has played a part in that. So long as we think we can make an inch of difference then I think we are doing our job. When links are made with outside groups and organisations, old and new, then that is fulfilling the ideal that has always been there as the beating heart of critical criminology. (Respondent 14)

There remain spaces for contestation and the realisation of our hopes. We must continue to engage in the battle for hearts and minds in the academy and beyond its walls. Let us provide scholarly and nuanced accounts of the problems we face today and let us work together to find ways to address them as best we can. Critical analysis remains intellectually powerful: understanding its implications can change people's lives and influence government policies. Critical criminological writings in the past have predicted, with somewhat disturbing accuracy at times, many of the problems we face in the here and now. Critical scholarship will continue to be acknowledged and have impact 'in the real world' and we should face the future not with trepidation, but with confidence that our arguments are strong and that collectively we can start to challenge problematic policies and practices of the corporate university.

Part B:

Iatrogenic Penal Harms
and
Visions of Justice

6.

Beyond Criminal Justice: 'It's a long road to wisdom, but it is a short one to being ignored'

This chapter is an edited and revised version of the introduction and conclusion to the book Beyond Criminal Justice *which was published by the European Group in June 2014. The chapter is co-written with J.M. Moore.*

> You see, if I look at my own experience [...] because I live for more or less a century. I am 84 now [...] when you have such a large space to see all the things [...] all the things you have seen change [...] When you look in such a sort of way on it then [...] you know that things can change very fast [...] I am firmly convinced that nobody knows about the future [...] We should certainly not think that criminal justice could not be abolished. (Louk Hulsman, cited in Roberts, 2007: 36)

The *European Group for the Study of Deviance and Social Control* (European Group) has for forty-three years provided opportunities for scholars, activists and students to critically engage with issues connected to state punishment, 'crime' and 'deviant' behaviour. At European Group conferences, state punishment has consistently been exposed as an instrument of dominance. From the very first European Group conference in 1973, the influence of penal abolition has been both clear and welcome. This influence has been both intellectual — how we see and understand the state's penal apparatus — and has defined the values of the European Group.

Abolitionism historically has had many forms; the most significant being the eighteenth- and nineteenth-century movements for the abolition of slavery and the continuing campaigns for the abolition of the death penalty. What characterises all abolitionist movements is a rejection of the possibility of reforming their target institutions. Neither slavery nor the death penalty needed reform. They required abolition. For penal abolitionists, the same principal applies to state punishment in general and prisons in particular. Marijke Meima (2014: 195) describes abolitionism as:

> The movement — grass-roots as well as academic — that tries to reach the diminishing and finally the abolition of the criminal law system, its rationale as well as its institutions.

Whilst reformers seek to find ways of making penal sanctions more effective, abolitionists represent a much more fundamental challenge; for us, the penal system is not malfunctioning but fundamentally flawed, it needs abolition. Included within the broader abolitionist movement are more specific abolitionist campaigns, including those arguing for an abolition of the imprisonment of women (Carlen, 1990), people with mental health problems (Hudson, 1993) and children (Goldson, 2005).

Penal abolitionism has a long history. For example, William Godwin's *Enquiry into Political Justice* "precluded all ideas of punishment or retribution" (1793: 237), whilst Edouard Desprez published his ground breaking text *De L'Abolition de l'emprisonnement* in 1868. Abolitionists recognise the reality that harmful acts, interpersonal conflicts, violence, problematic behaviours and a multitude of other troubles exist. What is distinctive about their thinking (and action) is the ways they chose to interpret and respond to such phenomena. By recognising that the way acts can be interpreted is socially constructed — for example, by being classified as 'crimes' — abolitionists offer the opportunity of seeing these acts in a variety of different ways. This in turn leads to the opening up of the possibility of a wide range of solutions (Hulsman, 1986).

Whereas the paradigm of 'criminal justice' funnels a wide variety of acts into the category of 'crime' — and thereby resolvable only through firstly the identification of someone to blame and secondly through the deliberate infliction of pain, what we popularly refer to as *punishment* — abolitionism seeks to understand each act in its own situational context and thereby offers the possibility of a multitude of possible resolutions (Hulsman, 1986). For abolitionists, the sanctions of the criminal justice system in general, and prisons in particular, neither addresses the underlying issues nor provides any restoration to victims. Instead, these 'solutions' are counterproductive, generate additional pain, produce social divisions and create further problematic behaviours (Christie, 1981; 1993). By returning conflicts to the parties involved, addressing them in their context and seeking to allow the participants to invent their own solutions, abolitionists offer a creative alternative to the crude infliction of blame and pain.

What's wrong with criminal justice?

Criminal justice language and thought has become embedded in our 'common sense' understanding of our world; it has, in a Gramscian sense, established its hegemony. But like much common sense, we only need to scratch the surface to see that its reality is far less impressive than its ideology. Criminal justice's *claims* are striking. It, in the name of the people, ensures fairness and 'justice'. It protects all equally and is enforced on all in society in a uniform manner. It protects society by controlling people who are dangerous, responding appropriately and proportionately to harmful and damaging acts. Through both its very existence and its operation, it prevents future problematic behaviour. Its operation benefits 'victims', who are portrayed as being at its core and is against 'offenders'. These two groups, who are at the centre of its focus, are portrayed as belonging in separate and distinct categories.

Central to abolitionist thought is a deconstruction of these claims based on an empirical observation of the *reality* of criminal justice practice. In its day-to-day operation, criminal justice reinforces the structural inequalities that characterise our socially unjust and unequal societies (Scraton, 2007). Its energies are focused predominately on controlling marginalised and powerless people whose 'crimes' are relatively harmless whilst failing to exercise control over powerful actors who are responsible for many of the most harmful behaviours (Hillyard and Tombs, 2004). With its focus on the infliction of pain as its ultimate outcome it is concerned with creating more not less harm (Christie, 1981). Despite its philosophical claim, in practice it fails to provide either security or protection for society (Mathiesen, 1990).

Whereas victims are a relative recent discovery for criminal justice, abolitionist critique has always taken victims seriously. A major part of the abolitionist project has been to return the conflict to the victim; to actually place them at the very centre of the conflict-resolution process (Christie, 1977). However, in so doing, it rejects the false dichotomy between the victim and the 'offender', recognising instead that often they have great similarities. Crucially, they share a common interest in successfully resolving their conflict. Abolitionist critiques have also highlighted the differential treatment of victims' experience — based around their class, 'race', gender, sexuality and age — at the hands of criminal justice agencies. They have also challenged claims that reforms have sought to address the needs of victims. These reforms have often focused on reducing the rights of the accused and increasing the severity of pain inflicted on the convicted; changes which do nothing to address the marginalisation of victims and their needs. In their implementation, such reforms purely exploit victims to justify enhancing the repressive capabilities of the state, which continues to be deployed to consolidate and extend unequal power relations.

So what, then, does the criminal process actually achieve? It is particularly good at damaging human beings and then 'Othering' them so that they become social outcastes. It creates false hierarchies, delivers pain and morally degrades the poor and powerless. Significantly, the criminal process is also a means of using people to demonstrate power — state power. It has also, as Sebastian Scheerer (2014: 88) has highlighted, proved to be very successful in the colonisation of the life world. The penal system, consumed by a "pathological over-criminalisation", has led to not only the rapid expansion of state bureaucracies and placed new populations of petty offenders under penal control but has also significantly increased the repressive capabilities of state power.

In their opposition to violence, abolitionists are particular concerned about the violence of the carceral state (Sim, 2009, 2014). For Jacqueline Bernat de Celis (2014), prisons are places of brutality, harm and *death*. The assertion that prisons are places of *death* — literal, civil and social death (Bernat de Celis, 2014; Scott, 2015) — threatens the legitimacy of penal institutions and this is especially so when it comes to corporeal death — the death of the body. Scraton and Chadwick (2014) firmly locate the cause of the deaths of prisoners in the violence of penal institutions. Those who take their own lives in prison, they argue, should not be seen as deficient. Rather, we should consider them as "responding *rationally* to inhuman policies and practices which are inherent in harsh regimes" (Scraton and Chadwick, 2014: 168, emphasis in the original). By recognising that prisons are difficult places for people to survive, Scraton and Chadwick challenged the individual pathology underscoring official discourses of deaths in custody. For abolitionists, self-inflicted deaths in prison are not the result of the failings of 'high risk inadequates' but of the iatrogenic harms of imprisonment.

Ida Koch (2014) has also exposed the iatrogenic penal harms, detailing how the long-term damage caused by the mental isolation of solitary confinement can destroy previous attachments and make future mutuality virtually impossible. The harms suffered by the prisoners are extensive and include: nightmares, anxiety, suicide attempts (sometimes successfully), self-injury, difficulties in concentrating, a loss of memory, fatigue, rage, declining physical health, hallucinations, and paranoia. The impact of isolation continues beyond release, with great difficulties being experienced in engaging in social interaction and with some reporting themselves "no longer (able to) cope with physical and emotional intimacy and contact" (Ibid.: 104). Koch's (2014: 104) conclusion is that detention in isolation is both unnecessary and "inhuman and cruel treatment"; a violation of human rights.

The importance of developing abolitionist theory

For Rene van Swaaningen (2014: 173–4), we should follow Michel Foucault's advice and avoid the mistake of "thinking we can present another — better — "law and order" so as to create a more righteous society". In examining the relationship between criminology and abolitionism, he highlights a major difference — abolitionism ultimately leads to the questioning of the legitimacy of the prison. One response is then to extend beyond criminology and its focus on 'crime' and punishment to one focused on social harms and the possibilities of penal abolitionism. The central premise of the abolitionism of Jacqueline Bernat de Celis (2014), the friend and collaborator of the great Dutch abolitionist Louk Hulsman (1986), is that for penal abolitionists the prison is "unacceptable" and must be rejected as a legitimate response to human conflict.

Penal incarceration should be rejected for three fundamental reasons: first, the prison is counter-intuitive to normal human values, ethical codes and commitments to human rights and well-being; second, the prison reflects an abstraction of humanity and its continued existence can lead only to further reification and alienation; and third, the prison has a clear political function in maintaining social inequalities (Bernat de Celis, 2014). The prison cannot be humanised and therefore a further central unifying theme of penal abolitionists is the demand for radical alternatives to prisons and non-penal forms of intervention. This requires radical transformation of the social system which perpetuates penal incarceration alongside pragmatic interventions for handling human conflict and problematic conduct that respect human diversity. To be an abolitionist means bearing witness to the violence of incarceration and being prepared "to stand up against it" (Bernat de Celis, 2014: 22).

Within abolitionist theory, the penal apparatus of the State is firmly located within its socio-economic, historical and political *contexts*. As Joe Sim (2009, 2014) has highlighted, prisons are 'warehouses for the poor' and thus, to remain both theoretically and politically potent, abolitionism must continue to engage with contemporary writings on the political economy of punishment and related disciplines (Scott, 2013). The increasing resort to the use of imprisonment is seen by Sim as a direct result of this political situation. However, the politics of imprisonment place considerable strain on the penal estate's capacity and have contributed to a deepening of the crisis within the prison. The English and Welsh prison system's expansion has accelerated and resistance within prison has, at least to date, largely been managed successfully. In a time of austerity for the majority of the population, Sim's (2014: 148) reference to "an increasingly fragile social order beset by economic decline, industrial stagnation and political conflict" seems highly relevant. In such a context, the abolitionist's challenge to the very legitimacy of the prison and penal system is particularly important.

It remains a truism, then, that the increasing authoritarianism in penal regimes and policing practices can only be understood when located within the wider drift towards a more authoritarian "law and order society" (Hall et al., 2013: 270). Raffaele Calderone and Piere Valeriani (2014: 116) have similarly argued that prisons are "theatres of class conflict" and it is therefore important, if anti-prison activists are to be successful, that they make connections with left-wing political organisations and other social movements promoting freedom, social justice and the recognition of common humanity. This is echoed by Heinz Steinert (2014), who has also called for abolition to be understood as part of a wider political struggle against repression, domination and inhumanity.

Pat Carlen (1983: 203) has observed that whilst the history of penology has been characterised by "the failure of punishment in general, and imprisonment in particular [...] [p]hilosophies of punishment, by contrast, have enjoyed a continuing success". Penal abolitionism represents a concerted assault upon the logic of the penal rationale and its current deployment in the institutions of the criminal law. It is therefore essential, as Willem de Haan (2014) has pointed out, for abolitionist analysis to be thoroughly grounded in social theory and moral and political philosophy. In a similar vein, Heinz Steinert (2014) has argued that it is important to explore the philosophical roots of penal abolitionism, and in particular a more considered debate about the philosophical connections between penal abolitionism and Marxist criminologies (Taylor et al., 1973). Indeed, for Heinz Steinert (2014: 26, 47-8), there is a "natural sympathy" between the two radical and emancipatory traditions — both penal abolitionism and Marxism have similar value bases and, to differing extents, draw upon the assumptions of a libertarian socialism that predates the emergence of both perspectives. Steinert (2014) draws attention to connections between critical criminologies and abolitionism and the values and principles of libertarian socialism, such as those around freedom, solidarity and socialist diversity. In this sense, abolitionism is a broad-based socialist liberation movement aiming to emancipate the powerless and dehumanised. Abolitionism is then the search for non-authoritarian ways in which the consequences of 'crime' and troublesome conduct can be minimised. As such, penal abolitionism must promote and be predicated upon an emancipatory politics and praxis.

Beyond criminal 'justice'

At the heart of abolitionist critique is a questioning of whether justice can ultimately be delivered through the criminal process (Hudson, 2003b). Abolitionists have argued that rather than contributing to the creation of a just society, criminal justice undermines it. In unequal societies, criminal justice reinforces social inequalities and focuses on inflicting pain on the least powerful (Mathiesen, 1990). Instead, abolitionists argue, to create a more just society and to meet the needs of both the 'victim' and the 'perpetrator', we need to develop alternative non-repressive conceptions of justice that can meet the needs of human beings (Hudson, 2003a). In other words, we must think *beyond* 'criminal justice'. Abolitionists must look beyond the criminal law and advocate alternative responses to conflicts, harms and disputes. Abolitionists must, in the words of Jolandeuit Beijerse and Renée Kool (2014) argue that we should avoid the 'traitorous temptation' of criminal justice.

Though punishment may well indeed have no moral defence, abolitionism must have one in order to survive and grow in contemporary societies. By engaging with contemporary social theory, abolitionism is not only given a new conceptual language and continued relevance in times of rapidly changing social (and penal) circumstances, but it also helps develop a new rationale and philosophical justification for abolitionism itself. Willem de Haan (2014) correctly argues that abolitionists should demonstrate not only that punishment is morally flawed but also that it is *possible* to imagine a world without prisons.

Drawing the abolitionist's attention to the value of philosophy, he calls for normative and 'utopian' thinking to show that punishment is not inevitable. For Willem de Haan (2014), abolitionism should present a rational challenge to the assumptions underpinning the incorporation of punishment as a social institution into philosophers' theories of justice and their attempts to reconcile punishment with a just social order.

Like a number of other abolitionists, most notably Barbara Hudson (2003a), de Haan (2014) argues that penal abolitionism should build strong connections with contemporary theories of justice. How can one person's rights be restored by inflicting pain on another person? Surely, de Haan (2014) argues, compensation or restitution are more effective expressions of justice than punishment. By separating out the concept of sanctions from that of punishment, de Haan provides for the possibility of just responses which are not based on pain infliction. His "plunge into moral and political philosophy" provides abolitionism with a much firmer theoretical grounding and shows how a just social order is not only possible without punishment but requires its rejection. Both Barbara Hudson (2003a) and Willem de Haan (2014) conclude that punishment is incompatible with justice — in other words, justice cannot be created or restored through the criminal law. That we must strive for justice without punishment is an important argument for abolitionists to make.

As Joe Sim (2009) points out, any solution to the penal crises must start by closing prisons and other penal institutions and not building new ones. To achieve this requires the creation of alliances with progressive social movements and especially with the people directly impacted by the excesses of the criminal law, such as prisoners' families and ex-prisoners. Willemien de Jongste (2014) and Marijke Meima (2014) make this point crystal clear, maintaining that abolitionists must also construct a progressive alliance with feminist, victim and other pro-justice groups based on shared concerns about the harm perpetrated against vulnerable groups. As well as the critique of iatrogenic penal harms, central to building this coalition must be the *positive moment* of abolitionism. As Angela Davis (2012: 52, 113) has recently argued:

> abolition involves much more than the abolition of prisons. It also involves the creation of new institutions that will effectively speak to the social problems that lead people to prison. [...] [It requires the] shifting of priorities from the prison-industrial complex to education, housing, [and] health care.

Social inequalities and social injustice are the most significant problems we face. Even when looking at interpersonal and relational conflicts, abolitionism points to the need to consider broader structural and political contexts. It is clear that we require solutions based upon equality, equity and social justice rather than penal repression. Abolitionism, therefore, combines the advocacy of change in the penal system with a demand for radical change at a societal level.

New non-penal ways of resolving conflicts, troubles and difficulties are needed not only for those problematic behaviours currently processed by the criminal law but also to address the harms of power and interpersonal abuses, such as sexual violence, corporate harms, environmental destruction and state-sanctioned killings — problems and conflicts which are largely neglected by the criminal law and penal system (Hillyard and Tombs, 2004). Abolition means adopting a different way of looking at the world — a different way of thinking. Central to this, as Louk Hulsman (1986) has highlighted, is the need to learn not to think about 'crime and punishment' — we need to decolonise ourselves of the language of penal repression, domination and authoritarianism. We must learn to take troubles, conflicts and individual and social problems seriously without falling into a punitive trap — to abolish repressive state apparatus and replace them with assistance for conflict resolution and other 'radical alternatives' that in the real world actually help people.

A number of key principles underscore these radical alternatives. Abolitionists acknowledge that most problematic and troublesome behaviours are dealt with outside the criminal process — interventions by the penal law are exceptions rather than the norm (Hulsman, 1986). Abolitionists also recognise human diversity and, at the same time, that 'offenders' are not exceptional and cannot be othered as 'them'. By recognising the nuances and diversity of struggles for justice, abolitionists recognise that there can be no one 'blanket alternative'. Abolitionist alternatives are based on a realistic assessment of what is possible; they engage with people's lived experiences and offer realistic ways in which human conflicts and problematic conducts can be managed.

For Marti Gronfors (2014), a leading member of the European Group, one possible alternative is mediation. Gronfors highlights the crucial distinction between resolving conflicts and solving problems — mediation can deal with communication between the parties to a conflict, but problems require more specialist interventions. Gronfors illustrates the strengths and weakness of mediation through an in-depth case study of the mediation scheme introduced in 1984 in the city of Vantaa in Finland.

The project had been set up on good abolitionist principles — recognition that conflicts are normal, best resolved quickly and between the people directly involved (Christie, 1977) — although it operated alongside criminal-justice interventions. This meant that some cases were both resolved in the mediation scheme and processed through the courts.

Gronfors's evaluation reaches some important conclusions. Firstly, mediation operates at its best when deployed to resolve a conflict between the parties. Where someone has a more general problem, expert advice is required rather than the communicative skills offered by mediators. Secondly, whilst the scheme was initially characterised by mediation resulting in creative solutions, it rapidly lost this aspect and, by the end of the two years, was exclusively trying to resolve disputes by financial compensation, often at levels far higher than would have been awarded by courts. Thirdly, participants reported high levels of satisfaction, with a significant proportion feeling they were getting 'justice'. Gronfors's final point is to raise the danger that such schemes, particularly when funded by the state, will be co-opted. There was evidence of this happening in Vantaa from its earliest days. An abolitionist vision of a future society would see the oppressive and authoritarian penal apparatus — based around repressive policing and pain-inflicting prisons — *replaced* perhaps by 'real utopian' alternatives such as 'Reconciliation and Conflict Resolution Service' and expert 'Problem Solving Services'. Compensation, support and redress for the person harmed could be the core functions of such services, leading to the use of 'sanctions' rather than punishments (Boonin, 2008; de Haan, 2014).

Significantly, *abolitionist alternatives* do not only seek to redirect the responses to conflicts and harmful acts away from the criminal process but also to critique the authoritarian nature of those alternatives (Sim, 2009). For real change, "punitive and repressive attitude[s]" need challenging as well as specific institutions (Swaaningen, 2014: 184). Central to this is the rejection of the "authoritarian idolatry" that comes from abdicating responsibility to the "professionals in charge" and state agencies. Ultimately, abolitionists are arguing for us all to reclaim our collective responsibility, or as Swaaningen (2014: 184) argues:

> If we want to put a stop to an undesirable situation, and we want our personal views and wishes to play a role in the settlement of the conflict, we should not just rely on some kind of authority to do it for us. We should take up our personal responsibility as well; before, during and after a criminalisable conflict.

Swaaningen's analysis touches on the way the campaigns of the women's movements against sexual violence have been 'defined in' by the criminal justice system. This theme is central to abolitionist insights into gendered violence and the possible responses. Common to abolitionist arguments from a feminist perspective is the seriousness of sexual and other gendered violence but also the abject failure of the criminal law to seriously address such problems. For Marijke Meima (2014), the criminal process has a number of fatal flaws. The most serious being the number of possibilities of escape offered — in the police investigation, in the decision to prosecute and in the trial; the ineffectiveness of the sanctions available in the event of a conviction; and the ways in which criminal justice formalises and removes the conflict from the parties. Neither the 'culprit' nor the 'victim', Meima (2014: 200) argues, "recognise himself or herself in the legal version of what has actually happened".

The absence of a single authoritative abolitionist approach is highlighted by Meima (2014). Instead, abolitionists argue for enabling people to find ways of resolving their own conflicts. This raises the obvious problem of the cooperation of the alleged perpetrator and the perceived inferiority of 'alternatives' to the criminal process (Hudson, 2003a, 2003b). However, by moving away from criminal justice's focus on blame and penal sanctions (and the associated legal protection of a defendant), an abolitionist approach promotes such mutual cooperation. Meima (2014) draws on the conferencing approach of restorative justice allowing for the parties to reach a resolution without the need for judicial intervention (although some form of civil judicial intervention may be necessary where agreement has not been reached). But does this mean that the 'rapist' will effectively get away with their sexual violence? For Meima (2014: 203), this is not the central question; instead she prioritises the objective of stopping sexual violence. She argues that under an abolitionist approach, not only is the necessary message about the unacceptability of sexual violence communicated, but also that:

> The chance that a rapist will learn from this procedure, being confronted with all the suffering and problems he has caused, is much bigger than the chance that he will learn from the distant, authoritarian and uniform procedure we know now.

For Jolandeuit Beijerse and Rene Kool (2014), the starting point in respect of responding to violence against women is the encounter between women as victims and the criminal justice system. They conclude, like most researchers, that criminal justice largely fails to hold perpetrators to account, and where it does it can only offer women "that the violator will be punished" (Beijerse and Kool, 2014: 211). This failure has led to a number of responses from the women's movements. Initially, their focus was firstly on a political understanding of sexual violence which located it within the context of power relations, and secondly on the provision of direct services to women victimised by this violence. This political understanding has led inevitably to a critique of criminal justice and its potential role in responding to sexual violence. For significant sections of the women's movements, this has led to calls for the reformation of criminal justice to make it more effective through, for example, revised legal definitions of offences and the training of police and prosecutors. The authors highlight how such moves have largely failed and will prove "a dead-end street" (Ibid.: 219). Such a failure is, they argue, inevitable when women rely on an institution whose primary function is the maintenance of social order. The women's movements, they conclude, must avoid "the traitorous temptation of criminal justice" (Ibid.: 207).

In a similar manner, Willemien de Jongste (2014) has sought to explore understandings of power underpinning feminist theory and the abolitionism of Louk Hulsman (1986). Like Beijerse and Kool (2014), de Jongste's (2014) analysis draws upon the experience of law reform and the women's movement in the Netherlands. She identifies a conflict between the movement's theoretical understanding of both sexual violence and the operation of criminal justice as strategies of patriarchal power, and the latter's increasing advocation of criminal law as the appropriate paradigm within which to respond to sexual violence. For de Jongste (2014), attempts to reform criminal law inevitably lead to the reinforcing of existing power relations: whatever success is achieved in changing the wording of the penal code with respect to sexual violence, the reliance on criminal justice leads to "an implementation of a dominant view of rape rather than a means of fighting against it" (de Jongste, 2014: 236).

Abolitionists recognise that the criminal law cannot provide safety and protection and we cannot achieve human liberation and emancipation through punitive means. Criminal processes always fail as they are about domination and, as such, are incapable of successfully responding to the terrible events and losses that human beings sometimes have to face. The criminal law is clouded in a great deception — that it exists to serve the people — but people are always subservient to the needs of the penal system, which itself serves its masters and the higher interests of the state. As Rene van Swaaningen (2014) maintains, we should be very wary of those who place the institutions of criminal law on a pedestal and, as Jolandeuit Beijerse and Rene Kool (2014) argue, be very sceptical of the apparent seductions of the criminal law

Finally, then, there is the problem of ensuring that abolitionist wisdom informs policy and practice in societies which deploy repressive and authoritarian means in response to 'criminality'. Abolitionists must walk a tightrope between being co-opted by state agencies and being defined out of the dialogue all together. In a crucial contribution to the debate, Thomas Mathiesen (1974) talked about the "competing contradiction" — an argument that could compete with dominant ideologies and discourses on 'crime' and punishment but which, at the same time, undermine and contradict their central logic. This idea is essential for abolitionist interventions in the present. As Joe Sim (2009) has argued, we must look to "exploit contradictions" in the existing system whilst engaging in counter-hegemonic struggles and forms of contestation that allow current 'common sense' on 'crime' to be turned into 'good sense'. To achieve this, abolitionism needs therefore to take three key steps:

1. *Ensure theoretical and political coherence* by developing an understandable counter-hegemonic set of principles that can challenge common sense and authoritarian ideologies.
2. *Build a social movement* by making alliances and constructing an alternative power base that could have political influence.
3. *Participate in struggles* whilst recognising that effective resistance must come from below and be determined by the people directly involved.

The goal should be to avoid being co-opted but follow the 'hard road' to greater understanding and wisdom without being 'defined out' and thus ignored. This challenge, expressed in papers delivered at the European Group conferences, continues to be central to debates in abolitionism today. Despite the last quarter of a century being characterised by a period of penal expansion, it is important that we, like Louk Hulsman in the quote at the start of this chapter, retain a belief in the possibility of penal abolition. Indeed, this expansion in the sheer number of people incarcerated (or otherwise supervised by criminal-justice agencies) and the growing punitive ideology underpinning many other aspects of social policy, makes abolitionist ideas even more essential in the struggle for social justice.

References

Beijerse, J. and Kool, R. (2014) 'The Traitorous Temptation of Criminal Justice: Deceptive Appearances? The Dutch women's movement, violence against women and the criminal justice system' in Moore, J.M., Rolston, W., Scott, D. and Tomlinson, M. (eds) (2014) *Beyond Criminal Justice* Bristol: EG Press

Bernat de Celis, J. (2014) 'Whither Abolitionism?' in Moore, J.M., Rolston, W., Scott, D. and Tomlinson, M. (eds) (2014) *Beyond Criminal Justice* Bristol: EG Press

Boonin, D. (2008) *The Problem of Punishment* Cambridge: Cambridge University Press

Calderone, F. and Valeriani, P. (2014) 'Prison Politics and Prisoners' Struggles in Italy' in Moore, J.M., Rolston, W., Scott, D. and Tomlinson, M. (eds) (2014) *Beyond Criminal Justice* Bristol: EG Press

Carlen, P. (1983) 'On Rights and Powers: Some notes on penal politics' pp 203–216 in Garland, D. and Young, P. (eds) *The Power to Punish* London: Heinemann Books

Carlen, P. (1990) *Alternatives to Women's Imprisonment* Milton Keynes: Open University Press

Christie, N. (1977) 'Conflict as Property' *British Journal of Criminology,* Volume 17, No. 1, pp 1–15

Christie, N. (1981) *The Limits of Pain* Oxford: Martin Robertson

Christie, N. (1993) *Crime Control as Industry* London: Routledge

Cohen, S. (1985) *Visions of Social Control* Cambridge: Polity Press

Davis, A.Y. (2012) *The Meaning of Freedom,* San Francisco: City Lights Books

de Haan, W. (2014) 'The Necessity of Punishment in a Just Social Order: A critical appraisal' in Moore, J.M., Rolston, W., Scott, D. and Tomlinson, M. (eds) (2014) *Beyond Criminal Justice* Bristol: EG Press

de Jongste, W. (2014) 'The Protection of Women by the Criminal Justice System? Reflections on feminism, abolitionism and power' in Moore, J.M., Rolston, W., Scott, D. and Tomlinson, M. (eds) (2014) *Beyond Criminal Justice* Bristol: EG Press

Desprez, E. (1868) *De l'abolition de l'emprisonnement* Paris: Librairie De E Dentu

Godwin, W. (1793) *Enquiry into Political Justice* London: G.G.J. and J. Robinson

Goldson, B. (2005) 'Child Imprisonment: A case for abolition' in *Youth Justice* Volume 5, No 2. pp 77–90

Gronfors, M. (2014) 'Mediation: an experiment in Finland' in Moore, J.M., Rolston, W., Scott, D. and Tomlinson, M. (eds) (2014) *Beyond Criminal Justice* Bristol: EG Press

Hall, S., Jefferson, T., Clarke, J. Critcher, C. and Roberts, B. (2013 [1978]) *Policing the Crisis* London: Macmillan

Hillyard, P. and Tombs, S. (2004) 'Beyond Criminology' in Hillyard, P., Pantazis, C., Tombs, S. and Gordon, D. (eds) *Beyond Criminology* London: Pluto

Hudson, B.A. (1993) *Penal Policy and Social Justice* London: Macmillan

Hudson, B.A. (2003a) *Justice in the Risk Society* London: Sage

Hudson, B.A. (2003b) *Understanding Justice* London: Sage

Hulsman, L. (1986) 'Critical Criminology and the Concept of Crime' in *Contemporary Crises,* Volume 10, No. 1, pp 63–80

Koch, I. (2014) 'Mental and Social Sequence of Isolation' in Moore, J.M., Rolston, W., Scott, D. and Tomlinson, M. (eds) (2014) *Beyond Criminal Justice* Bristol: EG Press

Mathiesen, T. (1974) *The Politics of Abolition* Oxford: Martin Robertson

Mathiesen, T. (1990) *Prisons on Trial* London: Sage

Meima, M. (2014) 'Sexual Violence, Criminal Law and Abolitionism' in Moore, J.M., Rolston, W., Scott, D. and Tomlinson, M. (eds) (2014) *Beyond Criminal Justice* Bristol: EG Press

Roberts, R. (2007) 'What Happened to Abolitionism?' Unpublished MA Thesis, London School of Economics

Scheerer, S. (2014) 'Dissolution and Expansion' in Moore, J.M., Rolston, W., Scott, D. and Tomlinson, M. (eds) (2014) *Beyond Criminal Justice* Bristol: EG Press

Scott, D. (ed) (2013) *Why Prison?* Cambridge: Cambridge University Press

Scott, D. (2015) 'Against Criminal Injustice, For Social Justice' in *European Group Newsletter,* May 2015

Scraton, P. (2007) *Power, Conflict and Criminalisation* London: Routledge

Scraton, P. and Chadwick, K. (2014) 'The Experiment That Went Wrong: The crisis of deaths in custody at the Glenochil Youth Complex, Scotland' in Moore, J.M., Rolston, W., Scott, D. and Tomlinson, M. (eds) (2014) *Beyond Criminal Justice* Bristol: EG Press

Sim, J. (2009) *Punishment and Prisons* London: Sage

Sim, J. (2014) 'Working for the Clampdown: Prisons and politics in England and Wales' in Moore, J.M., Rolston, W., Scott, D. and Tomlinson, M. (eds) (2014) *Beyond Criminal Justice* Bristol: EG Press

Steinert, H. (2014) 'Marxian Theory and Abolitionism' in Moore, J.M., Rolston, W., Scott, D. and Tomlinson, M. (eds) (2014) *Beyond Criminal Justice* Bristol: EG Press

Swaaningen, R. van (2014) 'The Image of Power: Abolitionism, emancipation, authoritarian idolatry and the ability of unbelief' in Moore, J.M., Rolston, W., Scott, D. and Tomlinson, M. (eds) (2014) *Beyond Criminal Justice* Bristol: EG Press

Taylor, I., Walton, P. and Young, J. (1973) *The New Criminology* London: RKP

7.

Constance Lytton: Living for a cause

This chapter was originally published in the European Group Newsletter *in March 2014. The chapter is co-authored with Faith Spear.*

Vision is often personal, but a cause is bigger than any one individual
People don't generally die for a vision, but they will die for a cause
Vision is something you possess, a cause possess you
Vision doesn't eliminate the options; a cause leaves you without any options
A good vision may outlive you, but a cause is eternal
Vision will generate excitement, but a cause generates power.
(Adapted from Houston (2001))

In *Prisons and Prisoners: Some Personal Experiences by Constance Lytton and Jane Warton*, published 100 years ago this month in March 1914, Lady Constance Georgina Bulwer-Lytton presented one of the most significant challenges to twentieth-century anti-suffrage politics. In so doing, she put herself forward as a 'champion of women' (Lytton, 1914) in the hope that one day women would attain political equality with men.[1] *Prisons and Prisoners* is a comprehensive and, at times, a harrowing personal account of her four prison sentences as a militant suffragette. The book is a compelling insight into the mind of a young woman consumed by a cause which would prove to be instrumental in prison reform and votes for women, as well as tragically being a contributory factor to her death.

Desperate to find some way of empathising with the other suffragettes, Constance Lytton had a desire to stand beside those who were fighting. She was with them not as a 'spare part' but as a comrade. Most famously, to avoid receiving special treatment and privileges as a result of her family connections, she took on the guise of 'Jane Warton' and in so doing personally experienced the horrors of prison, including

---

[1] For further details, see Lytton (1909).

force-feeding. Although her health suffered, her story is one which shows courage, determination and an undeniable dedication to equality and justice (Lytton, 1914).

Concentrating attention on political injustice and votes for women, Constance Lytton brought notice to class and gender disparities in punishment and the struggles for the rights of women, always maintaining that the suffragette's militant actions were *political* rather than *criminal*. All this from a woman who described herself as having an exaggerated dislike of society and of publicity in any form, and yet remarkably was at the same time a militant suffragette who took part in deputations to Parliament and prolonged periods of penal incarceration (Lytton, 1914; Haslam, 2008).

Constance Lytton is not the only woman from a privileged background who has written about her prison experiences. The famous Irish rebel, Countess Constance Georgine Markievicz (1927–1973), most well known for her participation in the 1916 Easter Rising, wrote extensively about her time in prison. Indeed, her *Prison Letters* were published to huge acclaim and are still considered today to be of great political significance. In more recent times (October 2013) Vicky Pryce, former joint head of the UK's government economic service, published her account of her three-and-a-half days incarcerated in HMP Holloway (12–15 March 2013) and eight weeks in HMP East Sutton Park Open Prison (15 March to 12 May 2013).[2] Her book, *Prisonomics*, which ultimately seeks to predicate penal change on an economic rationale rather than on humanitarian concerns, has not been so well received. The reaction is partly because it cannot be considered as representative of the lived realities of most women in prison,[3] partly because of the privileged status she was accorded inside prison and the vast economic resources at her disposal,[4] and partly because of the support she was given in writing the book and her failure to identify closely with the painful realities of other prisoners.[5] Yet

---

[2] HMP East Sutton Park is a Grade-II listed sixteenth-century building.

[3] Criticism addresses both the limited time she spent inside and her social background before and after prison.

[4] Undoubtedly, relationships were distorted as both fellow prisoners and prison officers knew who she was and that she writing a book. She also brought more than £1,490 in cash into prison. This level of economic resources can be contrasted to that of ordinary prisoners, whose weekly wage was around £10–15.

[5] Four researchers were paid to collect data for the second part of the book; much of the book refers to life outside the prison; and whilst she writes about 'lovely' people, things and places (i.e., pages 49, 68, 74, 79, 98) and 'kindnesses' (i.e., pages 18, 42, 84), she distances herself from acknowledging painful prison realities.

perhaps the most damning indictment comes when the book is compared to the prison writings of people like Countess Constance Markievicz or Lady Constance Lytton, for then it becomes evident just what is missing from *Prisonomics*.

Lytton's experiences of imprisonment

After being arrested for being part of a deputation marching to Downing Street on 24 February 1909, Constance Lytton was sentenced to four weeks' imprisonment in HMP Holloway. In *Prisons and Prisoners*, she provides extraordinarily rich descriptions of prison conditions, daily routine, fellow prisoners and prison wardresses in Holloway Prison at that time. Although initially held in the hospital wing because of her poor health, following acts of resistance which in effect amounted to self-harm, she was allowed to join other prisoners on "the other side" in the main wings (Lytton, 1914). She had a brilliant eye for detail and provides a number of clear and vivid accounts of sometimes overlooked aspects of prison life. For example, she describes how her prison clothes, with broad arrows stamped over them, were often ill-fitting, stained, unironed and looking unwashed even after they had been to the laundry. Further, the poor design and cut of her prison shirt was not just uncomfortable but so bad it "looked like the production of a maniac", whilst her prison shoes were too small and painful to walk in (Lytton, 1914: 105). The prison cells were small, bitterly cold and poorly ventilated, making it hard for prisoners to breathe, never mind stay warm. Beds were uncomfortable whilst pillows were "stuffed with thunder", making sleep and rest difficult under the best of circumstances and, when compounded by noise, impossible (Lytton, 1914: 114).

In *Prisons and Prisoners*, Constance Lytton draws the reader's attention to the lack of privacy, including the ironies of being in so many ways alone in prison yet at the same time not having the opportunity to retreat to a private space of one's own. She recounts the monotony of prison's daily routine where days collapse into each other and the general dragging of time engenders feelings of wastefulness. She complains about the rigid enforcement of petty rules and the judgemental opinions of wardresses, which make prisoners feel like they belong to "a race apart" (Lytton, 1914: 116). Insightfully, Constance Lytton also recognised the difficulties that wardresses had in understanding how the pains of imprisonment shape prisoners' experiences; such things the prison official can only "witness without sharing them" (Ibid.: 126). She rightly concludes that this results in a general failure on the part of prison officials to correctly read the feelings, meanings and actions of those they detain. When describing her interaction with the wardresses:

> I noticed that there was no inflection in the voice when speaking to prisoners, nor did the wardresses look at them when addressing them. As a prisoner, it was almost impossible to look in the eyes of my keepers, they seemed to fear that direct means of communication; it was as if the wardresses wore a mask, and withdrew as much as possible all expression of their own personality or recognition of it in the prisoner. At first, the impression received was as of something farcical. I remember that it amused me immensely and absorbed my attention with a sort of fascinated curiosity. But this soon went off, and made for a chilling deadening impression. (Lytton, 1914: 75)[6]

Constance Lytton acknowledged that her prison experience was mitigated somewhat by *who* she was. Despite the poor conditions she encountered, some improvements had been made on her arrival, including the supply of knives and forks which had not been available to prisoners in Holloway before her time there. As perhaps only an aristocrat would, she yearned for an authentic prison experience, and noted how other women prisoners seemed dejected, lifeless, listless, detached from each other and haunted by their own suffering, anxiety and bitterness (Lytton, 1914). On a number of occasions in her reflections on her time in Holloway Prison, she uses her pen to poetically describe the abnormality, pain, sadness and venomous nature of penal incarceration, leaving the reader in no doubt as to her repugnance of the penal machinery and its inevitably destructive results.

> The prison from here looks like a great hive of human creeping things impelled to their joyless labours and unwilling seclusion by some hidden force, the very reversal of the natural, and which has in it no element of organic life, cohesion, or self-sufficing reason. A hive of hideous purposes from which flows back day by day into the surrounding stream of evil honey, blackened in the making and poisonous in result. The high central tower seemed to me a jam

---

[6] We have drawn upon two sources of *Prisons and Prisoners*. This reference gives the page number from the Heinemann 1914 edition, whilst other references are from the manuscript edited and introduced by Haslam (2008), unless otherwise stated.

pot, indicative of the foul preserve that seethed within this factory
for potting human souls. (Lytton, 1914: 180)

Despite all the bleakness of the prison experience, Constance Lytton
emphasised above all those moments when humanity and the human
spirit were able to overcome the brutal indifference characterising daily
prison routines. She writes about the kindness and compassion of other
women prisoners (especially other suffragettes) and the brief glimpses of
humanity that she saw hiding behind the "masks" worn by wardresses
when performing their duties (Lytton, 1914). Indeed, for her such "rare
occasions of gladness outweigh from their importance the much more
numerous experiences of gloom, anxiety, anger and physical suffering"
(Ibid.). Yet she never became blinded by these brief moments of
"gladness", keeping her sights firmly upon carefully describing the
"nightmare of horror" of HMP Holloway and a dehumanising system
which trapped both prisoners and wardresses (Ibid.: 132).

Shortly after her release from Holloway Prison, Constance Lytton was
arrested and sentenced to imprisonment for a second time — this
occasion on Saturday 9 October 1909 for throwing a stone at the car of Sir
Walter Runciman in Newcastle upon Tyne. Once imprisoned, she
immediately went on hunger strike at HMP Newcastle. Although refusing
medical examination, her health condition was still officiously checked
and, after abstaining from eating food for three days of her one-month
sentence (Monday 11 to Wednesday 13 October 1909), she was released.
Her release was ordered, according to Home Secretary Herbert Gladstone,
because of concerns regarding her heart condition. Unlike working-class
women suffragettes on hunger strike in prisons, the aristocrat Constance
Lytton had not been force-fed. The belief that her class background had
shaped her treatment in prison led to a fundamental change in her tactics.

'Jane Warton, Spinster' and Walton Prison

The writings of Lady Constance Lytton on the prisons of Holloway and
Newcastle are undoubtedly worthy of commemoration in their own right,
but what she did next was truly remarkable, making *Prisons and Prisoners*
one of the most unique prisoner autobiographies ever written. After
hearing about the force-feeding of a working-class suffragette of her
acquaintance, Miss Selina Martin, and another named Miss Leslie Hall,
while on remand at Walton Prison in Liverpool, Constance Lytton hatched
a plan that would entail, if necessary, "sharing the fate of these women"

(Lytton, 1914: 214). Her intention was to transcend her class background in an attempt to understand the lived experiences of working-class women prisoners. In so doing, she hoped to express political solidarity with the suffering of the less fortunate and to use her own frail body as the central way of achieving this.

Whilst visiting Manchester in early January 1910, she disguised herself with a most ridiculous hair cut, cheap glasses and even cheaper clothes and then rejoined the WSPU (Women's Social and Political Union) as 'Jane Warton, Spinster' (Lytton, 1914). She had chosen her new name carefully: the first name was taken from Jeanne of Arc (Jeanne is translated as either Joan or Jane) whilst the surname was derived from her relatives the 'Warburtons' but shortened to 'Warton' to appear more ordinary. She hoped the real meaning of her name 'Jane Warton' would give her strength in what she anticipated would be difficult times ahead (Ibid.: 215).

'Jane Warton' was subsequently arrested on Friday 14 January 1910 after participating in a protest march about the force-feeding of working-class women suffragettes like Selina Martin in Walton Prison. 'Jane Warton' started her hunger strike in the police cells that Friday evening, a couple of days before she was to begin her sentence at Walton Prison. Just as she had done under her real name, when in prison 'Jane Warton' refused medical examinations. There was, however, to be no further investigation into the health of working-class suffragette 'Jane Warton' and, eighty-nine hours into her hunger strike, force-feeding began. Between Tuesday 18 and Saturday 22 January 1910, 'Jane Warton' was to have liquidised food poured into a tube forced into her stomach through her mouth on eight separate occasions.

At 6:00pm, Tuesday 18 January 1910, the force-feeding began. The medical officer and five wardresses entered her cell with the "feeding apparatus" (Lytton, 1914: 236). There was no attempt to medically examine 'Jane Warton' and the half-hearted attempts by the medical officer to induce her to eat unsurprisingly failed.

> I offered no resistance to being placed in position, but lay down voluntarily on the plank bed. Two of the wardresses took hold of my arms, one held my head and one my feet. One wardress helped to pour the food. The doctor leant on my knees as he stooped over my chest to get at my mouth. I shut my mouth and clenched my teeth [...] The sense of being overpowered by more force than I could possibly resist was complete, but I resisted nothing except with my mouth [...] He seemed annoyed at my resistance and he

broke into a temper as he plied my teeth with the steel implement [...] He said if I resisted so much with my teeth, he would feed me through the nose. The pain of it was intense and at last I must have given way for he got the gag between my teeth, when he proceeded to turn it much more than necessary until my jaws were fastened wide apart, far more than they could go naturally. Then he put down my throat a tube which seemed to me much too wide and was something like four feet in length. The irritation of the tube was excessive. I choked the moment it touched my throat until it had gone down. Then the food was poured in quickly; it made me sick a few seconds after it was down and the action of the sickness made my body and legs double up, but the wardresses instantly pressed back my back and the doctor leant on my knees. The horror of it was more than I can describe. I was sick over the doctor and wardresses and it seemed a long time before they took the tube out. (Ibid.)

When the force-feeding was over, the doctor slapped 'Jane Warton' on the cheek and left her cell (Ibid.).

I could not move, and remained there in what, under different conditions, would have been an intolerable mess. I had been sick over my hair, which, though short, hung on either side of my face, all over the wall near my bed, and my clothes seemed saturated with it, but the wardresses told me they could not get me a change that night as it was too late, the office was shut. I lay quite motionless, it seemed paradise to be without the suffocating tube, without the liquid food going in and out of my body and without the gag in my teeth [...] Before long I heard the sounds of forced feeding in the cell next to mine. It was almost more than I could bare. (Ibid.: 238)

'Jane Warton' continued to vomit following being force-fed on further occasions (Ibid.). Her physical frailty was noted by the medical officer but, remarkably, when her heart was checked by a junior doctor, he exclaimed "Oh ripping, splendid heart! You can go on with her" (Ibid.: 241). From her fourth to eighth feedings onwards, the doctor and wardresses were more gentle, for they had realised that 'Jane Warton' was someone else in disguise, even though they remained unsure of her true identity. Her physical and emotional strength was virtually broken and, at her feeding on Friday 21 January, she was "convulsed with sobs" (Ibid.). Following outside intervention from her family, she was released from HMP Walton on the morning of Sunday 23 January 1910.

Writing, reception and legacy of Prisons and Prisoners

When Constance Lytton ('Jane Warton') was finally released from Walton Prison on 23 January, a major political scandal immediately followed. The then Home Secretary, Herbert Gladstone, claimed that 'Lady Constance Lytton' had been released from Newcastle Prison when she went on hunger strike because she had heart disease, yet in her guise as 'Jane Warton' had been subjected to force-feeding and was released due to "loss of weight and general physical weakness"(Lytton, 1914: 265). Before Constance Lytton, some thirty-five other women suffragettes had been force-fed whilst on hunger strike, but none of these suffragettes were members of the ruling elite and their sufferings during force-feedings had largely been ignored. Lady Constance Lytton's treatment as 'Jane Warton' by contrast was a major political embarrassment, although the extent of the fallout from her revelations and the concerted petitioning of her brother and sisters remain unclear. Although Herbert Gladstone ended his tenure as Home Secretary shortly after the release of 'Jane Warton', it is debatable whether the two events were linked.[7]   The personal consequences for Constance Lytton of her 'force-feeding', sadly, are undoubted. Following her release, she was confined to her bed for six weeks because her heart was so weak, and in the autumn of 1910, a heart seizure temporarily paralysed her. Her health never fully recovered and although the initial paralysis eased, two more years of suffering from heart seizures followed (Lytton, 1914).

Remarkably, Constance Lytton somehow found the passion and energy to continue, as by this time she had achieved personal insight complete with understanding, but, most of all, a strategy; she was once more arrested and sent to Holloway between 21 and 28 November 1911. Although the sentence was for a month, members of her family paid the requisite sum for her release and so she served one week, only. Tragedy was to strike on 5 May 1912, when Constance Lytton suffered a stroke. In *Prisons and Prisoners* she wrote that she had:

---

[7] For discussion on this, see Haslam (2008).

had a stroke and my right arm was paralysed; also, slightly my right foot and leg. I was taken from my flat to my sister's house [...] from that day I have been incapacitated from working for the Women's Social and Political Union, but I am with them still with my whole soul. (Lytton, 1914: 284)

This remarkable and courageous woman wrote her book *Prisons and Prisoners* with her left hand as a result of the paralysis. She spent the final years of her life (1912–1923) as an invalid at Knebworth, cared for by her mother and hired nurses, one of whom she closely befriended. As the *Letters of Constance Lytton, Selected and Arranged by Betty Balfour* (Lytton, 1925) published posthumously in 1925 indicates, Constance Lytton was a prolific letter writer prior to her stroke in 1912, but following this was able to write only a very few personal letters, showing us just how much of a struggle it must have been to write *Prisons and Prisoners* with her left hand. Christabel Pankhurst wrote on 20 March 1914 that *"Prisons and Prisoners* is in itself a triumph of will — a great conquest of the spirit over bodily infirmity". Indeed it was.

The story of Constance Lytton as detailed by her own hand, and that of others, caught the imagination of both her peers and fellow suffragettes. Her story initially came out in a fictionalised form, as a thinly disguised character in the classic Gertrude Colmore (1911) novel *Suffragette Sally*.[8] Her struggle also had a far-reaching effect on legislation. This can be illustrated by the Prisoners (Temporary Discharge of Ill Health) Act, which became known as the Cat and Mouse Act. It was rushed through Parliament in 1913 to allow the discharge of hunger-striking suffragettes from prisons as a response to growing public disquiet about the use of forcible feeding. This Act allowed for the early release of prisoners who were so weakened by hunger striking that they were at risk of death. However, they were to be recalled to prison once their health was recovered, when the process would begin again. Though hardly a victory, political pressure continued to mount and finally, in Constance Lytton's lifetime, propertied women aged over the age of thirty got the vote in 1918.[9]

As a consequence of her actions "for this cause" (Houston, 2001), many were grateful to Constance Lytton for her sacrifices. Below are some of the many testimonies:

---

[8] For further details on this classic text, see Lee (2008).

[9] The struggle for the vote for working-class women continued until 1928, after Constance Lytton had died.

The Outlook (28 January 1910) "Whenever the annals of the human race are preserved, this deed of hers will be treasured up as a priceless possession".

Emmeline Pethick Lawrence (28 January 1910)
"[her act] will be written in letters of gold upon the tables of human history".

Mrs Coombe Tennant, (Visiting Justice, 1925, cited in Balfour, 1925) "prisons today are different from what they would have been had she not gone down into hell".

Constance Lytton died at the age of fifty-four. At her funeral, Emmeline Pethick Lawrence placed a palm leaf on the casket, with the statement:

Dearest Comrade — You live always in the hearts of those who love you and live forever in the future race which inherits the new freedom you gave your life to win (cited in Miles and Williams, 1999).

Critical appraisal

When looking back at *Prisons and Prisoners* 100 years on, it is clear that the book is not only an important historical artefact in terms of publicising the struggle for women's equality but also a remarkable testimony of one women's experience of imprisonment. *Prisons and Prisoners* provides insights neglected by some penological narratives of that time and directly contradicts official reports and documents — most famously those of the then Home Secretary, Herbert Gladstone (see Haslam, 2008). Undoubtedly, *Prisons and Prisoners* continues to humanise prison studies and to enrich understandings of prison life, both past and present.

It also provides an antidote for those drawn to the publicity-craving celebrity autobiographies of the political elite who are imprisoned for their own corruption. When contrasting Constance Lytton's *Prisons and Prisoners* with the more recent *Prisonomics* by Vicky Pryce (2013), it seems the two books provide almost a mirror image of each other. *Prisons and Prisoners* is a personally courageous attempt to uncover the terrible truth regarding the experiences of both ordinary prisoners and suffragettes. Deeply connected to radical suffragette politics, the book questions imprisonment because it is a dehumanising environment creating unnecessary human suffering. In comparison, *Prisonomics'* central focus is upon the economic, rather than human, costs of penal incarceration. But what distinguishes the two books more than anything else are the different moral and political commitments of the authors to their given cause. Whereas a strong commitment to her cause is evident in nearly every act undertaken by Constance Lytton (as described in her autobiography), in the main, this quality is noticeable only through its absence in the writings of Vicky Pryce. As such, it is difficult to imagine commemorating the publication of *Prisonomics* in the next century.

Nonetheless, *Prisons and Prisoners* and what it attempted to achieve are also not without difficulties. Despite her best efforts, it was always an impossible ambition for Constance Lytton to entirely transcend class boundaries and gain an experience that could reflect the lived realities of ordinary women prisoners. Even as 'Jane Warton' she could never experience the restricted choices and power differentials shaping pre- and post-incarceration for working-class women offenders. Her understanding of working-class women in prison was always informed by a pastoral and maternal ideology rather than by an ideology of political emancipation, and resulted in a tone which, in the main, sought to foster sympathy for prisoners through their 'victimhood' rather than actualising change motivated by an understanding of prisoners as free-willed autonomous agents (Scott and Spear, 2013). Consequently, whereas suffragette women prisoners (Constance Lytton included) are presented as engaging in acts of resistance, working-class criminal women prisoners are constructed as passive and unable to fight back against penal oppression (Ibid.).

Furthermore, Constance Lytton made little progress in providing a platform from which the actual voices of either working-class women suffragettes or 'ordinary' prisoners could be heard, although her stroke and subsequent paralysis in 1912 may have made such endeavours physically impossible. Nevertheless, in *Prisons and Prisoners*, and in the wider writings of Constance Lytton (Lytton, 1909, 1910a, 1910b), we only ever hear her privileged voice and, significant though this is, it can only provide us with a partial narrative of that historical moment. Despite these concerns, the courage, bravery and commitment of Constance Lytton to expose the brutal treatment of working-class women in prison, whatever the cost to her fragile health, must be recognised for the heroism it undoubtedly was. It represents a victory of the human spirit over what appear to be insurmountable odds and, 100 years on, is a story that can inspire those working *against* dehumanisation and *for* human equality in all of its rich and wonderful diversity.

References

Balfour, B (1925) 'Introduction' in Lytton, C. (1925) *Letters of Constance Lytton, Selected and Arranged by Betty Balfour* London: Heinemann

Colmore, G. (1911) *Suffragette Sally* Toronto: Broadview Press

Haslam, J. (ed) (2008) *Prisons and Prisoners: Some Personal Experiences by Constance Lytton* Toronto: Broadview Press

Houston, B. (2001) *For this Cause: Finding the Meaning of Life and Living a Life of Meaning.* Castle Hill: Maximised Leadership Inc.

Lee, A. (2008) *Suffragette Sally by Gertrude Colmore* Toronto: Broadview Press

Lytton, C. (1909) *'No Votes for Women': A Reply to Some Recent Anti-Suffrage Publications.* London: A.C. Fiefield

Lytton, C. (1910a) 'A speech by Lady Constance Lytton, delivered at Queen's Hall, 31st January 1910' pp 326–332 in Lee, A. (2008) *Suffragette Sally by Gertrude Colmore* Toronto: Broadview Press

Lytton, C. (1910b) 'The Prison Experience of Lady Constance Lytton' in *Votes for Women* 28 January 1910, pp 301–305 in Haslam, J. (ed) (2008) *Prisons and Prisoners: Some Personal Experiences by Constance Lytton* Toronto: Broadview Press

Lytton, C. (1914) 'Prisons and Prisoners: Some personal experiences by Constance Lytton and Jane Warton, spinster' in Haslam, J. (ed) (2008) *Prisons and Prisoners: Some Personal Experiences by Constance Lytton* Toronto: Broadview Press

Lytton, C. (1914) *Prisons and Prisoners: Some Personal Experiences by Constance Lytton and Jane Warton, Spinster* London: William Heinemann

Lytton, C. (1925) *Letters of Constance Lytton arranged by Betty Balfour* London: Heinemann

Markievicz, C. (1973 [1927]) *Prison Letters of Countess Markievicz* London: Virago Press

Miles, P. and Williams, J. (1999) *An Uncommon Criminal: The Life of Lady Constance Lytton, Militant Suffragette 1869–1923.* Knebworth: Knebworth House Education and Preservation Trust

Pankhurst, C. (1914) 'A Prisoner's Book' in *Suffragette*, 20 March 1914, pp 323–326 in Haslam, J. (ed) (2008) *Prisons and Prisoners: Some Personal Experiences by Constance Lytton* Toronto: Broadview Press

Pethick Lawrence, E. (1910) 'Lady Constance Lytton' in *Votes for Women* 28 January 1910, pp 314–315 in Haslam, J. (ed) (2008) *Prisons and Prisoners: Some Personal Experiences by Constance Lytton* Toronto: Broadview Press

Pryce, V. (2013) *Prisonomics* London: Biteback

Scott, D. and Spear, F. (2014) 'Constance Lytton/Jane Warton *Prisons and Prisoners*: 100 years on' in *Howard Journal of Criminal Justice,* July 2014

The Outlook (1910) editorial of *Votes for Women,* 28 January 1910 pp 311–314 in Haslam, J. (ed) (2008) *Prisons and Prisoners: Some Personal Experiences by Constance Lytton* Toronto: Broadview Press

8

Speaking the Language of State Violence:
An abolitionist perspective

This article was originally published in the European Group Newsletter *in February 2016.*

Of central concern for penal abolitionists today is the fostering of a coherent and politically plausible strategy that can facilitate a decisive shift away from the global expansionist penal trajectory of the last three and more decades. Prison populations in recent years have reached record highs in many countries (Scott, 2013b) and, at the time of writing in January 2016, the average daily prison population in England and Wales stood at just under 86,000 people, more than double the number of the early 1990s. Strategically, penal abolitionism requires a "name" (Critchley, 2012: 9) around which a new anti-prison "social imaginary" can be formulated that can capture the hearts and minds of the populace and, as a result, create a powerful, sustainable and effective mobilisation of counter-hegemonic oppositional social forces against hyper-incarceration (Laclau and Mouffe, 1985: 155). Contemporary abolitionist social movements must, in other words, operate like ideological cement binding together currently fragmented groupings of people struggling against domination and exploitation into a single unified alliance (Ibid.).

But how should abolitionists frame the issue? What is the best language to use? This chapter contends that the 'language of state violence' may be one way of 'naming the problem'. This is not to say that violence is the only way that prisons can be analysed and conceptualised, but it may be a politically significant way of expressing the iatrogenic harms of penal confinement and mobilising resistance. For the purposes of this discussion, violence is defined as physical/psychological pain, harm or death resulting from an individual action or a given set of structural arrangements (see further definitions by Cover, 1988: 203; Iadicola and Shupe, 2003: 23). Violence is the systematic "denial of need" (Galtung, 1994: 55) and pertains when the social production of suffering and harm are legalised, institutionalised and endemic within state policy and operational practices. State violence, then, is understood as a form of coercive power which produces violent outcomes.

The Capitalist State has the monopoly on the legitimate deployment of such coercive power (violence) and, consequently, the law performs an integral role in organising and structuring the *legal institutionalisation of physical repression* that we call the prison. For scholars such as Nicos Poulantzas (1978: 76) the assumed split between law and lawless terror is in fact "illusionary". Prison is terror. Lawful terror. It is a manifestation of institutional violence. That prisons are drenched in violence does not mean, however, that physical violence is constantly exercised. Physical violence may well be rare events in certain penal institutions, but this does not mean people live free from the shadow of violence. What is permanently "inscribed in the web of disciplinary and ideological" rules and practices of penal regimes is the fear of violence. As such, a *"mechanism of fear"* (Poulantzas, 1978: 83; emphasis in original; see also Scraton et al., 1991) underscores penal power. Prisons are places of (legal) *repression* (Poulantzas, 1978; Cover, 1988; Scraton et al., 1991). Such repression can be explicit, as for example through the structured humiliations and denials of dignity within the daily role of the prison officer — strip searches; control and restraint; locking people into a cell; and so on — or it can be implicit, where prisoners conform because they know physical violence will follow if they do not. In terms of everyday situations, *legal repression* shapes the conduct and acquiescence of prisoners (Cover, 1988). The acquiescence of prisoners can thus be understood in the context of the potential threat of an "overwhelming array" of practices of state violence and the *fear* of state violence: "prisoners walk into prison because they know that they will be dragged or beaten into prison if they do not walk" (Cover, 1988: 211).

Ultimately, to speak the 'language of state violence' is to insist that, irrespective of the conditions, architecture, or general resources available, the prison will always be a place that systematically generates suffering, harm, and death. Understanding prisons as a modus operandi of *state violence* may help abolitionists gain political momentum, for it leads to a focus on both 'institutional' and 'structural' violence (Scraton and McCulloch, 2009; Ritchie, 2012). Ultimately, it provides a name to mobilise around and makes connections between the prison and social inequities.

State violence and structural violence

By speaking the language of 'state violence' it may be possible for abolitionists to start building new networks and alliances beyond the prison walls. The problem the abolitionist opposes is violence: suffering, pain and death (Cover, 1988). Prisons are one institutional site of state violence. If we are against violence, then we should be against the prison, for they are places of suffering, pain and death. To reinforce this message, abolitionists can locate imprisonment within the broader context of *structural violence* and the harm it generates (Galtung, 1969). Structural violence refers to the harmful outcomes of an unequal society aiming to establish or reproduce a given "hierarchical ordering of categories of people" (Iadicola and Shupe, 2003: 31). Capitalist societies are structured in such a way that access to resources are restricted for certain groups of people which negatively impact upon life chances, health, intellectual, physical and spiritual development. The state, as the orchestrator of social relations, is directly implicated in the existence and consequences of 'structural violence'. Although he did not use the term 'structural violence', in *The Condition of the Working Class in England* (1844), Friedrich Engels gives us a clear indication of how pain and death can be systematically generated. In a well-known passage, Engels argues that the poor, marginalised and excluded find themselves:

> in such a position that they inevitably meet a too early and an unnatural death, one which is quite as much a death by violence as that by the sword or bullet; when it deprives thousands of the necessaries of life, places them under conditions in which they cannot live — forces them, through the strong arm of the law, to remain in such conditions until that death ensues which is the inevitable consequence.

Whilst such 'state violence' is "more one of omission than of commission", it nevertheless "undermines the vital [life] force gradually, little by little, and so hurries them to the grave before their time" (Ibid.).

Abolitionists in the UK have consistently argued that the role of the prison is interconnected with the broader structural inequalities of advanced capitalist societies (see, for example, Scraton et al., 1991; Sim, 1984, 2009; Scott, 2013b). Prisons house socially excluded people from impoverished social backgrounds. The language of state violence provides a clear conceptual framework through which the pain, harm and death created by social and economic inequalities can be directly linked to the application of penal confinement. It provides us with an interpretive frame and clear narrative that may help abolitionists connect further with socialists, feminists, anarchists, anti-poverty activists, and peace movements.

Prisons are not just about wasting life generally, but about wasting the lives of given segments of the population, for penal incarceration is shaped through complex intersections of class, 'race', gender and sexuality (Barton et al., 2006; Scott, 2013b). A drift towards a greater intensification in the control of the poor has spawned global hyper-incarceration and the substantial penal colonisation of welfare provisions and other sites of state detention. Prison has become a dumping ground for humans facing profound difficulties (Scraton and McCulloch, 2009). The language of state violence ties the expansion of the penal apparatus of the Capitalist State with the violence wreaked through poverty, for both reflect political and policy agendas of the Capitalist State. Here, abolitionists can engage with social movements that talk the language of 'state violence' and offer solidarity to the emancipatory struggles of those campaigning against other manifestations of 'structural violence'.

Operating independently of human actions, structural violence has a permanent, continuous presence which in the end produces "lethal effects" (Gilligan, 2000: 193). Today in the UK we find that the richest 10% of households holds 44% of its wealth. The poorest 50% in the UK possesses just 9% of marketable wealth and one in four live below the average national income. The bottom 10% of the population has less than £12,500 in total wealth, whilst the top 10% has £1 million or more in wealth. In 2015, 18 million people (30% of the UK population) lived in poverty. This is double the number of 1983 (Scott, 2013b; The Equality Trust, 2015). This is in the context of global hyper-inequalities in 2016, where the combined wealth of the sixty-two richest people is greater than that of the poorest 3.6 billion people on the planet (Hardoon et al., 2016). Structural inequalities weaken social bonds, generate false hierarchies, spawn intolerance, create anxieties and suspicion and promote moral judgments based on individual responsibility that subsequently lead to resentment and hostility to those classified as 'Other'. Unequal societies are highly conducive to the attribution of blame and the deliberate infliction of pain, and it has long been established that penal severity and income inequality are intimately connected. Prisons and poverty are tied through an umbilical cord of shared violent outcomes.

The extent of the poverty and disadvantages experienced by prison populations is staggering. Recent data compiled by the Prison Reform Trust (2015) inform us that 26% of the prison population (21,880 people) are from a Black or Minority Ethnic group; 33% of boys and 61% of girls in custody were formerly in care homes; 27% of men and 53% of women in prison have experienced emotional, physical or sexual abuse as a child; 46% of women in prison have experienced domestic abuse; 25% of women and 15% of men in prison have symptoms indicative of psychosis; 36% of prisoners have a physical or mental disability; 30% of prisoners have learning disabilities; 47% of prisoners have no formal qualifications; 15% of prisoners were homeless before custody (9% sleeping rough); 67% of prisoners were unemployed in the four weeks before custody (13% have never had a job); and 33% of prisoners do not have a bank account. Abolitionists must emphasise the counterproductive nature of a government policy attempting to address the structural violence of poverty through the institutional violence of the prison place. Prisons are filled with the neglected and the impoverished. Prisoners are confronted with violence in prison and through the organisation of society. We cannot address such violence by advocating institutional solutions grounded in violence. The overall message is clear: violence only breeds more violence.

Abolitionism: beyond penal reform

Whilst there is some overlap in what penal reformers and penal abolitionists understand by 'violence', there are a number of major differences, especially regarding the meaning of 'state violence' (See Table 1). Whereas penal reformers largely focus on interpersonal violence and advocate reforms they believe will lead to its reduction, for abolitionists, violence is an endemic and ongoing process institutionally structured within the day-to-day workings of the penal regime (Scott, 2015). For abolitionists, there are no simple solutions to the "violence of incarceration" (Scraton and McCulloch, 2009).

Speaking the language of state violence, within a broader understanding of the structural contexts and social and economic inequalities detailed above, clearly distinguishes prison abolitionists from penal reformers. Abolitionists and anti-prison activists in organisations such as *Critical Resistance* and *INCITE!* Women of Colour Against Violence in the US already follow the strategy of naming state violence as the

TABLE 1: The differences between reformist and abolitionist approaches to violence in prison

	PENAL REFORMISM	PENAL ABOLITIONISM
Conceptualisation of violence	Interpersonal/physical and cultural violence. Focus on violence of prisoners and prison staff.	Cultural, physical, institutional and structural forms of violence. State violence operates on a continuum and prisons are places of both direct physical 'interpersonal-institutional violence' and indirect 'institutionally structured violence'.
	Focus on intention and wilful actions of individuals.	Focus on harmful outcomes and acts of omission and commission. Individuals are not the only perpetrators of violence.
	Violence is an event/interaction that can be expressive, instrumental, rebellious or adaptive.	Violence is *also* an ongoing process permeating day-to-day relations and lived experiences. Violence can be physical and/or psychological harm. Violence is pain and death.
Causes of violence	Explanations linked to individual pathologies, defects and deficiencies and cultural codes of violence among both prisoners and staff. Poor prison design and architecture can lead to an exacerbation of interpersonal conflicts.	Explanations of all forms of violence focus on social and institutional, organisation and structural contexts. Prison cultures may naturalise (and thus fail to acknowledge) institutionally structured violence.
	The full extent of state violence is not always recognised. Rather, it is taken for granted as an integral part of the penal machine.	Interpersonal/physical violence by prisoners may be directly generated by penal confinement as a form of individual or collective resistance or rebellion.

Violence in prison	Violent behaviour is linked to illegal behaviours by individuals or groups.	Violence behaviour is linked to exploitative power differentials, structural constraints and hierarchies. Prisons are places of dehumanisation and the denial of need.
	Violence (sexual or physical) is defined by the law and may be remedied through the law and the penal system.	The law itself can be a form of violence. Prisons will always generate pain and death.
	Different prisons have different levels of safety, violence and moral performance.	All prisons are characterised by institutionally structured violence. Violence is a universal feature rather than something that can fluctuate relative to specific problematic or humane prisons.
Assumptions behind anti-violence strategies	Violence can be greatly reduced/eradicated in the prison by progressive reforms.	Violence (pain and death) is endemic to the prison place. The structures of confinement inevitably produce iatrogenic penal harms.
Examples of anti-violence strategies	Prisoner mediation and community forums; smaller and better designed prisons; restorative justice and alternative means of conflict resolution in prisons; challenging the prisoner code; challenging prison office culture; prison officers as peacekeepers; improving prison conditions.	Emancipatory humanitarian interventions which can reduce harm, and both contradict and compete with existing penal policies; human rights *for* prisoners, stressing acknowledgement of inherent dignity and hearing the voice from below; deployment of the attrition model as a strategy for de-penalisation; non-violent responses to human conflicts, troubles and problematic conduct *in place* of the prison; social justice responses at a societal level that can combat structural violence and meet human needs. Anti-violence political activism contesting hierarchies of power.

129

problem to be addressed (Davis, 2006; Ritchie, 2012; Oparah, 2013). American 'new abolitionists' turn conventional logic on its head: they argue that rather than offering excluded and marginalised communities safety and protection, the "penal industrial complex" in fact perpetrates harms and violence against them (Oparah, 2013). Through speaking the language of state violence, *Critical Resistance* and *INCITE!* have been able to connect with feminists, anti-racists, socialists, anti-capitalists and anti-violence activists to build a new, broad-based coalition against the penal apparatus of the Capitalist State. This approach in many ways transcends the divides between reformers and abolitionists — the objective is to visibilise critique and end violence. This strategy has also led to mainstream anti-violence activists becoming more conscious about the limitations of the penal law as a means of responding to violence, especially violence against women (Ritchie, 2012). Speaking the language of state violence does, though, mean moving beyond reformist strategies that try to tinker with the existing criminal processes. Instead of focusing on the limitations of the criminal process alone, speaking the language of violence helps to make important links between poverty, workplace harms, racial violence, sexual violence, imprisonment and other varieties of state harm. Naming 'the problem' as state violence demonstrates beyond any doubt that penal abolitionists take violence seriously and provides a language to articulate and critique domination, exploitation and subjugation in capitalist, patriarchal and neocolonial societies.

For abolitionists, the only way to end the "violence of incarceration" (Scraton and McCulloch, 2009) is by abolishing the prison. But reformers and abolitionists need not always be in opposition, for like reformers, abolitionists are compelled to promote emancipatory and humanitarian initiatives in the here and now. Critique of the prison place does not mean that the daily problems and difficulties of prison life are downplayed or neglected. Abolitionists, however, must be much more ambitious than aiming for a purely descriptive account and instead attempt to not only deepen and extend our understanding of prison violence but also aim to direct existing struggles towards abolishing violence in all its manifestations.

State violence and institutionally structured violence

Like penal reformers and indeed many penal practitioners, abolitionists are concerned about the nature and extent of interpersonal physical violence in prison (Scott, 2015). Accounts, like the testimony cited below from a prisoner recently released from HMP Liverpool in February 2015, are chilling.

> Everything is solved with violence. And if you're not of that attitude, then you're soft [...] There's an average of five fights every day. The showers are normally the place where disputes and debts are sorted out. I have seen inmates leave with bust lips, blood pouring from their nose and with other injuries [...] I have seen three inmates enter a cell, leave a few minutes later and watch as a prisoner comes out with cuts, slashes and stab wounds [...] The officers watch everything and are fully aware of what's happening, but do not get involved. Either because it makes their shift easier or they fear attacks on them [...] Violence is the fluent language of the prison. You have to learn to speak it quick at Walton or you will get eaten alive. (Ex-prisoner, cited in Siddle, 2015)

Much of the penological literature concentrates on physical violence, especially violence perpetrated by prisoners on other prisoners (Cohen et al., 1976; Edgar et al., 2003: Levan, 2012; Trammell, 2012), although there has for some time been considerable evidence of prison officer violence (Kauffman, 1988; Edney, 1997). Whilst the physical violence of prisoners should not be downplayed or ignored, it is only one kind of violence and is by no means the most harmful (Scott, 2015). One of the most pertinent moral, political and intellectual tasks of abolitionism is to move the debate beyond simply a focus on the physical violence of prisoners and, in so doing, help establish a new broader counter-hegemonic cultural understanding of penal violence.

Violence is considered by many people to be immoral and the perpetration of physical violence is considered problematic in most circumstances. Prisons, though, are distinct moral places where normal moral conventions can sometimes be neutralised in daily interactions between prisoners and penal authorities (Scott, 2008). There are, of course, official condemnations of prisoners' physical violence (see, for example, the special issue of *Prison Service Journal*, September 2015 on 'violence reduction'), but often the official critique of violence is reduced to explanations of individual pathology, alongside references to the deprived nature and inherent violence of the perpetrators (Levan, 2012). Such analysis dislocates physical violence from the permanent and irremovable situational contexts of penal confinement. Interpersonal physical violence by prisoners is taken most seriously by penal authorities and this may well be because it is the most visible form of violence and, as such, presents a direct threat to the state's monopoly on the use of force. By contrast, abolitionists should directly locate interpersonal prisoner and prison-officer physical violence within the organisational structures of penal institutions.

Interpersonal-institutional violence is often taken for granted as a part of prison life and it is routinely accepted that physical violence can and will be deployed by prison officers where and when it is deemed necessary (Iadicola and Shupe, 2003: 28). Prison officer violence is also connected to the asymmetrical hierarchies of the penal institution. Although staff cultures differ in intensity across and within prisons, the hierarchical nature of the prison place exacerbates the 'us and them' mentality. Further, through a narrow focus on specific objectives, such as key operational indicators, targets and outcomes, prison officers may fail to question or evaluate the ends of their given role or function. This clouding of the 'big picture' can lead to social separation, negative stereotyping and dehumanising classifications neutralising moral commitments to the prisoner. Bauman (1989) refers to those institutional practices eroding their membership of a shared moral community as "adiaphorization". Such social distancing can generate ill treatment and scenarios where exclusion of the Other is considered unproblematic: the Other is forgotten, invisibilised or met with cold indifference.

Dividing practices categorising people as either deserving or undeserving, worthy or unworthy, eligible for care and support or less eligible are often deeply ingrained in prison officer occupational cultures (Kaufmann, 1988; Scott, 2008). The 'superior' prison officer identify becomes reliant upon the debasing of the 'inferior' Other — the prisoner. The good, law-abiding and honourable prison officer should be treated with respect, whereas the inadequate prisoner should not. The prisoner is no longer perceived as a genuine victim but rather can be blamed for their own suffering. Johan Galtung (2013: 57) refers to this as the "Self Other gradient", for the badness of the prisoner (the Other) has to be emphasised so that the goodness of the prison officer (the Self) becomes more apparent.

Physical violence against prisoners is sometimes viewed by staff as not only necessary but also morally justifiable. Violence is used for the right reasons to control the less eligible prisoner, something which has been referred to as "righteous violence" (Edney, 1997: 291). Prisoners are placed beyond the realm of understanding and common humanity. They are Othered. Using violence against prisoners can be a means of gaining respect and status as well as providing "excitement" in the otherwise bleak and monotonous routine (Scraton and McCulloch, 2009).

For prison officers, the location and timing of physical violence is often carefully chosen (Edney, 1997). Sometimes it takes place in concealed and isolated spaces of the prison where the officer cannot be easily seen; at other times, officers may utilise the opportunities given to them by prisoners — such as targeting unpopular prisoners during prisoner disturbances or on the way to the segregation unit, or applying greater force than necessary when applying restraints (Dawkins, 2006). More indirectly, prison officers can facilitate prisoner-on-prisoner interpersonal violence by turning a blind eye, such as leaving the cell of a potential victim open; failing to patrol hot-spot areas known for prisoner assaults; or failing to intervene when physical violence erupts between two prisoners (Levan, 2012).

But this is not the only form of institutional violence. Another silent, invisible yet potentially deadly form of state violence is "institutionally-structured violence" (Iadicola and Shupe, 2003, emphasis in original; Scott, 2015). Rather than a perverse or pathological aberration, institutionally structured violence is an inevitable and thoroughly legal feature of prison life. Institutionally structured violence is constructed through the operation of the daily rules, norms and procedures of penal institutions and impacts upon how interactions are formed and performed. It pertains when autonomy and choices are severely curtailed; human wellbeing, potential and development are undermined; feelings of safety and sense of security are weak; and human needs are systematically denied through the restrictive and inequitable distribution of resources (Sykes, 1958; Sim, 1984; Galtung, 1994; Gilligan, 2000; Scraton and McCulloch, 2009).

Prisons are structured according to the dictates of domination and exploitation. Hierarchical and antagonistic relationships result in an 'unequal exchange' between people ranked differently. This creates a form of structural vulnerability. Systemic exploitation takes many different forms in the prison place, such as through the informal prisoner code or bullying. For prisoners, physical violence can be a way of acquiring goods and services, keeping face or fronting out problems. In social hierarchies there are always winners and losers, with the losers open to physical (and sometimes sexual) exploitation. Though the physical violence of prisoners is often relatively minor (there are only small numbers of prisoner homicides), victimisation and exploitation is routinised and part of the social organisation of the prison (Edgar et al., 2003).

A person can never be truly free in prison — everywhere they will be restricted by invisible (and sometimes quite visible) chains that place significant limitations upon human movement. Restrictions on prisoner contact and relationships are structurally organised and, whilst physical violence is relational and dependent upon a number of contingencies, it is embedded in, and socially produced by, the situational contexts of daily prison regimes (Cohen, 1976). Most obviously, we think of this in terms of prison conditions, crowding and the spatial restrictions created by the architectural dimensions of the prison place itself. Prisons are a specifically designated coercive spatial order controlling human freedom, autonomy, choices, actions and relationships (Sykes, 1958). External physical barricades regulate the conditions of social existence through sealing the prisoner off from their previous life, whilst internal control mechanisms apply constraints to the minutiae of the prison day. Security restrictions on prisoner movements — such as access to educational and treatment programmes; religious instruction; work and leisure provision — are carefully structured and regimented around predetermined orderings of time and space. The architecture of the prison place determines the location of events and distribution of bodies and, in so doing, also highly regulates relationships and, subsequently, physical violence.

The general lack of privacy and intimacy; the 'forced relationality' between prisoners sharing a cell; insufficient living space and personal possessions; the indignity of eating and sleeping in what is in effect a lavatory; living daily and breathing in the unpleasant smells of body odour, urine and excrement; the humiliation of defecating in the presence of others, these are all institutionally structured situational contexts (Nagel, 1976). Yet if these visible and daily spatial constraints were all there was to institutionally structured violence then prison reformers' calls for improved prison conditions, greater forms of autonomy and enhanced resources allowing prisoners to choose how they live their lives might be considered sufficient. But they are not.

In one way or another, the sense of loss and wasting of the prison place affects all prisoners (Medlicott, 2001). The acute pains created through saturation in time consciousness can be overwhelming and, as a result, prisons become places of death. The literal death of a person — corporeal death — has haunted the prison place throughout its history. For centuries, hundreds of people have died in prison every year (Sim, 1990). In recent times, deaths in prisons have once again taken an upward turn. Between 2012 and 2013, self-inflicted deaths rose from sixty to seventy-four deaths — a 23% rise — and this number increased to eighty-three self-inflicted deaths in 2014. There were 242 deaths in total in prison in 2014, approximately one third of which were self-inflicted (MoJ, 2015: 7). The picture was even worse in 2015; 257 prisoners died this year, eighty-nine of whose deaths were self-inflicted (Bowcott, 2016). The deadly outcome of a self-inflicted death needs not the intentional hands or actions of another. Rather, it is a penal harm directly produced by the structural arrangements of the prison place. This constrains prisoners so much that some literally suffocate.

Historically, prisons have produced two other forms of 'death': civil death and social death. Civil death means a person is 'dead in law'. Talk of the legal or civil death of prisoners inevitably draws parallels with slavery, for which the concept was first deployed (Guenther, 2013). Though the removal of the legal rights of prisoners is no longer entirely complete in English law, prisoner rights are still very restrictive (Scott, 2013a). Since the 1970s, the legal recognition of prisoner rights has been placed on 'life support' and though the judicialisation of penal power has allowed access to the courts and has strengthened prisoners' due-process rights, successful prisoner petitions are still relatively rare, especially with regards to living conditions (Scott, 2013a). The continued denial of prisoners' right to vote,[1] and the political controversy that calls for political enfranchisement have engendered, is evidence that the legal death of prisoners still holds some weight and that the prison sentence continues to define the person. As former Prime Minister David Cameron put it on 3 November 2010 (cited in Horne and White, 2015: 25):

> It makes me physically ill even to contemplate having to give the vote to anyone who is in prison. Frankly, when people commit a crime and go to prison, they should lose their rights, including the right to vote.

Civil death has become entwined with the third form of 'death' produced through imprisonment: social death. Social death is 'symbolic death' rather than physical death, where the former self is consciously extinguished as a worthy and moral subject. Social death is about the 'death' of human relationships, status and moral standing and, at its extreme, refers to the non-recognition of the prisoner as a fellow human. Whilst in prison, the prisoner is treated like an outcast (Guenther, 2013).

---

[1] See the decision of the European Court of Human Rights on 6 October 2005 in *Hirst v United Kingdom* (No. 2).

The prison sentence is a moral judgement that leads to the construction and distancing of a perceived morally inferior person. The person imprisoned is denounced and censured. The prisoner label is a category of blame, shame and humiliation — and, irrespective of their offence, the label of 'prisoner' carries with it the weight of social and moral condemnation. In a hierarchical and antagonistic environment, the prisoner is a subject whose views, opinions and voice can be refused or ignored, making them increasingly vulnerable to exploitation. The former self has died. Consequently, the prisoner may be required to find new ways to secure respect.

The long-term harmful consequences of social death come from the literal severing of the prisoner from previous relationships in the wider community. An individual's self-identity is shaped through relations with other people, and a person can only recognise themselves through engagement with fellow humans. Prisons remove the existing positive foundations of personhood. Living relationships become dead ones. The elimination of relationships constituting self-identity can result in the demolition of the former personality (Scott and Codd, 2010). The estrangement of imprisonment removes mechanisms of support and mutual aid, undermines family life and damages the ability to live in normal human society. It takes people out of their familiar situational contexts and subsequent damage to the self can prevent re-socialisation (Guenther, 2013). For abolitionists, the long-term harmful consequences wrought by social death are further evidenced by high recidivism rates and difficulties in successful resettlement.

Prisons, then, are places of enforced estrangement. They will always be places that take things away from people: they take a persons' time, relationships, opportunities, and sometimes their life. Prisons are places which constrain human identity and foster feelings of fear, *alienation* and emotional isolation. For many, prisons provide lonely, isolating and brutalising experiences. Prisons are places of dull and monotonous living and working routines depriving prisoners of their basic human needs (Sykes, 1958; Galtung, 1969). For prisoners, this can lead to a disintegration of the self and corporeal death. For prison officers, this can lead to a culture of moral indifference (Scott, 2008). Such indifference is socially produced in a culture where prisoner humanity is neutralised and pain ignored. Through distantiation and institutionalised "adiaphorization" (Bauman, 1989), the prisoner is no longer considered a member of our shared moral community. To be sure, the institutionally structured violence of the prison place is much more conducive to producing indifference and neglect than a commitment to an ethics of care (Scott, 2008).

Abolish violence

Abolitionists need to build a political powerbase which can effectively challenge penal expansionism. This chapter has called for abolitionist activists to strategically adopt the language of state violence as a first step towards building a new anti-prison counter-hegemony. Abolitionism must build links with socialist, anarchist, feminist and anti-violence peace activists and connect with social justice, pro-democratic and human rights groups and organisations. By speaking the language of state violence, political alliances joining together the above mentioned grassroots movements and NGOs can be built.

The starting point for a new abolitionist counter-hegemonic social movement is to name the prison place for what it actually is — an institution of legalised and officially sanctioned violence. This entails denaturalising the taken for granted deprivations that are organisationally structured within daily penal regimes. Abolitionists must debunk current myths around the *virtuous* and *morally performing prison* and instead acknowledge that prisons produce a specific moral climate that is more likely to dehumanise and dehabilitate than positively transform an individual. Articulating the brutal mundaneness of everyday prison life that is so corrosive to human flourishing and wellbeing can help facilitate a new culture that can assist in making state violence more visible.

Abolitionists must emphasise how prisons are the enemy of the people, not their protectors. Prisons are a human tragedy for all those caught up in exploitative and oppressive relations. Focusing on prisons as state violence also highlights the tensions around promoting the criminal law as a means of responding to social harms such as rape and sexual violence. Indeed the punishment of sexual violence has not only led to the reinforcement of state legitimacy, but, in the US at least, to further expansion of the penal net among poor, disadvantaged and marginalised women (Ritchie, 2012). The belief that prisons can be used to 'control' male violence and create greater safety and public protection are today key ways of legitimating the prison place: by focusing on the violence of penal confinement it is possible to challenge this logic. The prison is unlikely to provide a means of increasing the safety and well-being of anyone, be they 'victims', 'offenders' or 'bystanders'.

This does not mean that current patterns of interactions in the prison place cannot be challenged at all. Prison authorities and prison officers should be encouraged to talk openly about the harmful consequences they see on a daily basis: they, alongside prisoners, can bear witness to the truth of current penal realities and should be allowed to do so without negative consequences (i.e., with impunity). Whilst it is impossible to change all the structural arrangements of the prison place, there are still everyday operational practices and cultures that can transformed. Emancipatory humanitarian changes can be introduced to mitigate the worst excesses of institutionally structured violence. Some needless deprivations can be removed and many daily infringements of human dignity can be greatly reduced. Cultural changes can be made to the prison place: a democratic culture providing first a voice to prisoners, and then a commitment to listen to that voice with respect and due consideration, can enhance recognition. Finding new non-violent ways of dealing with personal conflicts and troubles in prison would reduce the extent of physical violence and would help de-legitimate cultures of violence.

Abolitionism must be a movement of both deconstruction and reconstruction: providing a challenge to the penal system and demanding the social, economic and political emancipation of all people. Abolitionism must contribute to fostering an emancipatory politics and praxis. This requires political changes in the distribution of the social product so that society is organised in a way that can meet human needs. It means naming all forms of violence — including those of imperialism (colonialism), gendered violence, slavery, racism, neoliberal capitalism, poverty and war — and acknowledging how these forms of violence mutually reinforce each other. The united call must be for the *abolition of violence.*

Yet there remain potential pitfalls with this strategy. Adopting a broad-based approach to violence may lead to a decentring of focus away from prisons and punishment, especially if numbers of people with knowledge or experience of imprisonment are small. Further, when focusing on 'institutional structures', abolitionists must be careful that their argument is not reduced to a crude form of social pathology. There is also always the danger that structural analysis can lead to the denial of human agency. Human choices are constrained by social circumstances, not determined by them. Finally, recognising that prisons are spaces of legalised violence systematically producing pain, suffering and death privileges 'consequentialist' ethics. But the moral frameworks

138

underscoring penal abolitionism must not be reduced to consequentialism alone. Abolitionists must continue to make principled 'deontological' critiques, noting that 'two wrongs don't make a right'; emphasise the 'virtue' of 'turning the other cheek'; and draw upon the 'ethics of alterity' when proposing alternative ways of dealing with the violent actions of others (Hudson, 1996, 2003).

Prisons can never free themselves from violence entirely. Prisons systematically generate pain, suffering and death — they are places of iatrogenic penal harm. We must once again urgently, vigorously and robustly call for a radical reduction in the use of prison. Quite simply, violence cannot be used as a weapon against violence. But perhaps abolitionists can utilise the language of state violence as a way of connecting with like-minded people to form a new emancipatory politics and praxis.

References

Barton, A., Corteen, K., Scott, D. and Whyte, D. (eds) (2006) *Expanding the Criminological Imagination* London: Routledge

Bauman, Z. (1989) *Modernity and the Holocaust* Cambridge: Polity Press

Bowcott, O. (2016) 'Deaths and self-harm in prison rise sharply' in *Guardian,* 28 January 2016

Critchley, S. (2012) *The Faith of the Faithless* London: Verso

Cohen, A.K. (1976) 'Prison Violence: A sociological perspective' in Cohen, A.K., Cole, G.F. and Bailey, R.G. (eds) (1976) *Prison Violence* London: Lexington Books

Davis, A. (2005) *Abolition Democracy* California: Seven Stories Press

Dawkins, J. (2006) *The Loose Screw* Essex: Apex Publishing Ltd

Edney, R. (1997) 'Prison Officers and Violence' in *Alternative Law Journal* pp 289–292

Edgar, K., O'Donnell, I. and Martin, C. (2003) *Prison Violence: The Dynamics of Conflict, Fear and Power* Devon: Willan

Engels, F. (1844) *The Condition of the Working Class in England* (unpaginated) https://www.marxists.org/archive/marx/works/1845/condition-working-class/ch07.htm (consulted 6 May 2015)

Galtung, J. (1969) 'Violence, Peace, and Peace Research' *Journal of Peace Research* Volume 6, No. 3 pp 167–191

Galtung, J. (1994) *Human Rights in another Key* Cambridge: Polity Press

Galtung, J. (2013) 'Cultural Violence' pp 41–58 in Galtung, J. and Fisher, D. (2013) *Johan Galtung: Pioneer of Peace* London: Springer

Gilligan, J. (2000) *Violence: Reflections on our Deadliest Epidemic* New York: Jessica Kingsley

Guenther, L. (2013) *Solitary Confinement: Social Death and its Afterlives* London: University of Minnesota Press

Hardoon, D., Fuentes-Neva, R. and Avele, S. (2016) *An Economy for the 1%* London: Oxfam http://policy-practice.oxfam.org.uk/publications/an-economy-for-the-1-how-privilege-and-power-in-the-economy-drive-extreme-inequ-592643

Hillyard, P. and Tombs, S. (2004) 'Beyond Criminology' in Hillyard, P., Tombs, S., Pantazis, C. and Gordon, D. (eds) (2004) *Beyond Criminology* London: Pluto Press

Horne, A. and White, I. (2015) *Prisoners' Voting Rights* (last updated 11 February 2015) House of Commons Library http://researchbriefings.files.parliament.uk/documents/SN01764/SN01764.pdf (consulted 10 May 2015)

Hudson, B.A. (1996) *Understanding Justice* Buckingham: Open University Press

Hudson, B.A. (2003) *Justice in the Risk Society* London: Sage

Iadicola, P. and Shupe, S. (2003) *Violence, Inequality and Human Freedom* (second edition) Oxford: Rowman & Littlefield Publishers

Kauffman, K., (1988) *Prison Officers and Their World* Cambridge, MA: Harvard University Press

Laclau, E. and Mouffe, C. (1985) *Hegemony and Socialist Strategy* London: Verso

Levan, K. (2012) *Prison Violence: Causes, Consequences and Solutions* Aldershot: Ashgate

Medlicott, D. (2001) *Surviving the Prison Place* Aldershot: Ashgate

Ministry of Justice (MoJ) (2015) *Safety in Custody Statistics England and Wales: Deaths in Prison Custody to March 2015 — Assaults and Self-Harm to December 2014* London: MoJ

Nagel, W.G. (1976) 'Prison Architecture and Prison Violence' in Cohen, A.K., Cole, G.F. and Bailey, R.G. (eds) (1976) *Prison Violence* London: Lexington Books

Oparah, J. (2013) 'Why No Prisons?' in Scott, D. (ed) (2013) *Why Prison?* Cambridge: Cambridge University Press

Prison Reform Trust (2015) *Prison: The Facts — Bromley Briefings Summer 2015* London: PRT

Ritchie, B. (2012) *Arrested Justice: Black Women, Violence and America's Prison Nation* London: New York University Press

Scott, D. (2008) 'Creating Ghosts in the Penal Machine' in Bennett, J. and Crewe, B. (eds) (2008) *Understanding Prison Staff* London: Routledge

Scott, D. (2013a) 'The Politics of Prisoner Legal Rights' in *Howard Journal of Criminal Justice*

Scott, D. (2103b) 'Unequalled in Pain' in Scott, D. (2013) (ed) *Why Prison?* Cambridge: Cambridge University Press

Scott, D. (2015) 'Eating your Insides Out' in *Prison Service Journal*, September 2015, No. 221, pp 68–72

Scott, D. and Codd, H. (2010) *Controversial Issues in Prisons* Buckingham: Open University Press

Scraton, P. and McCulloch, J. (eds) (2009) *The Violence of Incarceration* London: Routledge

Scraton, P., Sim, J. and Skidmore, P. (1991) *Prisons under Protest* Milton Keynes: Open University Press

Siddle, J. (2015) 'The punishment at Walton is not being in jail — it's surviving there hour by hour' in *Liverpool Echo,* 15 February 2015

Sim, J. (1984) 'Violence in Prisons' in *Emergency*, No. 1, Winter 1983/4 pp 18–21

Sim, J. (2009) *Punishment and Prisons* London: Sage

Sykes, G. (1958) *Society of Captives* New Jersey: Princeton University Press

The Equality Trust (2015) 'The Scale of Economic Inequality in the UK' http://www.equalitytrust.org.uk/about-inequality/scale-and-trends/scale-economic-inequality-uk (consulted 30 May 2015)

Trammell, R. (2012) *Enforcing the Convict Code: Violence and Prison Culture* London: Lynne Rienner

9

Against Criminal Injustice, For Social Justice: Reflections and possibilities[1]

This chapter was originally published in the European Group Newsletter *in May 2015.*

At the time of writing, April 2015, the general election in the UK is only a few weeks away. We are in urgent need of plausible and radical alternatives to the neoliberal rhetoric of mainstream political parties and the formulation of new social policies that can rewrite the old story of the 'rich getting richer and the poor getting prison'. We need to start with an honest appraisal of the limitations of contemporary political and penal governance in our times (in the UK and across many other countries in Europe) and formulate a new libertarian socialist vision promoting social solidarity, human emancipation and genuine equality for all. In this chapter, I wish to make some progress in this direction by discussing the problem of 'criminal injustice' — that is, the injustices and inequalities exacerbated by the criminal process — and the urgent need to tackle such 'criminal injustice' through radical interventions grounded in the principles of social justice. Let me start, though, by thinking about the nature and extent of 'criminal injustice'.

Against criminal injustice

When thinking about 'criminal injustice', we first must focus on the people processed by the institutions of the criminal law. Exclusive focus on criminal acts renders invisible the social backgrounds of people who have been criminalised and the very real human costs of economic and social inequalities. Most people, in some way or other, operate through

---

[1] This paper was originally delivered at the 'Sites of Resistance' conference organised by the new Resisting 'Crime' and Criminalisation Group at Manchester Metropolitan University, 25 March 2015.

stereotypes, but when it comes to how the law is enforced it is essential that special attention is given to investigating discriminatory stereotyping. By examining *who is criminalised* (individual biographies and social backgrounds) rather than just *what they have done*, we gain a picture of how criminalisation works within a structurally unequal society. Critical criminologists and abolitionists have argued for many years that the application of the criminal label in the UK is determined not by what you do, but by who you are, and how closely you conform to stereotypes of respectability or un-respectability (Sim et al., 1987; Scraton and Chadwick, 1991; Hudson, 2003; Scott, 2013b; Bell, 2015).

Smokescreens
People belonging to social classifications labelled as high risk with low respectability are the ones most likely to come under police suspicion and surveillance. Stereotyping of group characteristics, around 'race', class, gender, age, disability and sexuality, alongside current social constructions of 'crime', result in common-sense perceptions of particular individuals as 'threats' to the social order. These 'suspect communities' (Hillyard, 1994; Pantazis and Pemberton, 2009), comprising largely poor people, are not necessarily more criminogenic than the middle classes, but their 'illegalities' do become the main focus of the institutions of the criminal law. Despite the widespread prevalence of 'illegal activities' across all social classes, it is the poor and disadvantaged — those raised in care; those unemployed or on benefits; victims of sexual violence; or those who have difficulties in reading and writing — who are most likely to be Othered, criminalised and then penalised. It is the poor who are subject to 'categorical suspicion': people regarded as dangerous and problematic not because of what they have done "but because of the groups to which they belong" (Hudson, 2003: 61).

My focus on 'criminal injustice' today concerns primarily the criminalisation of poverty and the demonisation of the poor. Criminalisation and penalisation are means of conveying an image of a concerned government taking vigorous action to alleviate troubles faced by the poor, marginalised and socially unequal. Thomas Mathiesen (1990) calls this the *action function* of the criminal law: the government, through policing and punishment, appears to be taking action against a pressing social problem — 'crime' in impoverished communities. But in doing so, criminalisation can create a 'smokescreen', hiding the brutal and harmful realities of poverty (Box, 1983). Especially in times of economic crisis or decline — such as the period in Britain since the financial crisis of 2008 —

lawbreakers from socially marginalised and excluded backgrounds are presented as a menace to law-abiding communities. Indeed, for Barbara Hudson (1993), such a strategy of 'blaming the poor for their poverty' and associated difficulties is absolutely necessary: anything other than their inherent criminality and individual inadequacies might lead to questions being asked as to *why* the economically powerful did not do more to help ease their predicament. In other words, criminalisation becomes a means of justifying the neglect of the poor, whose difficulties in life can now be passed off as individual pathologies.

Such demonisation and monstering falls most heavily upon those from Black and Minority Ethnic (BME) groups. This scapegoating has long been noted (Hall et al., 1978). Paul Gilroy (1987) some thirty years ago talked about the 'myth of black criminality', where BME groups in the UK are mythologically constructed as having a greater propensity to lawbreaking when compared to 'white' populations. The 'myths' of Black lawbreaking provide a way to 'explain away' the abandonment and neglect of impoverished and marginalised BME communities. The current UK coalition government's strategy is undoubtedly one of blaming the poor for their poverty, thus creating a smokescreen around its systemic neglect of these same groups via social policy and welfare provision.

We cannot understand criminalisation without also reflecting upon social inequalities and social injustice. The bigger the social distance between individuals, the easier it is to use the criminal label (Scott, 2013b). Growing social and economic inequalities result in the social production of moral indifference, psychic distance and dehumanisation. 'Us and them' mentalities that are highly corrosive for solidarity, cooperation and trust pertain. Inequalities provide a hotbed for practices of Othering and the application of the criminal law as a means to deal with social problems. Through such a focus on a person's illegalities, we can lose sight of the human being and the difficulties and troubles they face in everyday life; the harms and traumas they have experienced; their impoverished social backgrounds and their impoverished future life chances. 'Us and them' mentalities lead to the targeting of the 'incorrigible' and 'undeserving'. This scapegoating may or may not deliver increased security and safety for the rich and powerful but what it definitely does do is exacerbate existing forms of social exclusion. Through Othering processes, we inevitably lose sight of the common humanity of those people who are struggling to just survive in modern Britain.

In this context, we should not be surprised to learn that the criminal law is a central means of regulating poverty. The management of poverty via the criminal process has increasingly become a key governmental strategy following successive political administrations' embrace of neoliberalism from the late 1970s in the UK and elsewhere. Whatever terms we use to describe the criminalised poor — 'scroungers', 'layabouts', 'enemies within', 'risk posers', and so on and so forth — what is undoubtedly true is that it is the people who are most disadvantaged that are being targeted by the contemporary 'risk control' policies and repressed by the penal apparatus of the Capitalist State (Scraton and Chadwick, 1991; Hudson, 2003; Scott, 2013b).

Human wrongdoing and the application of the criminal label must be understood within wider social contexts and the social constraints shaping people's lives. The game is fixed — we are not all playing the game of life with the same rules or on the same kind of playing surface. The extent to which a wrongdoer deserves to be punished must be linked to levels of culpability, individual responsibility and blameworthiness because the application of the criminal law does not have equality of impact or provide equal justice in unequal societies. Where an individual's social situation may not only leave them more vulnerable to offending but also, whatever their behaviour, more vulnerable to criminalisation, culpability must be evaluated. Punishment sends a moral message that conveys blame, but obligations to obey 'white middle class man's law' (Hudson, 1993) are not something possessed equally by all. In a materially unequal society, we do not all have the same life opportunities or attachments. A person's choices are constrained by their socially situated set of lived circumstances (Box, 1983). Poor offenders will have less attachment to society and, as Joe Sim (1991) has argued, "if you ain't got nothing, you ain't got nothing to lose". Many of the risk posers sentenced by the courts have little chance of respecting the conditions imposed by their penalties. Indeed, the criminal process simply creates a new set of hurdles for offenders to fall over. In socially unequal societies we must reflect carefully on the current distribution of both benefits and pains, and on what this means in terms of justice and injustice.

The perfect storm

This leads us to consider the nature and extent of social injustice, poverty and social exclusion in the UK and acknowledge how daily choices and lived realities are constrained by such structural inequalities. We also need to recognise that these pressures and constraints have been intensifying over the last four decades. Since 1979, we have witnessed a concentration of wealth and power at the top of society and an erosion of power, status and opportunities for the rest of us, especially those at the bottom of society. A great storm called neoliberalism has hit the shores of the UK, and the lives of many poor people have been shipwrecked in the interests of the rich and powerful.

As the gap between the rich and the rest has grown, social solidarity has weakened. Ultimately, the rich believe they deserve to be rich because of *who they are* — that is their riches are based on their own personal merits, aptitudes and worth. As a direct consequence of this they believe that the poor deserve to be poor based upon *who they are* — their personal inadequacies, weaknesses and moral degeneracy. The greater the inequality gap, the fewer opportunities to share the lived realities of those struggling for daily bread, the harder it is to undermine such assumptions. Inequalities breed psychic distancing and Othering, which allow people to neglect the needs of fellow humans. It leads to anti-poor rhetoric and the monstering of the working classes. The distinction between the 'respectable'/'deserving' and the 'unrespectable'/'undeserving' poor finds fertile ground in Britain today. In today's parlance, this 'us and them' mentality is expressed in terms such as 'workers and strivers' vs. 'shirkers and skivers' (Lansley and Mack, 2015: 121). Those on benefits are hardest hit — they are seen as 'pulling the rope' and scrounging benefits from the respectable and law-abiding taxpayer. The principle of less eligibility — that the living standards of those on benefits should be lower than the waged labourer — is alive and well, and its influence is growing. Yet, despite claims of mass benefit fraud, government statistics show that the levels of benefits being fraudulently claimed is less than 1% and that people are more likely to not claim benefits they are entitled to than to falsely claim for benefits (Ibid.).

The popular media, government policies in recent years and neoliberal labour-market realities perpetuate stigmatising myths and exacerbate social exclusion. People want to work, but there are just not enough good jobs out there. There are a significant number of bad jobs (but, even here, not enough to meet the demand of two million unemployed) and these bad jobs are characterised by low pay; insecure work; increased forms of surveillance and competition in the workplace; demanding targets around productivity; and unsocial hours. 'Zero-hour contracts' have grown exponentially in recent times, and Lansley and Mack (2015) note that in 2014 there were 1.4 million people on "no guaranteed hours" contracts. The government's response has not been promising. What we are witnessing is a growing punitiveness of welfare provision. The 'penalisation of poverty' is no longer just restricted to the criminal process: 'criminal injustice' has spread beyond criminalisation, with its presence now increasingly evident in the policies and practices of welfare institutions. The end result is the same: the blaming, stigmatising and 'punishing of the poor'.

Government welfare policies now aim to responsibilise and sanction the poor rather than provide help, aid and assistance. Last year, one million people receiving either Jobseeker's Allowance (unemployed) or Employment and Support Allowance (disabled) were sanctioned by the welfare agencies for infractions such as missing an interview or refusing to take a job (including those with zero-hour contracts) (Ibid.). The *Guardian* journalist Patrick Butler (2015) gives us some indication of some of the reasons why benefits have been withheld:

1. Man who missed appointment due to being at hospital with his partner, who had just had a stillborn child.
2. Man sanctioned for missing an appointment at the jobcentre on the day of his brother's unexpected death. He had tried to phone Jobcentre Plus to explain, but could not get through and left a message which was consequently not relayed to the appropriate person.
3. Man who carried out sixty job searches but missed one which matched his profile.
4. Man had an appointment at the jobcentre on the Tuesday, was taken to hospital with a suspected heart attack that day, missed the appointment and was sanctioned for nine weeks.
5. Man who secured employment and was due to start in three weeks. He was sanctioned in the interim period because Jobcentre Plus told him he was still duty bound to send his CV to other companies.
6. Young couple who had not received any letters regarding an appointment that was thus consequently missed. Their address at the Department for Work and Pensions was wrongly recorded. They were left with no money for over a month.
7. One case where the claimant's wife went into premature labour and had to go to hospital. This caused the claimant to miss an appointment. No leeway given.
8. One man sanctioned for attending a job interview instead of Jobcentre Plus — he got the job so did not pursue a grievance against the JCP.
9. Man who requested permission to attend the funeral of his best friend; permission declined; sanctioned when he went anyway.

10. A diabetic sanctioned and unable to buy food was sent to hospital by GP as a consequence.

There may well be thousands of deaths related to benefit cutbacks and austerity measures in recent times, and forty-nine deaths directly related to benefit sanctions have been officially investigated. One of the biggest problems people face is that for two weeks following the suspension of benefits there is no financial support available (Butler, 2015).

Since 2013, benefits have been capped; the Social Fund (emergency loans) has been abolished and the recently introduced 'Universal Credit' (replacing six previously existing different benefits) has proved to be an administrative nightmare. The targeting of people who are disabled has been one of the most repugnant aspects of the current government's welfare reforms. Severely disabled people are likely to lose around £8,000 per person per year under the new policies; the Disability Living Allowance is being phased out and the new Personal Independence Payment could see around half a million people lose benefits; whilst the Work Capability Assessments — exploring what people can do and what work they could undertake — have been traumatic, unrealistic in their assessments of capacity and have led to tens of thousands losing benefits and many more being involved in a convoluted appeals process (Lansely and Mack, 2015).

Britain isn't eating
The intensification of the principle of less eligibility in welfare policies and the increasingly stringent and punitive means-testing and surveillance of benefits is leading to rising debts and desperate measures to find basic essentials. In the UK today, the average personal debt for those at the bottom of society stands at around 160% of their personal income. There has also been a massive rise in the use of food banks. In 2009, the Trussell Trust organised twenty-eight food banks in UK. In 2014, this number exceeded 400 (Lansley and Mack, 2015: 207). This alarming trend goes hand in hand with the growing inequalities blighting Britain today. Incomes at the top are rising at four times the rate of those at the bottom. The top 2.4 million households own assets worth around £1,300 billion, while the bottom 12 million own assets of around £150 million. The top 1% of the UK population owns around 23% of the UK's marketable wealth and, if housing is excluded, this rises to 33%. More broadly, the top 50% owns 91% of the wealth whereas the bottom 50% owns only 9% of the wealth (Scott, 2013b).

Poverty means not being able to participate fully in society. It prevents someone from feeling like they belong. Poverty is best understood as a "necessary need" (Heller, 1976) that develops and reflects the social norms of a given society at a given time. As such, necessary needs are not static but reflect the levels of material production (Ibid.). This understanding is reflected in the 'Poverty and Social Exclusion' and 'Breadline Britain' surveys (Lansley and Mack, 2015), which focus upon the extent of 'deprivation poverty' — a term which refers to people who are not able to afford *three or more basic necessities*. In 2015, 18 million people (30% of the population) live in poverty in the UK. This is double the number of 1983 (Ibid.). The financial squeeze is also being felt by those with middle-range incomes, who are gradually being dragged to the bottom. We are witnessing an increasing polarisation between those at the top and the rest of the population, something which Karl Marx predicted would happen some 150 years ago (Heller, 1976).

Economic inequalities intersect with and compound other social inequalities linked to gender, age, 'race', and as we discussed earlier, disability. It has long been noted that women in financial difficulties provide a human shield to protect their children from the worst excesses of poverty, and in recent times we have seen the emergence of the *'feminisation of poverty'* (Lister, 2003, emphasis in original). Young people in the poorest areas struggle to achieve success in formal education. Schools in the poorest areas have 10–25% of pupils achieving five GCSE passes at grades A–C, against a national average of just under 50%. Seventy per cent of people from BME backgrounds live in the eighty-eight most deprived local authority districts and over 30% of Pakistani and Black pupils and 50% of Bangladeshi pupils are eligible for free school meals. These children may well be eating, but those children who are entitled to free school meals do less well at gaining GCSEs (Child Poverty Action Group, 2015). According to Lansley and Mack (2015), over half of Black or Black British households and 42% of Pakistani or Bangladeshi households are in poverty, whilst on average African/Caribbean and Pakistani men earn £6,500 less than white men with similar qualifications (Lansley and Mack, 2015).

Poverty engenders Othering practices and processes of differentiation and demarcation, determining where the line is drawn between 'us and them'. Othering operates as a 'strategy of symbolic exclusion', which makes it easier for the rich to blame the poor for society's problems. The monstering of the poor also acts as a warning to others. Poverty leads to the denial of choices and opportunities; mental-health and physical-health problems; violations of dignity; inferior education; shorter life expectancy; susceptibility to violence; and general feelings of powerlessness. Yet poverty cannot be understood purely in material terms. Both as a concept and as a lived reality, it has to be understood also as a social relation — primarily between the poor and the non-poor. It is one of the greatest harms facing humanity today (Lister, 2003). Poverty crushes hope, undermines self-esteem, breeds ignorance and resentment, and not only damages health but can also considerably curtail life expectancy. It is a breeding ground for dividing practices of 'us and them', which not only demonise the 'have nots' but also engender fear and insecurity among those that have (Scott, 2013b).

Knowing we've taken the wrong path
Abolitionists and other critical criminologists must not remain silent about such 'criminal injustice'. It is important that critical criminologists give priority to highlighting the human costs, harms, injury and damage caused by neoliberalism, and its obsession with penalisation. The lived realities and experiences of those on the margins of society are too often hidden or ignored. They are invisibilised by the smokescreens created in advanced capitalist societies. The poor are forgotten and their claims to legal rights ignored. We need to make their lives visible — telling truth to power. We must recognise the inherent limitations of the aims of the 'criminal justice system'. Justice is aspirational and shaped by equal respect and non-hierarchal relationships, whereas criminal law is characterised by hierarchies of power, inflexible rules, violence, pain and death (Scott, 2013b). There is no path to justice via the penal law. The harms and problems that we have discussed above cannot be adequately addressed by the criminal process. As the late Barbara Hudson (1993, 2003) argued on many occasions, *there can be no legal justice in a socially unjust society.*

We should not forget that pain infliction is directed against the human being rather than the wrong perpetrated. Pain infliction, stigmatisation, suffering and harm creation — the core dimensions of penalisation — are morally problematic. Punishment cannot deliver *justice* but it can exacerbate existing forms of *injustice*. Punishment is a tragedy and its justifications a farce. Pain delivery is always a sign of failure — a reflection of injustice. The harmful implications of social inequality are warning signs. We need to act now to stop the damage that is being wrought by neoliberal political economy. Inequalities foster resentment, insecurity and despair. Growing insecurities leave too many with a sense of injustice.

Alongside this there are increasing concerns over yet more privatisation, more criminalisation, and more punitive responses to people who need help and assistance. Because they create so much political disillusionment, social and economic inequalities are a major threat to democracy itself (Bell, 2015).

We need to acknowledge that we have taken the wrong path and start thinking about radical alternatives. What we need is the strength and courage to take a different path and look for solutions grounded in the principles and values of *social justice*.

For social justice

We need to embrace a social justice agenda that can adequately address the problem of 'criminal injustice'. I think that this will entail recognition and respect for irreducible differences and an equitable redistribution of the social product. Alongside this, social justice calls for freedom from the dominance and oppression of the majority, and solidarity with, and responsibility for, sufferers. Principles of social justice are grounded in the assumption that other people should always be regarded as our equals, and we should avoid constructing false hierarchies that either superficially raise an individual's sense of importance or degrade another human. Majorities should not be allowed to dominate but ought to negotiate and hear the voices of minorities with equanimity. They must also be prepared to interrogate their own values and assumptions, and demonstrate a willingness to pay attention to the voices of 'concrete others'. To be treated the same is not equivalent to being treated equally. As Barbara Hudson (1993: 194) argued some twenty years ago:

> to do justice, we need to be alert not just to disparities arising from the unlike treatment of sameness, but also to discrimination in the like treatment of difference.

What is required, then, is a commitment to a social-justice normative framework that can recognise the fluidity and contingency of categorisations; demonstrate a willingness to pay attention to the voices of 'concrete others'; and acknowledge that each voice comes from a specifically situated position, standpoint or worldview rather than a generalised and abstract universalism.

The principles of social justice demand the deconstruction of hegemonic white-male power and its reconstruction, with the recognition of human diversity and justice. Drawing upon the insights of Paul Gilroy (1987), we can see that rather than being neutral, the law reflects existing discriminatory power relations: the presuppositions of the law are male, white and middle class, and reflect their material and property interests. Given the extent of human diversity and that we are not all the same, genuine *equality for all* is impossible under the assumptions of white male hegemony. The criminal law has failed to adequately protect Black and Minority Ethnic groups and migrant populations and, as described above, the enforcement of law is often blatantly discriminatory. Equality will be complex but we must somehow find a way in which it can encompass the diversity of human subjectivities.

An abolitionist real utopia

Critical analysis should draw attention to alternatives to capitalism and the punitive rationale that are ripe in our current historical conjuncture — what I have described elsewhere as an 'abolitionist real utopia' (Scott, 2013a). Building on the insights of Erik Olin Wright, this approach calls for radical alternatives that can (in effect) abolish poverty and the worst aspects of 'criminal injustice'. A good place to start would be the introduction of a Universal Basic (Minimum) Income (UBI) that is guaranteed for *all*. The UBI is a universal benefit that is not means-tested. It could abolish poverty and undermine less eligibility. It is also a 'competing contradiction' (Mathiesen, 1974) in that it undermines the logic of capitalist exploitation but, at the same time, works on the same logic as that of state benefits. The UBI would be a hugely radical change in the nature of helping and assisting those in dire need. It would also lead to increased freedom in terms of choosing whether to participate or not in the labour market for other people on middle incomes. The UBI would have a positive impact on the lives of most of the UK's population. It changes power relations in the labour market, for it shifts the balance of power away from multinational corporations and back to the workers (Scott, 2013a).

How would we pay for this? The answer is simple but not easy: tax the rich. If we increased taxation against the 120,000 richest people in the UK rather than penalise 120,000 poorest people in our prisons we would have enough money to pay for the UBI (Ibid.). Funds could also be generated by clawing back money from offshore tax avoidance schemes and legal loopholes. It has recently been estimated that £25 billion has been lost in tax revenues in the UK in recent years through such schemes (Lansely and Mack, 2015).

An even more radical funding proposal for the UBI would be the call to 'abolish inheritance now!' This is an idea that goes back to the great socialist thinker Emile Durkheim (cited in Scott, 2013a). Abolition of inheritance and would effectively not only abolish poverty but also economic inequalities. Significantly, it is something that can be done in our times (Scott, 2013b). There are a number of other key aspects of a social justice approach. These include creating full-time, permanent and meaning-creating work; a renewed focus on deep-seated learning at *all* levels, in effect moving from common sense to 'good sense' on core societal health; promoting the renationalisation of public utilities; improving the current transport networks and providing free public transport (trains and buses) where possible; supporting the NHS and demanding free physical and mental healthcare for *all*.

Human relationships must be at the very heart of justice, for justice and injustice are always more than simply processes: they are intimately tied to human outcomes and lived realities. Justice should be pursued via conflict-handling processes, reparation and reconciliation as the *norm* rather than *exception*. We must treat each other without violence, hostility or negative stereotyping, and with recognition of the other person's dignity and respect for their differences. When responding to wrongdoing, this means promoting interventions which locate the victim at the centre of the response; providing a voice to all parties, including the voice of the wrongdoer; downplaying or removing coercive solutions; making relationships the focal point of the reaction to a given problematic or troublesome act; focusing on positive and constructive outcomes and emphasising fixing, compensating and repairing acts or restoring balance; and ensuring that appropriate legal safeguards and forms of democratic accountability are in place for all parties (Hudson, 2003; Scott, 2013a; Scott, 2013c).

Rather than following a punitive logic, we need to explore how our responses to wrongdoing can best meet basic human values of kindness, compassion and care. We need interventions that are grounded in an 'ethic of care' that will encourage friendship, support and solidarity with those in need, whether they have broken the law or not. But we must also be closely attuned to the realities around disparities in power and wealth. Where there are economic equalities there will be power differentials, and where there are deposits of power there will be exploitation, domination and corruption. For too long have the powerful been able to act without consideration of responsibilities. We need to invert the logic of neoliberalism and call for the responsibilisation of the powerful with immediate effect (Bell, 2015).

Towards social justice

Let me bring this discussion to some kind of conclusion. What we need is a clear agenda for challenging 'criminal injustice' that is grounded in the values and principles of libertarian socialism and visions of social justice. First of all, we need to challenge neoliberal political economy and try to find a path towards social and economic equality. Equality is not the same as treating everyone the same but is about meeting each person's individual needs (i.e., equity). It is also about ensuring that everyone can maximise their potential so that they can fully participate in and contribute towards a just and decent society. Equality will inevitably be rather complex but it must involve a *recognition of human diversity*. We must learn to accept differences, but also acknowledge what we share — common humanity (Cohen, 2001). It is important that rather than focus on the 'enemies within', we should look to find new suitable friends (Scott, 2013b). Our responsibilities to other humans stretches way beyond our close family, friends and community to include those not known to us directly or those who do not share similar characteristics or social backgrounds. This is the true meaning of social justice (Cohen, 2001).

Justice involves thinking beyond the criminal process and repressive means of handling individual troubles and conflicts. We need to reappropriate the word 'security' and rearticulate it in a way that is once again focused on 'social security' and security against social harms. We also need to recapture the debate on 'freedom' — loosening it from its attachment to the 'market' and once more highlighting the importance of freedom from authoritarian policies and practices. To achieve such a goal, critical criminologists and penal abolitionists must strengthen ties with progressive social movements. We need solidarity and fidelity with grass-roots activism. As Thomas Mathieson has argued on a number of occasions, we must restore our faith in the power of local grass-roots resistance. This means direct engagement, and the building of movements which enshrine democratic participation. Following Lansley and Mack (2015), what we need in the North of England today is a 'Northern Truth and Social Justice Commission' to shed new light upon contemporary injustices in the north-east and north-west of England. Such a commission would be a means of facilitating the bearing of witness to the terrible hardship which is being created by the social and penal polices of the coalition government. A 'truth and social justice commission' is also something that could be replicated in other parts of the UK, across different regions in Europe and indeed in many other countries all around the world.

Finally, let me return to the penal apparatus of the Capitalist State and the punitive means-testing and sanctioning welfare policies of the current government, to which I have only one thing to say — *a plague on both your houses.*

References

Bell, E. (2015) *Soft Power and Freedom under the Coalition: State Corporate Power and the Threat to Democracy* Basingstoke: Palgrave

Box, S. (1983), *Power, Crime and Mystification* London: Routledge

Butler, P. (2015) 'Benefit Sanctions: The 10 trivial breaches and administrative errors' *Guardian* 24 March 2015

Child Poverty Action (2015) 'The Facts' http://www.cpag.org.uk/child-poverty-facts-and-figures (consulted 24 March 2015)

Cohen, S. (2001) *States of Denial* Cambridge: Polity Press

Gilroy, P. (1987) 'The Myth of Black Criminality' in Scraton, P. (ed) (1987) *Law, Order and the Authoritarian State* Milton Keynes: Open University Press

Hall, S., Jefferson, T., Critcher, C., Clarke, J. and Roberts, B. (1978) *Policing the Crisis* London: Macmillan

Heller, A. (1976) *Theory of Need in Marx* London: Allison & Busby

Hillyard, P. (1994) *Suspect Community* London: Pluto

Hudson, B.A. (1993) *Penal Policy and Social Justice* London: Macmillan

Hudson, B.A. (2003) *Justice in the Risk Society* London: Sage

Lansley, S. and Mack, J. (2015) *Breadline Britain: The Rise of Mass Poverty* London: Oneworld Publications

Lister, R. (2003) *Poverty* Cambridge: Polity Press

Mathiesen, T. (1974) *The Politics of Abolition* Oxford: Martin Robertson

Mathiesen, T. (1990) *Prisons on Trial* London: Sage

Pantazis, C. and Pemberton, S. (2009) 'From the Old to the New Suspect Community' in *British Journal Criminology* Volume 49, No. 5 pp 646–666

Scott, D. (2013a) 'Visualising an Abolitionist Real Utopia' in Malloch, M. and Munro, B. (eds) (2013) *Crime, Critique and Utopia* Basingstoke: Palgrave

Scott, D. (2013b) 'Unequalled in Pain' in Scott, D. (ed) (2013) *Why Prison?* Cambridge: Cambridge University Press

Scott, D. (2013c) 'Justifications of Punishment and Questions of Legitimacy' in Hucklesby, A. and Wahidin, A. (eds) (2013) *Criminal Justice (2nd Edition)* Oxford: Oxford University Press

Scraton, P. and Chadwick, K. (1991) 'The Theoretical and Political Priorities of Critical Criminology' in Stenson, K. and Cowell, D. (eds) (1991) *The Politics of Crime Control* London: Sage

Sim, J. (1991) 'You ain't got nothing you ain't got nothing to lose' in Bottomley, K., Fowles, A., Reiner, R. (eds) (1992) *Criminal Justice: Theory and Practice* London: British Society of Criminology

Sim, J., Gordon, P. and Scraton, P. (1987) 'Introduction' in Scraton, P. (ed) (1987) *Law, Order and the Authoritarian State* Milton Keynes: Open University Press

Part C:

Abolitionist Real Utopia

10.

Reimagining Citizenship:
Justice, responsibility and non-penal real utopias

This chapter was originally published in the European Group Journal Justice, Power and Resistance *in September 2016. The chapter is co-authored with Emma Bell.*

As has long been recognised, any attempts to develop alternatives to current penal practices are seriously hindered by the social distance created between offenders and a mythical law-abiding majority. The commonplace treatment of the majority of offenders as non-citizens precludes meaningful dialogue and debate with 'the citizenry'. In recent years, debate about penal issues amongst those who are seen to be worthy of citizenship has often been reduced to base populism (Pratt, 2007). Consequently, if we wish to move beyond exclusionary responses to 'crime' and social harm, the very notion of citizenship needs to be 'reimagined' in such a way that is genuinely pluralist and inclusive, incorporating all those affected by harmful behaviour, whether they are regarded as victims or offenders. This will entail rejecting all forms of penal fatalism in favour of a 'real utopian' approach (Wright, 2009) which seeks to recreate citizenship based on the principle of mutual responsibility and social action within institutions of 'the common'. Following Pierre Dardot and Christian Laval (2014), the 'common' is understood here as emancipatory praxis, as the shared activity through which people come together to develop alternatives to social problems, different from those proposed by either the State or private interests. It is a useful concept in that it is genuinely inclusive and encourages shared responsibility, thus enabling us to go beyond exclusive communities and penal policies generative of irresponsibilities. Rather than de-responsibilising citizens regarding their responses to social harm, as occurs when criminal justice issues are captured by the State, a real utopian conception of citizenship, based on this idea of the common would allow individuals and communities to play an active role in finding solutions to shared problems.

This chapter begins by discussing how exclusive notions of citizenship are detrimental to the very existence of a moral community based on mutual responsibility. It then explores how citizenship may be reimagined following the logic of 'considered utopianism' (Bourdieu) to foster a genuinely 'common' approach to problems of social harm. Drawing on the work of radical social theorists such as Proudhon (2011) and Dardot and Laval (2014), it is argued that a 'reimagined citizenship of the common' should foster both justice and responsibility. It is a citizenship that goes beyond communitarianism which, while fostering responsibility, often fails to promote justice, focusing as it does on the level of community rather than of state institutions. It is recognised that practices of the common will not emerge naturally and spontaneously but must be instituted (Dardot and Laval: 227). The final part of the chapter aims to demonstrate how constructing non-penal real utopias may both result from and help to institute a reimagined citizenship of the common. Picking up on Enrique Dussel's (2013) notion of 'liberation praxis', it suggests that citizenship must not be merely inclusive but also transformative if it is to be truly just. Transformative justice is thus promoted as a means of instituting a genuinely new non-penal rationality through emancipatory praxis.

Exclusive citizenship and irresponsibility

Conditional citizenship
As Reiner has pointed out, "the term 'citizenship' is now more often used in political discussion in exclusive, nationalistic, and particularistic terms, focusing on barriers to the status of citizen, with the stress on hurdles, testing, pedigree, and desert" (Reiner, 2010: 244). This trend has largely coincided with the rise of neoliberalism, with its emphasis on the need for individual citizens to become more 'active' in dealing with their own problems, rather than relying on the State. Consequently, citizenship has become increasingly conditional upon behaviour (Dwyer, 1998), upon an individual's capacity to accept personal responsibility. Those who are seen to have flouted the rules of the game are excluded from the normal rights of citizenship, notably 'social citizenship' (Marshall, 1950), as they find their social-security benefits withdrawn. Access to political citizenship is also increasingly restricted: for foreign nationals, it is increasingly subject to formal testing and economic status — for example, citizens or settled

foreign nationals wishing to sponsor their partner or spouse to join them in the UK must prove that they have a minimum gross annual income of £18,600. The civil rights of citizenship are also hard to enforce, as individual freedoms are threatened by new surveillance technologies and strengthened police powers.

Renewed focus on the responsibilities rather than the rights of citizens has been a useful way for neoliberal governments to scapegoat individuals for social problems whilst simultaneously justifying reductions in state spending. Yet the focus on the individual over the State has been much criticised, notably by New Labour seeking to build a 'third way' between the excessive individualism of the Thatcher years and the statism of the post-war period, and by Cameron seeking to 'detoxify' the Conservative Party of its 'nasty' (May, 2002), uncaring image. For both, the active citizen was not to be regarded solely as an individual but as a member of a wider community. What Jean and John Comaroff describe as the "Second Coming of Civil Society" was to be "the ultimate magic bullet in the Age of Millennial Capitalism" (2001: 44), capable of providing the necessary social glue to hold together societies fragmented by the ravages of neoliberalism, whilst enabling successive politicians to rebrand their politics. For New Labour, civil society was to be boosted by communitarianism which would ensure that individuals assumed responsibility, not for their own ends, but in the best interests of the community as a whole. For Cameron's Conservatives, the 'Big Society' was to enable individuals to work together to create "communities with oomph — neighbourhoods who [sic] are in charge of their own destiny, who feel if they club together and get involved they can shape the world around them" (Cameron, 2010a). In both cases, individuals and communities were to be liberated from the State and all of its coercive capacity, yet this vision ignored the coercive power of communities themselves.

Coercive communities and de-responsibilisation
For Barbara Hudson, communities can be extremely coercive, especially when they seek to enforce values, often imposing "a constriction of freedom of choice about how one lives" and grouping together to exclude those who fail to conform (Hudson, 2003: 91). Erik Olin Wright has also drawn attention to the fact that communities can foster "exclusionary solidarities" as well as "universalistic ones" (Wright, 2009: 267). The problem is often one of responsibility as the onus tends to be placed on individuals to integrate into the community rather than on the community

to integrate individuals: responsibility is often "a one-way street" (Hudson, Ibid.: 107).

Even more problematic is the fact that communities habitually divest themselves of responsibility altogether for individuals they deem to be unworthy of citizenship. Offenders in particular are often cast out of the community, both physically — in prison — and symbolically — by loss of the basic rights of citizenship. This is illustrated by the loss of the right to vote. As Duff has explained, the law can no longer bind us as citizens, as it is no longer "the law of an 'us' to which [offenders] unqualifiedly belong": it becomes the law of a 'we' from which they are excluded (Duff, 2005: 213). Yet a former Prime Minister regarded stripping offenders of such essential civil rights as entirely normal. David Cameron, commenting on the issue following the European Court of Human Rights' declaration that the UK's current blanket ban on voting is incompatible with Article 3 of the European Convention on Human Rights, declared, "when people commit a crime and go to prison, they should lose their rights, including the right to vote" (Cameron, 2010b). The exclusivity of communities is thus supported, and even encouraged, by the State, demonstrating the importance of moving beyond the State when developing real utopias, a point we shall return to below.

Once communities exclude 'undesirables' from their midst, they are effectively exempt from further responsibility for them, despite the government rhetoric of community responsibilisation. Such de-responsibilisation is regarded as legitimate once the community is accorded the status of victim. Indeed, as crime is always seen as being perpetrated against the community rather than being produced *in and by* the community, responsibility is seen to lie solely with offending individuals. This line of thinking helps to construct offenders as 'Other', as lying outside the moral community. As Zygmunt Bauman has so eloquently explained, once such social distance is created, undesirables can be dehumanised and "moral inhibition" regarding their treatment suspended (1989: 25). Using the work of Helen Fein, he effectively demonstrates how they are placed outside the "universe of obligation", cast into a world in which moral precepts do not bind. Punitive rather than welfarist responses to social harm are thus favoured.

The failure of liberal penal policies

Liberal penal polices have attempted to foster the development of more inclusive communities underpinned by the notion of responsibility. Communities have been encouraged to take more responsibility for dealing with harmful behaviour and reintegrating offenders, whilst wrongdoers themselves have been encouraged to take more responsibility for their own actions. One of the most influential liberal penological approaches in this mould is the "responsibility and justice paradigm" (Scott, 2001). Primarily influential in the 1990s and 2000s, this approach accepts the legitimacy of state punishments but advocates a new, more inclusive relationship between the prison and community (King and Morgan, 1980; Woolf, 1991). Prisons should be more like the community with "permeable walls" and stronger "community ties" (Woolf, 1991, para 1.148). Prisons should also be normalised in the sense that basic living standards and legal protection ought to be the same for all citizens, whether they reside inside or outside prison. Yet even this liberal rhetoric can be misleading. The prisoner is to be treated with 'respect' only if they make responsible choices whilst inside (Woolf, 1991; Scott, 2001). The community's responsibility to reintegrate offenders is only to be activated once offenders deem themselves worthy by demonstrating their own capacity to take responsibility. In recent times, the new Conservative government has sought to get communities involved in the rehabilitation of prisoners. The former Justice Secretary, Michael Gove, exhorted ordinary citizens to "help the hungry, the sick and the imprisoned" by playing a role in prisoner rehabilitation (Gove, 2015) whilst the then Prime Minister encouraged businesses to offer former prisoners a second chance by providing them with employment (Cameron, 2016). Prisoners themselves are to be responsibilised for their own rehabilitation, with privileges and earned release determined by participation in educational activity, in particular (Gove, 2015). Yet, in continuity with other 'liberal' reforms, community responsibility is conditional and selective: only those wrongdoers who are considered responsible are deemed worthy of reintegration into the moral community. As Cameron put it, the aim is to find the "diamonds in the rough and [help] them shine" (Cameron, 2016). The 'irredeemables' can legitimately be kept apart from society, preferably behind bars.

The possibility of the moral inclusion of wrongdoers is thus generally predicated on a logic of exclusion. The current focus on the normalisation of prisons through education, as promoted by Gove, can be understood as playing a role in shaping hegemonic understandings of the most appropriate responses to 'crime' and social harm. However, imprisonment is profoundly unnatural. Without doubt, prisons are cruel, lonely and destructive places. Confinement within such painful, isolating and brutal institutions is compounded by the constant menace of systematic abuse, maltreatment and, ultimately, dehumanisation. Threats to dignity, self-respect, personal safety and other prerequisites of humanity seem endemic to the largely hidden world of the prison. The problem is that current policies and initiatives aimed at reform and education are defined and defended on the terrain of the state. The prison aims to coerce offenders into being responsible citizens, ignoring the fact that prisons are hardly the appropriate environment for such purposes. There is, then, an urgent requirement to develop non-penal real utopian interventions, grounded in non-state understandings and practices of responsibilities and justice, which may effectively responsibilise *all* citizens, whether they are offenders, victims or potential victims of crime. It is necessary to reimagine the very concept of citizenship on which inclusive communities may thrive. We propose a real utopian vision of citizenship based on responsibility and justice, which we hope may invite non-penal real utopian interventions to deal with offending behaviour. Rather than embedding 'penal utopias', it is hoped that these visions may open up possibilities for real *non-penal* utopian alternatives to the penal rationale.

Towards a real utopian citizenship of the common

Citizenship as real utopia
Reimagining citizenship entails abandoning fatalism — the idea that only exclusionary responses are appropriate for problematic behaviour — in favour of a 'considered utopianism'. Following Ernst Bloch, Pierre Bourdieu described this strategy as one whereby we "work *collectively* on analyses able to launch realistic projects and actions closely matched to the objective processes of the order they are meant to transform" (Bourdieu, 1997: 128, emphasis in original). This idea fits closely with Wright's notion of real utopia: "utopian ideals that are grounded in the real potentials of humanity, utopian destinations that have accessible waystations, utopian designs of institutions that can inform our practical tasks of navigating a world of imperfect conditions for social change" (Wright, 2009: 4). With regard to developing a more inclusive notion of citizenship on which non-penal real utopian solutions might be based, this entails delineating the actually existing principles which would inform such a notion and exploring the real potentialities of collective action. Non-penal real utopias are about thinking differently, visualising new possibilities and realities and facilitating transformative change (Scott, 2013). They involve enhancing life and promoting human flourishing, and showing that another world is possible (Wright, 2009). Yet they must be

feasible and desirable, they must be possible in our historical conjuncture and also meet the demands of justice — that is, be democratic, be rights-regarding and facilitate (or are at least be consistent with) an equitable distribution of the social product and the meeting of human need (Dussel, 1985).

Key principles for inclusive citizenship

The first key principle which should inform an inclusive notion of citizenship is that of horizontality. Citizenship is commonly understood as a vertical relationship with the State whereby the latter determines the terms of that relationship in a top-down manner. Indeed, citizenship has been historically tied to the nation state under whose authority associated rights and obligations are determined (Isin and Turner, 2002: 3). Although the State claims to delegate greater power to communities, it is essentially the State which determines which citizens should have access to which rights. Following John Hoffman, it is necessary to go beyond the State when thinking about citizenship, since its monopoly on the 'legitimate' use of force means that those subject to force are necessarily prevented from exercising the rights and duties of citizenship (Hoffman, 2004). Furthermore, and this point is particularly relevant with regard to penal policy, "the use of force is inimical to conflict resolution: only negotiation and arbitration can resolve conflicts of interest, since force crushes agency, and the agency of all the parties is essential if a dispute is to be successfully tackled" (Hoffman, 2004: 173).

Agency is the second key principle which must underpin inclusive citizenship. As suggested above, agency is effectively denied in mainstream notions of citizenship as communities are divested of responsibility for 'undesirable' citizens. Those who are excluded from citizenship, whilst deemed responsible for their own exclusion, are also denied the opportunity to exercise agency in terms of determining how reparation can be made for harmful behaviour. As Hoffman underlines, the agency of *all* parties in a dispute is essential. This leads us to the third key principle supporting inclusive citizenship: the idea that citizenship should be plural, excluding no one. This means including those on the margins and periphery of society, as well as those in the centre.

Fourthly, all should be included on equal terms. As Nancy Fraser has explained, there must be "parity of participation" based on "social arrangements that permit all (adult) members of society to interact with one another as peers". The principle of equality is best upheld by affirming basic human rights, not limited to narrowly defined, and often conditional, citizenship rights. We thus suggest that it is necessary to go beyond "remarshalling citizenship", as Robert Reiner (2010: 261) advises, calling for a restoration of the political, social and civil rights of citizenship. Whilst this would certainly lead to a more inclusive notion of citizenship than that which currently exists, it is a version of citizenship which is understood primarily vis-à-vis the State rather than as solidaristic interaction with other citizens.

A citizenship of the common

These key principles ought to underpin what we describe as 'an inclusive citizenship of the common', based on an ethics of justice and responsibility. This idea finds its origins in commonism. Commonism is a form of socialism promoting communities of mutual care and support and the collective organisation of the relations of production so that it can meet human needs for all. The concept has a long tradition. It finds its origins in the ideas of early English socialists such as Gerrard Winstanley (2010 [1649]) whose writings and activism aimed to emancipate "common land" for the people and liberate the "spirit of community", and the French socialist tradition of 'mutualism' promoted by Pierre-Joseph Proudhon (2011).[1] Yet it is as a contemporary social movement that it has recently attracted renewed attention (Dardot and Laval, 2014), expressing its aims to build non-authoritarian partnerships and networks of cooperation and collaboration in everyday settings such as the workplace, the family, and the wider community (Shantz, 2013). Symbolically, commonism is a means of identifying our "common heritage", recognising each person's "common humanity" and facilitating "meaningful participation in decision-making processes around housing, work, education and food" (Ibid.: 11). Of central concern is the development of anti-capitalist, real utopian practices in the here and now, but there is also interest in non-penal means of resolving conflicts and addressing social harms.

Commonism questions the legitimacy of authoritarian power, structural inequalities and institutionalised practices of domination, exploitation and dehumanisation. Commonism morally condemns coercion and violence in all their manifestations, promoting instead non-authoritarian ways of organising human life through free agreements,

---

[1] Whilst we give a positive appraisal of the writings of Proudhon on justice, responsibility and non-penal real utopias, we distance ourselves from his notoriously anti-emancipatory writings on women and gender issues.

voluntary associations and the political ideal of mutual reciprocation and symmetrical relationships. Rather than cajole, control and destroy, commonism is life-affirming and promotes what Jun (2010: 56) calls 'vitality': the point is to help people live. Commonism is radically egalitarian with a strong emphasis on ethical judgement, diversity, freedom, direct participation in decision-making and the democratisation of political representation. As a basic principle of human dignity, ordinary people should be able to speak for themselves and democratic procedures ought to ensure that their voice is both heard and listened to (Scott, 2016a, 2016b).

For Dardot and Laval, 'the common' is not just about ideals or institutions; it is about social action and praxis. This is what gives the notion of "an inclusive citizenship of the common" its real utopian dimension: it is utopian in the sense that it goes beyond what actually exists, beyond a mere reformist agenda, yet it is real to the extent that it can only exist as lived experience. Commonism must therefore emerge from the common actions of *all* citizens. Dardot and Laval (2014) imagine a "federation of commons" that is not limited to the boundaries of a nation state but one which is plural and decentred, based not on formal rights granted by the State but instead on practice. It aims to be 'popular' without being 'populist', guided by commonly held principles such as dignity, solidarity, equity and freedom. It is also emancipatory in the sense that it enables individuals to participate directly in bringing about social change. Indeed, emancipatory praxis occurs when an individual consistently acts directly in accordance with the normative values and principles of human liberation — that is, integrating their broader ethical worldview within daily practice. Fundamentally, this entails taking on responsibility to act in the common good and the interests of others.

Concretely, in terms of developing a citizenship of the common, commonism may encourage collective practices such as "associational democracy", whereby collective organisations come together to take decisions and directly influence the political process (Wright, 2009). This would certainly encourage an active, emancipatory politics of the common, provided that these organisations remain as porous as possible, avoiding an exclusive membership ethos. In the current neoliberal context in which many different states are facing the same problems of inequality and injustice caused by transnational corporate power networks, it is also necessary that these groups do not confine themselves to the nation State but join together across borders to seek common solutions. Associational approaches are particularly attractive, addressing as they do the problems of irresponsibility highlighted above by allowing citizens to take joint responsibility for social problems and engage in a common endeavour to institute new practices.

Commonism thus directly challenges state power from below through everyday collective actions and praxis. *Contra* Proudhon, we cannot assume that these practices of the common will emerge naturally and spontaneously (Dardot and Laval, 2014: 227). It is necessary to think strategically about how to institute the common. In other words, the utopia of the common must be *real*. In the next section, we will attempt to show how constructing non-penal real utopias may be regarded as both emerging from and helping to construct a truly common notion of citizenship.

Non-penal real utopias of the common

Non-penal real utopianism should draw upon both a radical imagination that steps outside of the assumptions of the penal rationale and currently existing community-based interventions that engage with human troubles and problematic conduct. Exploring alternatives to exclusionary penal practices should be regarded as social action, as part of exercising citizenship as praxis. This entails reclaiming the issue from the State in order to develop alternative forms of justice firmly rooted in inclusive communities: from stateless citizenship it may perhaps be possible to imagine forms of stateless justice, a genuine 'justice of the common'.

The dangers of community responses to social harm
Moving beyond the State will entail citizens assuming real responsibility for the social problems that affect them, engaging in collaborative practices to address these in a meaningful way. It is not about communities getting involved in the existing institutions of the State, such as assuming a sense of 'ownership' of the prison (Faulkner, 2003: 306), but about communities being genuinely 'active' in developing inclusive, non-penal solutions. So far, attempts to resolve issues arising from harmful behaviour in the community context, notably restorative justice initiatives, have frequently been captured by the State (see, for example, Convery et al., 2008). Restorative justice, in placing the victim at the centre of analysis; providing a voice to all parties, including the voice of the offender; downplaying or removing coercive solutions; placing relationships at the heart of the response to a given problematic or troublesome act; focusing on positive and constructive *outcomes* and

emphasising fixing, compensating, repairing or restoring balance, can certainly be deployed as forms of non-penal intervention. Yet, in practice, restorative justice is often punishment under a different name. Whatever the definition or benevolent intentions of practitioners, the application of pain infliction continues, but, disturbingly, its reality is now disguised (Scott, 2009). Restorative justice remains a vague and illusive concept. On a practical level, the concern is that the Capitalist State is still given penal power, but that legal rights, safeguards and protections of wrongdoers are in effect removed, resulting in potentially heavier pain infliction than that occurring through the penal law. Restorative and shaming interventions, whilst non-penal in nature, have been and are used in addition to existing penal responses. Non-custodial responses to wrongdoing *must never* follow the logic that there must be a strengthening of community punishments in order to appear politically plausible. Finally, they do nothing to address structural inequalities and imbalances in power. There is no consideration of the implications (or harms) of the inequitable distribution of the social product or how life choices, including the perpetration of wrongs and harms, are shaped by structural contexts. This example of restorative justice demonstrates that there is no guarantee that the community response/stateless justice will be free from domination and coercion, especially when applied in profoundly unjust contexts. Non-penal real utopian solutions to social harm must therefore seek, above all, to promote genuine justice and responsibility for the Other.

Justice, responsibility and non-penal utopias
In his work on mutualism, Proudhon (1989) addressed the issue of justice and social harm. He grounded his notions of justice in respect, inherent dignity and guaranteed, mutually reciprocating relations. Citizens had a duty to protect the dignity of their neighbour and ensure that there was "natural harmony". However, Proudhon also recognised that conflict and troubles would be inevitable. Proudhon, himself imprisoned for three years where he experienced solitary confinement and 'forced relationality' and where his health was, in the long term, broken, was an early penal abolitionist. For him, no authority had the right to punish: punishment has nothing to do with justice, only with "iniquitous and atrocious vengeance". He was against penal servitude and argued that punishment was symbolic of the moral problems regarding inequality and injustice. Justice required that conflicts be handled through non-violent

methods, such as reparations. There was, for Proudhon, a need to replace penal discipline with the morality of justice (Hyman, 1979).

Yet Proudhon's vision of justice is limited to the extent that it fails to focus on the wider context in which injustice may occur. Enrique Dussel (2013: 413), on the other hand, though his vision of 'liberation praxis', demonstrates how we might broaden this focus by showing us how exactly justice may replace penal discipline. Central to the liberation praxis of Dussel (2013) is the "paradigm of life". Without ensuring that there are appropriate material conditions, there can be no justice. Both his understanding of responsibilities and justice are predicated on "an ethics of life" (Dussel, 2013: 108), a "community of living beings" where the "ethical duty [is] to reproduce and develop the life of the human subject" (Ibid.: 217). For Dussel, there is an ethical responsibility to ensure that those who are in an "asymmetrical" position to us — that is, they have less power and resources than we do — are treated with dignity and that their basic needs are met. Such a responsibility does not have to be demanded by another person, but rather arises automatically through the appearance of 'the face'. Through an encounter with, or knowledge of, a weaker person, we are compelled to abandon reciprocity and undertake non-reciprocal acts of hospitality. Praxis "is this and nothing more" (Dussel, 1985: 170): praxis is to make the stranger, the lost, the outcast and misbegotten part of our moral universe, and to respond actively in aid of their plight.

Dussel (2013: 207) refers to such people, who are excluded, marginalised denied dignity and "affected by a situation akin to death", as "victims". Liberation praxis entails not only recognising that such victims of social injustice are ethical subjects who have legitimate demands upon us in terms of meeting their needs but also ensuring that their voices and opinions are acknowledged (Scott, 2016b). Victims are often silenced or their voices cannot be heard, and liberation praxis demands that we challenge the validity of such denials from the perspectives of the victim themselves. This means listening and learning in order to *learn from* victims. Whilst there is "no single voice of all human kind", and to be treated the same is not equivalent to being treated equally, we must recognise the fluidity and contingency of categorisations; demonstrate a willingness to pay attention to the voices of "concrete others"; and acknowledge that each voice comes from a specifically situated position, standpoint or worldview rather than a generalised and abstract universalism (Hudson, 2003; Scott, 2016a). Equality will be 'complex' (i.e., equity) but we must somehow find a way in which it can encompass the diversity of human subjectivities. For real justice, there is a need for reflexivity and the promotion of freedom and autonomy; to hear different voices; and reconstruct a notion of universality that is sensitive to social contexts (Hudson, 2003).

A crucial analytical and normative innovation of liberation praxis is to view the world from the 'exterior' — to look at the world from the outside, through the eyes of the marginalised and excluded victim (Scott, 2106a). The engagement with community, then, is through an external lens. Liberation praxis looks at life from its negation (Dussel, 2008). Ethical responsibility and principles of justice are based on the experiences of those on the outside of the system: the Other. More than this, Dussel (2008) develops a clear set of normative political principles upon which community values and attitudes can be externally evaluated. The "formal principle" allows procedural safeguards, ensuring the promotion of the voices of all people (including 'victims'), so that a community is genuinely based on participatory democracy. The "material principle", as detailed above, notes that the social organisation of any society must be grounded in principles of distributive and social justice. Finally, the "feasibility principle" looks to promote and foster the most appropriate ways of delivering justice in the here and now.

The key question is not simply 'is this just?' but also 'who is granted justice and to whom is justice denied?' (Hudson, 2003). Those who most lacked justice (and, indeed, also security) are the poor, powerless and disadvantaged. Too often their sufferings are neglected or marginalised; too often their voice delegitimated; and too often their claims to equal respect denied. For Dussel (1985: 65), liberation praxis should result in "liberative justice":

> Liberative justice, which does not give to each what is due within the law and the prevailing order, but grants to all what they deserve in their dignity as others. Thus liberative justice is not legal justice, whether distributive or communicative, but real justice — that is, subversive: subverting the established unjust order. (Ibid.)

An ethics of justice requires acknowledgement and respect towards people not like us — it means respecting differences (Hudson, 2003). Justice as alterity demands that we meet the Other without violence and this approach, in effect, translates into *love of the other*. In terms of slogans, whilst equality, liberty and fraternity still pertain, we could perhaps articulate them today in terms of recognition and respect for irreducible differences; freedom from dominance and oppression of the majority; and solidarity with, and responsibility for, sufferers. Like Dussel (2013), critical scholars such as Barbara Hudson (2003) have also argued that our responsibilities to other humans stretch way beyond our close family, friends and community to also include the 'stranger', 'outcast' and others not known to us directly or not sharing similar characteristics or social backgrounds. We must learn to accept differences, acknowledge the existence of the stranger/'victim', but also to recognise what we share — *common humanity*.

> Far too often, in the real rather than the theoretical world, the response to the presence of the stranger — the application for entry, the beggar, the disorderly and disreputable — is to confine them, to segregate them, or to exclude them altogether. Prisons, detention centres, ghettoes and gated estates demonstrate the refusal of hospitality and the desire to avoid encounters with strangers, rather than to respond to their claims and needs. (Hudson, 2011: 120)

Drawing on the insights of Hudson (2011) and Dussel (2013), Scott (2016a) has argued that liberative praxis leads us down an emancipatory path that intimately connects debates around justice and responsibilities with the promotion of human rights. From an abolitionist perspective, Scott (2016a) argues that such a human rights agenda will always be "unfinished" for it must be forged through emancipatory struggle and acts of defiance. An 'abolitionist human rights agenda' from below will continuously evolve and should be focused on making more visible the institutionally structured violence of incarceration alongside broader structural inequalities that blight human life. Such abolitionist critiques should aim to reveal the ideological closure of the existing foundations of legal rights and reignite their more emancipatory potential. Abolitionist human rights agendas, therefore, move beyond a merely humanitarian approach reflecting the content of international covenants and grounded in the amelioration of suffering. Theirs is an agenda that reflects the liberation struggles of the powerless and contributes towards emancipatory and transformative praxis. Consequently, for Scott (2016a), the aspiration of those struggling for justice and human rights must be for freedom from domination and the removal of the causes of human suffering.

For abolitionists such as Hudson (2003, 2011) and Scott (2016a), human rights must reflect our responsibilities *for* the Other rather than for the self. To protect human rights, society must learn to hear and learn to learn from the voice of the estranged Other, recognise their inherent dignity, and meet them with non-violence (Scott, 2016b). Radical alternatives should be historically immanent, in place of an existing sanction and not be grounded in authoritarian forms of domination (Scott, 2013). Non-penal interventions must reflect the normative frameworks of human rights, democratic accountability and social justice. In this sense, the 'abolitionist real utopia' perspective maps directly onto the concerns of Wright (2010) and Dussel (2013).

For Dussel (2013), liberative justice is not just about creating freedom for victims, but also responsibility for the social, economic and political transformation of the conditions and structures which create victimhood in the first instance. In an argument reminiscent of that found in commonism, the aim of the praxis of liberation is to create symmetrical relationships resulting in mutual aid and responsibility. There is an "ethical obligation of 'transforming' the reality that produced victims" (Dussel, 2013: 288) and the creation of a new 'mutual responsibility' (Ibid.: 281).

> The excluded should not be merely *included* in the *old* system — as this would be to introduce the Other into the Same — but rather ought to participate as equals in a new *institutional* moment [...] This is a struggle not for *inclusion*, but for *transformation*. (Dussel, 2008: 89, emphasis in the original)

Transformation must entail direct engagement with the 'victim'. For the purposes of non-penal utopian justice, the victim here must be understood widely to include *all* victims of social injustice, whether or not they have broken the law and caused harm. The encounter with the victim, for Dussel (2013: 352, emphasis in original), is the "*possible utopia*". We must work day in, day out with the people of the "present utopia: the peripheral peoples, the oppressed classes" (Dussel, 1985: 48) Emancipatory politics and praxis must then exercise an "*ethical-utopian reason*" (Dussel, 2013: 223, emphasis in original) and draw upon the "feasibility" principle to build upon interventions that are real and viable in our historical moment.

Unleashing transformative justice
When developing non-penal responses to social harm, we therefore have a responsibility to work with all those affected, in a common endeavour

to develop a just response in opposition to the often unjust responses of the State. It is an opportunity to create a counter-revolution in response to these exclusionary responses by proposing a new non-penal rationality that is genuinely transformative. A citizenship of the common, for an emancipatory politics and praxis, ought therefore to favour transformative justice. Ruth Morris (2000: 3) describes transformative justice as such:

> Transformative justice uses the power unleashed by the harm of crime to let those most affected find truly creative, healing solutions. Transformative justice includes victims, offenders and their families, and their communities, and invites them to use the past to dream of a better future [...] Transformative justice recognises the wrongs of all victims, and recognises also that sooner or later, we are all both victims and offenders.

Transformative justice means handling conflicts and troubles by listening, acknowledging the victim's injury and hurt, and finding ways that can lead to healing and just settlements for all. Transformative justice is victim-focused, but it recognises equally the victims of problematic and troublesome interpersonal harms, and the 'victim' (Dussel, 2013) of the harms generated by 'distributive' and social injustices, multinational corporations and state domination (Morris, 2000: 5). The focus is justice and the transformation of contexts and situations characterised by injustice and the facilitation of more caring, cooperative and inclusive communities. Only transformative social justice can lead to transformative non-penal justice: transformative justice is impossible in unjust contexts. Justice means responding to harms in a non-violent manner and trying to "correct mistakes" (Dussel, 2008).

This goal of social transformation leads to an emphasis on finding answers, recognising wrong done, providing safety and security, providing an appropriate form of redress and helping the victim to find new meanings and understandings (Morris, 2000). But it also means meeting needs — housing, relational, therapeutic — and reaffirming life. Transformative justice is about restoring 'world' for victims, providing them with a voice and helping to create or rebuild 'vitality' — the paradigm of life (Dussel, 2013). The struggle for transformative justice is at the heart of our daily lives — interventions, direct action, writing, speaking, engaging with people about the issues that matter — living a life that connects with our principles and responsibility for Others: emancipatory politics and praxis.

Conclusion: commonism, real utopias and transformative justice

In neoliberal societies, individualism and competition constantly undermine the 'common' as the ties that bind us become weakened. As society becomes increasingly atomised, collective participation in social, institutional and political structures is limited, allowing power to become evermore concentrated at the top. In a context of 'decollectivisation' and profound social inequality (Dardot and Laval, 2014: 15), attempts to reinvigorate communities have been unsuccessful. The discourse of individual responsibilisation has paradoxically justified the irresponsibility of communities with regard to individuals who are thought to have failed in their duties to the community. Once de-responsibilised in this way, communities have allowed the State to exercise its repressive power with regard to those who are deemed unworthy of citizenship.

A reimagined citizenship of the common offers a possibility to citizens to become genuinely active in imagining alternative social structures. Faced with the significant hegemonic power of the neoliberal model, such a concept of citizenship is unlikely to emerge spontaneously. Conscious efforts need to be made to get citizens involved in common projects to radically reimagine the way that society is currently ordered, thus ultimately fostering mutual responsibility. Dussel's concept of "liberation praxis" allows us to imagine how we may assume responsibility for developing a *just* social order and meeting our ethical obligations to the Other. It suggests that citizen action needs to be transformative, capable of overturning hegemonic rationalities of all kinds. In that sense, it is utopian, but it is also real, grounded in the praxis of collective action. It is through working collectively to develop common responses to social problems such as 'crime' that the notion of a citizenship of the common can go beyond the ideal to become a practical, transformative reality, capable of generating non-penal responses to social problems.

References

Bauman, Z. (1989) *Modernity and the Holocaust* New York: Cornell University Press

Bourdieu, P. (1997) 'A Reasoned Utopia and Economic Fatalism', Speech of acceptance of the *Ernst-Bloch Preis der Stadt Ludwigshafen*

Braithwaite, J. (1989) *Reintegrative Shaming* Cambridge: Cambridge University Press

Cameron, D. (2010a) Speech on the 'Big Society'
http://www.telegraph.co.uk/news/politics/david-cameron/7897445/David-Cameron-launches-his-Big-Society.html

Cameron, D. (2010b) HC deb 3 November 2010, Volume 517, col. 921

Cameron, D. (2016) 'Prison Reform', speech to the Policy Exchange, London, 8 February

Comaroff, J. and Comaroff, J.L. (eds.) (2001) *Millennial Capitalism and the Culture of Neoliberalism* Durham: Duke University Press

Convery, U., Haydon, D., Moore, L. and Scraton, P. (2008) 'Children, Rights and Justice in Northern Ireland: Community and custody' in *Youth Justice* Volume 8, No. 3 pp 245–263

Dardot, P. and Laval C. (2014) *Commun: Essai sur la révolution au XXIe siècle* Paris: La Découverte

Duff, R. A. (2005) 'Introduction: Crime and citizenship' in *Journal of Applied Philosophy* Volume 22, No. 3 pp 211–16

Dussel, E. (1985) *Philosophy of Liberation* Oregon: Wipf and Stock

Dussel, E. (1998) *The Underside of Modernity* New York: Humanity Books

Dussel, E. (2008) *Twenty Theses on Politics* Durham: Duke University Press

Dussel, E. (2013) *The Ethics of Liberation* Durham: Duke University Press

Dwyer, P. (1998) 'Conditional Citizens? Welfare rights and responsibilities in the late 1990s' in *Critical Social Policy* Volume 18, No. 4 pp 493–515

Etzioni, A. (1995) *The Spirit of Community* London: Fontana Press

Faulkner, D. (2003) 'Taking Citizenship Seriously: Social capital and criminal justice in a changing world' in *Criminal Justice* Volume 3, No. 3 pp 287–315

Gove, M. (2015) 'The treasure in the heart of man — making prisons work', speech delivered to the Prisoners' Learning Alliance, London, 17 July

Hoffman, J. (2004) *Citizenship beyond the State* London: Sage

Hudson, B.A. (1993) *Penal Policy and Social Justice* London: Macmillan

Hudson, B.A. (2000) 'Punishing the Poor: Dilemmas of justice and difference', in Haffernan, W. and Kleinig, J. (eds) *From Social Justice to Criminal Justice* New York: Oxford University Press

Hudson, B.A. (2003) *Justice in the Risk Society* London: Sage

Hudson, B.A. (2011) 'All the People in all the World: A cosmopolitan perspective on migration and torture' in Baillet, C. and Franko-Aas, K. (eds) (2011) *Cosmopolitan Justice and its Discontents* London: Routledge

Hudson, B.A. (2012) 'Who Needs Justice? Who Needs Security?' in Hudson, B.A. and Ugelvik, S. (eds) (2012) *Justice and Security in the 21st Century* London: Routledge

Hyams, E. (1979) *Pierre-Joseph Proudhon* London: John Murray

Isin, E.F. and Turner B.S. (2002) 'Citizenship Studies: An introduction' pp 1–10 in Isin, E.F. and Turner, B.S. (eds) *Handbook of Citizenship Studies* London: Sage

Johnstone, G. (2003) 'Restorative Approaches to Criminal Justice' pp 1–18 in Johnstone, G. (ed) (2003) *A Restorative Justice Reader* Devon: Willan

Jordan, B. (1993) *Theory of Poverty and Social Exclusion* Cambridge: Polity Press

Kelly, D. (1994) 'Introduction' in Proudhon, P.J. (1994) *What is Property?* Cambridge: Cambridge University Press

King, R. and Morgan, R. (1980) *The Future of the Prison* Farnworth: Gower Publishing Ltd

Marshall, T.H. (1963 [1950]) *Citizenship and Social Class*; reprinted in Marshall, T.H. (1963 [1950])*Sociology at the Crossroads* London: Heinemann Educational Books

Mathiesen T. (1974) *The Politics of Abolition* New York: John Wiley & Sons

May, T. (2002) 'Speech to the Conservative Party Conference', http://conservative-speeches.sayit.mysociety.org/speech/600929

Morris, R. (2000) *Stories of Transformative Justice* Toronto: Canadian Scholars Press

Proudhon, P.J. (1989) *General Idea of Revolution in the Nineteenth Century* London: Pluto Press

Proudhon, P.J. (2011a) 'Justice in the Revolution and in the Church' in Mckay, I. (ed) (2011) *Property is Theft* Edinburgh: AK Press

Proudhon, P.J. (2011b) 'What is Property?' in Mckay, I. (ed) (2011) *Property is Theft* Edinburgh: AK Press

Reiner, R. (2010) 'Citizenship, Crime, Criminalization: Marshalling a social democratic perspective' in *New Criminal Law Review* Volume 13, No. 2 pp 241–261

Scott, D. (2001) 'Prisoners' Rights and the 'Responsibilities and Justice' Paradigm': Which rights? Whose responsibility? What justice?' in *Strangeways* Volume 4, August 2001 pp 8-11

Scott, D. (2009) 'Punishment' in Hucklesby, A. and Wahidin, A. (eds) (2009) *Criminal Justice* Oxford: Oxford University Press

Scott, D. (2013) 'Visualising an Abolitionist Real Utopia: Principles, policy and praxis' in Malloch, M. and Munro, B. (eds) *Crime, Critique and Utopia* Basingstoke: Palgrave

Scott, D. (2016a) 'Regarding Rights for the Other: Abolitionism and human rights from below' in Weber, L., Fishwick, E. and Marmo, M.(eds) (2016) *Routledge Handbook of Criminology and Human Rights* London: Routledge

Scott, D. (2016b) 'Hearing the Voice of the Estranged Other: Abolitionist ethical hermeneutics' *Kriminolosches Journal*, Fall 2016,

Shantz, J. (2013) *Commonist Tendencies* New York: Punctum Books

Swaaningen, R. van (1997) *Critical Criminology* London: Sage

Winstanley, G. (2010 [1649]) *The New Law of Righteousness* London: EEBO Editions

Woolf, L.J, (1991) *Prison Disturbances* London: TSO

Wright, E.O. (2009) *Envisioning Real Utopias*,

http://citeseerx.ist.psu.edu/viewdoc/download?doi=10.1.1.152.6099&rep=rep1&type=pdf

11.

Otherwise than Prisons, Not Prisons Otherwise: Therapeutic communities as non-penal real utopias

This chapter was originally published in the European Group Journal Justice, Power and Resistance *in September 2016. The chapter is co-authored with Helena Gosling.*

Prisons are profoundly dehumanising institutions filled with socially disadvantaged people who have experienced multiple forms of social exclusion. Despite the best of intentions of those hoping to find some virtue in the current incarceration binge, the punitive rationale, which underscores prisons' very existence, inevitably undermines humanitarian attempts to bring about desired personal transformations or tackle social exclusion (Scott, 2008). What we urgently require is recognition that the prison as a place not only reflects, but perpetuates, social inequalities. At the same time, we need plausible and historically immanent radical alternatives that can reach beyond hegemonic neoliberal and penal logics currently informing policy, and offer a new way of responding to troubled individuals. Such radical alternatives must engender both the humanitarian impulse *to engage right now* with the tragedies of imprisonment and social injustice, but also be something that maintains fidelity with, and commitment to, the wider idealised aspirations of living in a world without prisons and the deep-seated social inequalities they mirror.

There are many difficulties when attempting to promote alternatives to prison, varying from net widening, where alternatives become add-ons to existing sentences, to falling through the net, where people are abandoned and neglected and nothing is done to help them. Radical alternatives must be able to incorporate engagement with the problems and possibilities of our historical moment, whilst simultaneously disrupting punitive and other ideologies which facilitate social inequalities. They must also be *genuine alternatives*, for only then, when coupled with policies promoting social inclusion and social justice, can they meet the criteria of an abolitionist non-penal real utopia (Scott, 2013).

In this chapter, we consider whether Therapeutic Communities (TCs) can be promoted for substance-using lawbreakers as part of a wider abolitionist strategy aiming to reduce social harms and challenge social and economic inequalities. The chapter starts by outlining the normative framework of an abolitionist real utopia, before moving on to critically explore the historical and theoretical contexts of TCs. The discussion then turns to the existing literature on TCs as an alternative to penal custody. At that point, we evaluate whether TCs are compatible with the values and principles of an abolitionist real utopia. The chapter concludes that whilst there is no blanket alternative to prison, and no single answer to the way society responds to lawbreakers whose offending behaviour is influenced by substance use, TCs can be part of the solution, but they must be coupled with other interventions tackling structural inequalities grounded in the principles of social justice.

An abolitionist real utopia

Prisons are inherently problematic institutions; they are places of interpersonal and institutional violence, and legal, social and corporeal death — and these terrible outcomes are structured within the very fabric of penal institutions (Scott and Codd, 2010; Scott, 2015). It is possible for prisons to offer a place of reflection and refuge for a few people when all other options have failed but, given the deprivations, pains and iatrogenic harms that underscore daily prison regimes, these cases are the exceptions that prove the rule. Yet, for penal abolitionists, critique is never enough. Abolitionists must be prepared to advocate constructive and radical alternatives to the penal rationale. Such alternatives must be realistic and pragmatic, whilst at the same time be consistent with idealistic and utopian visions — a position which has been referred to as an 'abolitionist real utopia' (Scott, 2013).

In short, an abolitionist real utopia promotes visions of radical alternatives grounded in the following five normative principles that build upon continuities and possibilities in our historical conjuncture. A radical alternative must:

1. Compete with a prison sentence
Radical alternatives must implicitly or explicitly compete with, and contradict, current penal ideologies, discourses, policies and practices

(Mathiesen, 1974). Alternatives must compete with the institutions of the criminal process by promoting interventions that are grounded in historically immanent potentialities, whilst simultaneously possessing an emancipatory logic that contradicts current practices of repression and pain infliction. Those in power must find it difficult to ignore or dismiss the proposed radical alternative but, at the same, it must be impossible for them to reappropriate the alternative within the logic of the penal rationale. The justification of a radical alternative must also be strong enough so that it can be considered a genuine alternative to a prison sentence.

2. Be otherwise than prison

To avoid net widening, the radical alternative must directly replace a punitive sentence of the criminal courts. Interventions should not be considered 'add ons' or initiated alongside existing penal practices. They must be deployed in place of a prison sentence that would otherwise have been sanctioned against a given individual.

3. Be a non-coerced intervention allowing meaningful participation

In conjunction with the below human-rights standards, genuine radical alternatives must be non-coercive and demonstrate that they can be productive and meaningful ways of addressing problematic behaviours, conflicts and troublesome conduct. As such, radical alternatives must adhere to democratically accountable values and principles requiring unhindered participation; recognition of all voices' validity; and facilitate decision-making processes.

4. Safeguard human dignity and minimise human suffering

Radical alternatives must have a non-punitive ethos aiming to uphold, respect and protect the intrinsic worth and value of human beings. There must be no violations of human dignity, nor should the intervention create stigma, injury or harm. The radical alternative must therefore be *better* than prison, which is a place of pain, blame and death. These human-rights standards place certain ethical boundaries upon interventions and help steer us towards alternatives that can reduce rather than create unnecessary human pain and suffering. To avoid an unintentional or hidden escalation of harms, radical alternatives must have sufficient transparency, procedural safeguards and be rooted in the principles of fairness, openness, equality and legal accountability. Care should therefore be taken to ensure that any proposed alternative intervention for handling conflicts does not become a form of punishment in disguise. Importantly, the alternative must be otherwise than prison, not a prison otherwise.

5. Promote (or, at the very least, not inhibit) social justice

A radical alternative must look to facilitate, and not prevent, the promotion of social justice. An abolitionist real utopia is a form of emancipatory knowledge that challenges inequality, unfairness and injustice. This requires not only problematising the current application of the criminal label, which overwhelmingly punishes the poor, disadvantaged and vulnerable, but also actively promoting interventions which reduce social inequalities and aim to meet human needs (Scott, 2013). Radical alternatives to prison must (at the very least) not impinge upon such interventions.

The following analysis explores whether TCs can be advocated as a form of abolitionist real utopia. In so doing, we appraise the reality and potential of the TC to meet the five normative values outlined above, by considering the following key questions: Can TCs incorporate both an engagement with the problems and possibilities of our historical moment? Do TCs possess an emancipatory logic contradicting institutions and practices of penal repression? Are TCs genuine alternatives to penal custody? Do TCs adhere to values and principles safeguarding human dignity and reducing human suffering? And do TCs facilitate or hinder social justice? To answer these questions, we will first explore the meanings, origins and theoretical priorities of TCs.

Origins of the TC

Generally speaking, each TC forms a miniature society in which staff and clients are expected to fulfil distinctive roles that are designed to support the transitional process on which individuals embark during their residency (Gosling, 2015). Although day-to-day activities vary depending on the population served and the setting of the programme, all TCs use a holistic approach based on principles of self-help and mutual aid.

The origins of the TC can be traced to two independent movements: the 'democratic' and the 'hierarchical'.[1] The democratic TC was developed

---

[1] Although it is becoming increasingly difficult to distinguish between the two traditions, the hierarchical TC typically provides a more 'hierarchical' and structured treatment

at Henderson Hospital, England during the 1960s, and specialised in supporting individuals with moderate to severe personality disorders, as well as those with complex emotional and interpersonal issues. Generally speaking, the democratic TC provides a psychosocial approach, which is intended to help troubled individuals understand and, as far as possible, lessen or overcome their psychological, social and/or emotional issues and difficulties (Stevens, 2013).

The hierarchical TC is derived from Synanon, San Francisco, which comprised a self-help community for substance users, established by Charles Dederich in 1958. The hierarchical TC is a psychosocial intervention which uses self-help and behaviour modification techniques to help individuals address underlying issues and difficulties that surround their substance use (Perfas, 2004). Given our focus on substance use, we explore only the priorities and values found in the hierarchical TC.

At first glance, the TC's historical origins do not look overly promising. Charles Dederich practiced a highly confrontational brand of therapy built on an autocratic, family-surrogate model that required a high level of self-disclosure (Perfas, 2004). An individual's needs were met through total participation in Synanon, and individual roles and responsibilities evolved to serve the maintenance of the Synanon community. Clients were required to conform to rules, norms and expectations that detailed how to behave, and to uphold predetermined values that applied to everyday life: from getting up in the morning to relaxing in the evening (Kennard, 1998).

A wide range of methods, such as reward and sanction systems, peer pressure and encounter groups were employed to introduce conformity and commitment to the rules and regulations. Rather problematically, in the late 1970s, completion of Synanon was abolished as Dederich redefined addiction as a terminal disease that could only be arrested by sustained participation in the community (White, 1998). This shift marked the beginning of the end of Synanon, as its earlier ethos gave way to the development of a community that introduced a greater degree of coercion and a series of loyalty tests which drove out all but the most committed residents (White, 1998). The authoritarian communitarian nature of Synanon and other early TCs has quite rightly evoked much criticism (Waldorf, 1971; Sugerman, 1986; Kooyman, 1986, 1993; White, 1998; Gosling, 2015). It is the alternative models which subsequently

---

environment, whereas the democratic tradition prioritises a more collective 'democratic' treatment approach.

evolved in the TC movement that offer a firmer ground for its inclusion within an abolitionist real utopia manifesto.

In 1968, Dr Ian Christie converted a ward of St. James Hospital, Portsmouth into Europe's first hospital-based TC for substance use. At around the same time, Professor Griffith Edwards of the Maudsley Hospital Addiction Unit established the Featherstone Lodge TC and Dr Bertram Mandelbrote created a TC in the Littlemore Hospital in Oxford. Hospital-based TCs were a result of a group of British psychiatrists who had been inspired by visits to Daytop Village and the Synanon-influenced Phoenix House in New York. Although essentially inspired by the American movement, European TCs went on to develop their own identity due to strong opposition to the harsh confrontation of residents and demoralising learning techniques that had taken place in Synanon. This dissatisfaction led to the development of a European TC that provided a more balanced and supportive dialogue between clients and staff (Broekaert, Vandevelde, Schuyten, Erauw and Bracke, 2004; Broekaert, 2006; Goethals et al., 2011; Vanderplasschen et al., 2014), and thus was much more in line with the normative framework of an abolitionist real utopia.

The residential TC identifies itself as an abstinence-based programme, providing a stark contrast to programmes available during the 1970s that sought to limit the harm that emerged from substance use.[2] During this time, heroin use, which was associated with American jazz music and Hollywood films, was at the centre of British public and political concern. It is perhaps unsurprising, then, that an American programme, such as the TC, was integrated into the British alcohol and drug treatment system with relative ease, accounting for approximately half of the 250 residential beds in Britain by the end of the 1970s (Yates, 1981, 2002, 2003).

When the hierarchical TC first emerged, the notion that a group of substance users could manage and control their own recovery was greeted with scepticism by mainstream alcohol and drug services (Yates, 2003; Broekaert et al., 2006; Yates, 2012). Despite initial and continuing scepticism from Europe's mainstream alcohol and drug treatment culture, the TC survived the test of time. The programme is a well-established self-help modality in countries such as Italy, Greece, Spain, Portugal, Lithuania, Hungary and Poland, with more than 1,200 TCs across Europe alone (Vanderplasschen et al., 2014).

---

[2] For example, substitute prescription programmes and needle-exchange schemes.

Despite divergent origins, philosophies, clientele and settings, the democratic TC and hierarchical TC are considered to be vanguards of new and alternative therapies for individuals who have mental-health or substance-use issues (Rawlings and Yates, 2001). Since the inception of the TC there has been great debate about whether hierarchical TCs are similar to or significantly different from their democratic cousin (Glaser, 1983; Sugarman, 1984; Lipton, 1998; Lipton, 2010; Stevens, 2013). There is, however, a general agreement that TCs:

> share an encouragement of residents' active involvement in, and responsibility for, the day-to-day running of the TC; a respect for the social learning and behavioural reinforcement that occurs naturally in the course of communal living. (Stevens, 2013: 14)

We now turn to a discussion of the TCs' theoretical and methodological priorities, and their relationship to the normative framework of an abolitionist real utopia.

The theoretical priorities of the TC

For George DeLeon (2000), the first research director at Phoenix House New York and foremost evaluator of the TC for substance use, the theoretical priorities of the day-to-day workings of a TC can be separated into three distinct parts.

1. View of the disorder
For DeLeon (2000), substance use is a disorder of the whole person affecting some, if not all, areas of functioning. Although substance users cite a variety of reasons and circumstances as to why they use substances, TCs emphasise that individuals must recognise how they have contributed to the problems that they are experiencing and develop coping strategies to manage potential future problems.

2. View of the person
According to DeLeon (2000), substance users characteristically display a variety of cognitive deficits such as poor awareness, difficulty in decision-making and a lack of problem-solving skills. In addition to these cognitive characteristics, substance users commonly display difficulties in how they see themselves in relation to their personal self-worth and as members of society with self-regulation, as well as how they communicate and

manage feelings. Although the origins of an individual's experienced and displayed trust issues are multifaceted, they typically reflect social and psychological influences such as histories of unsafe and abusive families, poor parental models of trust and negative socialisation. The problem is not only in an individual's inability to trust others, but the inability to trust themselves and their own feelings, thoughts and decisions (DeLeon, 2000).

3. View of recovery and right living

Despite the various social and psychological backgrounds that substance users have, the fundamental goal of recovery in a TC remains the same: to learn or relearn how to live without substances. According to the TC perspective, recovery is a gradual process of multidimensional learning involving behavioural, cognitive and emotional change (DeLeon, 2000). 'Behavioural change' refers to the elimination of asocial and antisocial behaviour and the acquiring of positive social and interpersonal skills. 'Cognitive change' refers to gaining new ways of thinking, decision-making and problem-solving skills. 'Emotional change' refers to the development of skills necessary for managing and communicating feelings. 'Right living' means abiding by community rules, remaining substance free, and participating in daily groups, meetings, work and therapeutic interventions. According to the TC perspective, the daily practice of 'right living' not only provides a positive prototype that can be referred to after separation from the TC but, given time, will evolve into a change in lifestyle and identity (DeLeon, 2000).

The term 'community as method' refers to the self-help approach used within a TC, where it is the community itself that brings about change (De Leon, 2000: 92). Community as method means encouraging residents to use their time constructively by teaching them how to learn about themselves and bring about personal change. These strategies and interventions place demands on the individual by expecting them to participate, behave appropriately and respect the rules of the programme. Being a member of a TC means that every individual is expected to monitor, observe and provide feedback on other people's behaviour, attitude and personal change. Residents are part of the programme twenty-four hours per day, seven days a week, and are observed in everything that they do: work, leisure, peer interactions, group participation, and so on. It is through these observations that a picture emerges of residents' behaviours and attitudes, which need to be challenged and developed. The fundamental assumption that underlies the community as method approach is that residents obtain maximum therapeutic and educational impact when they meet community expectations and use the peer community to change themselves (DeLeon, 2000).

TCs as a radical alternative to prison

We have explored the historical foundations and theoretical assumptions underscoring the TC. What is now required is some consideration of the evidence that the TC can be a plausible (effective) and historically immanent alternative to custody. The first thing to note is the relative scarcity of research exploring the possibility of the TC as an alternative to prison for people with substance-use issues. Below is a brief overview of the literature over the last few decades.

Exploring the importance of interventions other than prison, a longitudinal study by Bale et al. (1980) compared the effectiveness of three residential TCs and an outpatient methadone-maintenance programme for 585 male veterans addicted to heroin. The study's conclusions confirmed that therapeutic interventions could be much more progressive and appropriate than a prison sentence. In short, Bale et al. (1980) discovered that when compared to those who received either no treatment or only limited forms of detoxification, those who had been in a TC or methadone treatment for over seven weeks were not only less likely to be convicted of a serious crime, use heroin or subsequently receive a prison sentence, but were also more likely to be in education or employment. A few years later, Wilson and Mandelbrote (1985) conducted a ten-year follow-up study on the Ley Community in Oxford (UK). Rather than using control groups, the authors compared the demographic data, criminal careers and substance usage of admissions from 1971 and 1973 with an analysis of the lengths of time that people resided in the TC. On this basis, they found that programme involvement was the most significant factor in recidivism rates, arguing that residents who stayed for over six months had a reconviction rate of 15%, whereas for those who stayed for under a month, the figure rose to 85%. The most obvious and recurring problem with outcome measures such as (re)conviction and programme completion is the fact that such measures cannot provide definitive answers as to whether an individual has reverted back to substance use and/or participated in criminal activity.

In a similar vein, Nemes et al. (1999) have examined the efficacy of providing either enhanced abbreviated or standard inpatient and outpatient treatment for substance users. The experiment randomly assigned 412 clients to two TCs, which differed primarily in planned duration. Findings suggest that a twelve-month course of treatment, including at least six months in a TC followed by outpatient treatment, can produce marked reductions in substance use and 'crime' among persons who complete both phases. An additional study by Messina et al. (2000) compared factors that predicted outcomes in men and women randomly assigned to two TCs differing primarily in the length of inpatient and outpatient treatment. The results here showed that the predictors of outcomes for men and women were the same regardless of gender. Results further suggested that longer residential programmes had a particularly beneficial impact on women. Furthermore, Farrall (2000) found that women participants of the CREST programme (n = 41) were statistically less likely to relapse on alcohol than the women in a work-release programme or 'control group' (n = 37).[3] Of the women participating in the CREST programme, only 39% relapsed. Taking specific drugs into account, women in CREST were significantly less likely to relapse on alcohol. Women in CREST were also more successful at forging some sort of social support system in the community.

Literature exploring the option of the TC as a substitution for a prison sentence is very limited, particularly in the UK, but one such study was conducted by Lamb and Goertzel (1974) who undertook a detailed review of the Ellsworth House rehabilitation programme in the US in the 1970s. Residents of Ellsworth House gained employment in the community whilst participating in a therapeutic programme. For the study, offenders already sentenced to a prison term of four months or more were randomly assigned to either Ellsworth House or to a comparison group which remained in prison. Although the conclusions reached by Lamb and Goertzel (1974) were not decisively in favour of the TC over the prison (as recidivism rates were comparable for the two cohorts), the authors did find that the Ellsworth House group had a higher rate of employment upon release.

There is a little more literature examining whether referral to a TC is an option that is better than a prison sentence. For example, Dynia and Sung (2000) provided a detailed review of the Drug Treatment Alternative to

---

[3] Although little insight is provided into the characteristics of the control group, it is important to recognise that the heterogeneity of the population served by a TC besides programme adaptation and modification means that establishing a true randomised control group is a complex, if not impossible, task.

Prison (DTAP) programme in Brooklyn, New York in the 1990s. The DTAP runs from fifteen to twenty-four months and follows a traditional TC structure. The DTAP includes individual, group, and family counselling sessions; vocational and educational courses; and relapse prevention. Residents are helped to find a job and accommodation before they leave. The aim of this TC is to divert non-violent drug users over the age of eighteen away from prison and into residential services. The DTAP works on a 'sentence deferral system' so that, rather than being used as a replacement for a prison sentence, the accused must plead guilty before a referral is given. The guilty plea is conditional upon the offender completing the DTAP programme, for only then can it be withdrawn and the case dismissed. Belenko and colleagues (2004) also conducted longitudinal research on the DTAP in New York, finding that, in comparison to the control group of prisoners, DTAP residents were 56% less likely to be rearrested; 60% less likely to be reconvicted; and 65% less likely to receive a new prison sentence.

Additional research by Zarkin and colleagues (2005) focused on the financial benefits of the DTAP in comparison to a prison sentence. The authors argued that while the DTAP costs on average $40,718 per resident, and $50,886 per resident for those who complete it, the financial outlays of the DTAP were much lower than the average $124,995 incurred in criminal-justice costs. Zarkin et al. (2005) argue that over a six-year period, $7.13 million would have been saved if everyone in their comparison group had joined the DTAP. It is also worthwhile mentioning here the study conducted by French et al. (2002) which compared the economic benefits and costs of a modified TC for homeless and 'mentally ill chemical abusers' (MICAs) relative to a comparison group. Data from the period twelve months pre-admission to the modified TC were compared to data from twelve months post-admission across three outcome categories: employment, criminal activity and the utilisation of health-care services. The economic costs of the average 'modified' TC episode was $20,361. The economic benefit generated by the average 'modified TC client' was $305,273 (French et al., 2002).

Despite the limited set of data available, there appears to be some evidence that TCs are cheaper, more humane and more effective in addressing substance use than prison. Whilst we acknowledge that such findings are provisional, they are promising and raise the question as to what findings might emerge if more substance users in England and elsewhere went to a TC rather than a prison. Yet we must caution against an overly optimistic appraisal. The vast majority of the problems facing substance-using lawbreakers are not due to personal inadequacies or failures of individual responsibility, but rather are structurally generated through the social and economic inequalities of neoliberal capitalist societies. The divisions that really matter exist with regard to housing, health, transport, work, income and wealth. We must not be seduced into a medicalised illusion about the causes of distress, suffering and discontent, which then obfuscates the broader structural contexts generating social harms (Illich, 1977; Scott and Codd, 2010; Rapey et al., 2011). Accordingly, the effectiveness of any therapeutic intervention, including the TC evaluation studies we have discussed above, must be contextualised within the hurt, trauma and injury generated by social inequalities and poverty; the notoriously weak and methodologically inconsistent scientific analysis of the treatment efficacy of therapy; and the fact that there is much evidence which indicates that those who need help the most appear to benefit from therapy the least (Moloney, 2013). As Paul Moloney (2013: 93) pessimistically concludes:

> There is no consistent, good quality evidence that any type of therapy can outperform a well-designed placebo, that any approach is reliably superior to another, or that any given set of curative ingredients outdo their competitors. Only one observation is upheld: that confident and emotionally warm professionals are more appreciated by their clients, and get better results, a statement that applies equally to politicians, salespeople and prostitutes.[4]

Can a TC be an abolitionist real utopia?

The commentary above has raised a number of questions which require further attention and deliberation. Of particular pertinence here is

---

[4] We would like to reiterate the point made above regarding the limitations of evaluations on therapeutic interventions. Critics have identified that evaluative studies of treatment efficacy, such as those regarding people who have sexually offended, have tied themselves in knots by trying to deploy positivistic methodologies (for a critical review of literature on the effectiveness of treatment programmes for prisoners from a number of different social backgrounds, see Scott and Codd (2010) Controversial Issues in Prisons Buckingham: Open University Press). Yet we would not wish to be overly pessimistic. We would draw attention to voluntary programmes in the community that have been adopted throughout Europe for people who sexually offend, such as the interventions by the late Ray Wyre at the Gracewell Clinic in Birmingham in the 1980s; the work of the Lucy Faithful Foundation in UK; and the Prevention Project Dunkelfeld (PPD) in Germany.

whether TCs can be promoted as part of a wider manifesto of an abolitionist real utopia. In other words, does the TC provide a historically immanent alternative that can move beyond the existing punitive rationale and help to challenge social inequalities? Do they provide a genuinely different way of working alongside individuals who end up in the criminal process as a result of substance use? Are they better places in comparison to prison and can they protect human dignity and minimise human suffering? Can they respect and define clients as human beings who need to be consulted and whose voices are heard, rather than merely entities that need to be managed and risk assessed? And do they facilitate or inhibit the requirements of social justice? Let us now reflect upon these questions in more depth.

1. The TC as a historically immanent challenge to the punitive rationale
TCs are predicated upon helping the individual rather than punishing them. It should be remembered that TCs developed during the 1960s when communal living and notions of peace making were advocated on a social level. In some ways, the TC is part of the legacy of the radical, emancipatory and utopian social movements of this time. In this sense, the TC has a similar historical countercultural foundation to that of penal abolitionism (and, consequently, to the abolitionist real utopia). Importantly, the TC is an intervention which is deeply rooted in our historical conjuncture, and thus can provide a plausible and immanent alternative to imprisonment. Although there is some evidence (see below) that the TC can still be deployed in an oppressive and authoritarian manner, a genuine TC is rooted in compassion, mutual aid and the ethic of care. The TC draws upon a therapeutic rather than punitive rationale, and whatever the limitations of therapy (Moloney, 2013), at its best, this justification endeavours to alleviate, rather than inflict, pain. Undoubtedly, a genuine TC provides a progressive and contradictory space that undermines the logic of penalisation because its overriding philosophy is fundamentally grounded in humanitarian values such as empathy, respect for oneself and respect for others. Ultimately, the TC advocates individual and social forms of inclusion.

Government agendas focusing upon 'community values' and 'reintegration' ignore the harmful consequences of imprisonment post-release: notably, the legacies of civil and social death and the further embedding of social inequalities. Evidence indicates that TCs can help reduce harms and may be more 'efficient, effective and economic' than penal custody. Therapeutic interventions can perhaps tap into official discourses around evidence-led policy and thus be attractive to governments wishing to really break the links between substance use, criminalisation and penalisation. TCs could also fit into a localised agenda and even potentially have some resonance with populist governmental slogans such as the 'Big Society', albeit offering a very different form of intervention than that envisaged by Conservative politicians in England and Wales. There is also the argument which governments may find attractive, regarding the TC as an intervention prior to incarceration. Imprisonment creates its own individual and social harms, and can lead to prisonisation and dehabilitation. For those who genuinely wish to see a rehabilitation revolution, the TC is both revolutionary and grounded in rehabilitative and restorative principles. This all means that a case can be made for TCs to be considered a plausible and politically defensible option in a time of penal excess.

2. TCs can be a genuinely alternative way to work alongside substance users

TCs have an alternative conception of individuals who are deemed to be problematic, one that is much more positive than current dominant beliefs about substance users. TCs work with the person, not the socially constructed problems that surround them, such as criminal and deviant labels. TCs do not rely on, nor support, the use of diagnostic categories or proposals which suggest that substance users have a disease or some kind of faulty thinking that requires adaptation and modification. In theory, the ethos which underpins all day-to-day activities that take place in a TC is based upon recognising a person as an individual, not a problem, number or risk. In practice, however, we have found that this is somewhat diluted as there is a recurring tension among staff and residents when it comes to the admission of individuals with a history of imprisonment. This illustrates the need to divert substance users away from the criminal process.

There then remains the very real possibility that a TC can operate in a similar way to that of the prison, or perhaps even inflict more pain. There is no guarantee that an intervention which calls itself a TC will automatically be *better than* prison (Scott and Gosling, 2015). In one large Italian TC that we observed in November 2015, where members were compelled to reside for four years, the daily regime was rooted in exploitive labour practices. This 'TC' appeared to hide behind the claim that work is therapeutic and educational. From day one, residents were allocated to workshops producing goods for local, national and multinational capitalist corporations without recompense. This seems tantamount to a form of servitude. Community membership ranged from fourteen to twenty-five year olds and, whilst selection criteria may have been based on the likelihood of desistance and malleability for change, at this age, members are likely to be more flexible in developing skills to ensure that they are economically productive. The division of labour in these workshops was also profoundly masculinist, with the role of men and women reflecting a gendered hierarchy of male and female work, ensuring the separation of men and women working in the community. An authoritarian communitarian ethos pertained — there was a rigid and dominating structure that was grounded in extensive supervision. Residents were supervised for their first year by a long-serving peer, which even included being observed and escorted to the bathroom (Scott and Gosling, 2015). Care must be taken, therefore, to ensure that any proposed alternative intervention does not become a form of "punishment in disguise" (Hannah-Moffatt, 2001) or a "prison without walls" (Cohen, 1980). We are calling for genuine alternatives and any proposed TC must not resemble "semi-penal institutions" (Barton, 2005).

3. TCs facilitate meaningful participation and acknowledge residents' voices

Genuine TCs reject autonomy-sapping and power-abusing characteristics of total institutions in favour of supportive relationships between the service provider and client, described as evocative rather than didactic, as individuals can begin to understand themselves and their relationships with society through an ongoing interaction with their peer community, rather than some form of expert truth or knowledge about the situation in which they may have found themselves.

As we have identified, there can be a tension regarding the 'TC sentence' and the importance of voluntary engagement. This could perhaps in some cases be overcome, but the need for individuals to, in some way, choose the TC as an alternative sentence seems crucial. Inevitably, this concern places an increased burden on ensuring that democratic participation is at the heart of TC practices. Fitting the TC within the existing sentencing and criminal process can also result in problems of organisation, with tensions resulting from different working credos, orientations and assumptions (i.e., treatment, punishment or welfare logics).

There remains, of course, the question of what should happen if an individual chooses not to enter a TC and what would be the most appropriate responses under such conditions? We know that coercive therapeutic interventions are much less successful than their voluntary counterparts (Scott and Codd, 2010) and, therefore, the issue of voluntary participation remains paramount. We would suggest that alongside the TC there must also be spaces available, perhaps places which in the past have been called sanctuaries, where an individual could reflect upon the possible options available to them. Thus, alongside opportunities for substance users to carefully consider the right path at this moment in their lives, we would reiterate the point that the TC is only one of a raft of non-penal radical alternatives promoted in an abolitionist real utopia. If an individual was to refuse to voluntarily participate, then perhaps other non-penal interventions would be more appropriate in its place (for examples, see Scott, 2013).

4. TCs can protect human dignity and minimise human suffering
TCs are based on promoting human dignity, respect for all members of society and human liberation, rather than moral condemnation. In other words, they operate alongside individuals, enabling them to work through their problems and to challenge boundaries rather than constructing a neoliberal 'responsibilised subject'. Instead of "governing from a distance", TCs provoke questioning the self, but in so doing, also provide an "invitation to change" (Gosling, 2015), which involves a safe and supportive environment in which longitudinal support, friendship and recognition of one's own and others' struggles and needs are embraced in the journey away from substance use and related harms.

To avoid an unintentional or hidden escalation of pain, the TC envisaged as an abolitionist real utopia must have sufficient transparency, respect procedural rights, and be rooted in the principles of fairness, equality and legal accountability. TCs can minimise harm on an individual and local community level, which is something of great significance, but we must recognise that they are unable to combat effectively the hurt, injury and suffering generated by structural inequalities and social injustices.

5. TCs do not inhibit strategies of social justice
The vast amount of people who are imprisoned in England and Wales are from socially marginalised and excluded backgrounds (Scott, 2008). In the focus groups we undertook with TC practitioners and clients, there was a general consensus that TCs can be used in place of a prison sentence for substance users who have committed a non-violent offence.[5] The

emphasis here on 'non-violent' offenders is strategic. Focusing on such substance users in the TCs may be a good way to introduce the TC to a sceptical audience, but in the long term we would advocate the importance of challenging violence in all of its manifestations, including interpersonal violence. We do not have space to explore the issue of violence and related issues like 'community safety' in depth, but we recognise that not only may the TC be a non-violent means of responding to interpersonal violence, but that we must also promote policies which seek to challenge other forms of violence, most notably 'institutional violence' and 'structural violence' (Scott, 2015). Here, we understand violence in its broadest sense as harmful outcomes damaging human potential through the organisational structures of an institution such as a prison, and the structured inequalities of advanced capitalist societies. We have argued throughout this chapter that the TC cannot adequately address such harms and injuries, nor can it sufficiently provide 'community safety'. Community safety and reductions in violence can only be achieved by challenging hierarchies of domination and inequitable structures of power, and by promoting policies grounded in social justice.

We have noted elsewhere that we often found in the focus groups caution surrounding "how many prisoners" a programme could accept before "they had an impact" on day-to-day therapeutic interventions (Scott and Gosling, 2015). Although this provides a stark contrast to the TC ethos we briefly touched upon earlier, it provides a perfect illustration as to how a substance user's involvement with the criminal process simply adds further pressures and strains when it comes to accessing help and support. With this in mind, we suggest that using TCs alongside the criminal process is ineffective as the context of the intervention compounds inequalities that lead people to prison in the first instance: dehumanising rather than humanising people.

More broadly, we need to locate the focus on the TC as a solution within consideration of broader socio-economic and political contexts, shaping both the application of the criminal label and the focus of the criminal process on impoverished and marginalised communities, which may reinforce individual pathological explanations of 'crime'. An overemphasis on TCs as a solution may mystify the structural contexts and so must not be separated from a wider commitment to promote

---

[5] Focus groups took place between August and November 2014 and were carried out in five residential TCs for substance use in England, France, Denmark, Italy and Australia. The number of participants in total was sixty.

other radical alternatives and wider emancipatory changes in how we deal with wrongdoers and social injustice.

Conclusions

Voluntary engagement remains vital, and the need for individuals to in some way choose the TC as an alternative sentence seems crucial. Inevitably, this concern places an increased burden on ensuring that democratic participation is at the heart of TC practices. Fitting the TC within the sentencing and criminal process can also result in problems of organisations, with tensions emerging from different working credos, orientations and assumptions that may prove difficult to overcome. We also remain concerned that through individualising problems, attention may be distracted from how the individual troubles and social problems are generated in the first instance. An overemphasis on TCs as a solution may obscure the material constraints shaping individual choices. We must never lose our focus on challenging economic and social inequalities. As Moloney (2013: 208) argues, if problems:

> are caused by material things happening to material bodies: on one side, traumatic abuse and persecution; and on the other, soul-deadening labour, squalid impoverishment, the boredom of joblessness, the moralising sermons of the privileged [...] then it seems sensible [...] to change the world [through] a concerted effort to take the plight of the poor and marginalised seriously, to redistribute wealth [and] to give them more say over their own future.

Yet, despite the fear that the TC may only be able to provide a 'plaster for a broken leg', this intervention remains a politically plausible one in the UK, where talk of rehabilitation continues to have resonance with public opinion and is a radical alternative to the prison sentence, albeit one that cannot hope to fully address all of the problems which its clients face in a structurally unequal society.

A TC is something that exists right now and could be implemented immediately in place of a prison sentence in England and Wales. The TC is an alternative that would not be automatically ruled out of the debate — it is a radical alternative for substance use lawbreakers that can compete with the punitive logics of our time. Its logic of support is the antithesis of the punitive trajectory and, so long as it is deployed beyond the criminal process, should also be able to avoid co-option, although, as we highlighted earlier, this is something that must be monitored closely.

There are a number of existing examples from across Europe where TCs are currently being utilised as alternatives to prison, albeit this option is still, in the main, relatively underused. There is (some) evidence that TCs are more likely to be effective interventions in terms of preventing recidivism for substance-use law breakers, but, importantly, the principles and practices of genuine TCs also allow us to focus upon human need and human growth as a rationale for their promotion. The evidence suggests the TC is better than the prison and, though this may not be the best of all possible solutions (as David Small (2011) has argued, we require a political approach challenging existing material power relations rather than therapy), the TC may yet offer a non-penal real utopian alternative to the current incarceration binge (Scott, 2013; Scott and Gosling, 2015). The TC, when promoted as part of wider strategy to tackle social inequalities and social injustice, may be an intervention that can help ameliorate, rather than exacerbate, some of the worst harms, pains and injuries generated in advanced capitalist societies. On these grounds, TCs can be promoted as a non-penal abolitionist real utopia.

References

Bale, R., Van Stone, W., Kuldau, J., Engelsing, T., Elashoff, R. and Zarcone, V. (1980) 'Therapeutic communities versus methadone maintenance. A prospective controlled study of narcotic addiction treatment: design and one-year follow-up' in *Archives of General Psychiatry* Volume 37, No. 2 pp 179–193

Barton, A. (2005) *Fragile Moralities, Dangerous Sexualities* Aldershot: Ashgate

Belenko, S., Foltz, C., Lang, M., Hung-En, S. (2004) 'Recidivism among high-risk drug felons: a longitudinal analysis following residential treatment' in *Journal of Offender Rehabilitation* Volume 40, No. 112 pp 105–321

Broekaert, E., Vandevelde, S., Schuyten, G., Erauw, K. and Bracke, R. (2004) 'Evolution of encounter group methods for substance abusers' in *Addictive Behaviours* Volume 29, pp 231–244

Broekaert, E., Vandevelde, S., Soyez, V., Yates, R. and Slater, A. (2006) 'The third generation of therapeutic communities: the early development of the TC for addictions in Europe' in *European Addiction Research* Volume 12, pp 1–11

Cohen, S. (1980) 'Preface' in Dronfield, L. (1980) *Outside Chance* London: Null

DeLeon, G. (2000). *The Therapeutic Community. Theory, Model and Method* New York: Springer.

Dyna, P. and Sung, H. (2000) 'The safety and effectiveness of diverting felony drug offenders to residential treatment as measured by recidivism' in *Criminal Justice Policy Review* Volume 11, No. 4 pp 299–311

French, M. McCollister, K., Sacks, S., McKendrick, K. and DeLeon, G. (2002) 'Benefit-cost analysis of a modified therapeutic community for mentally ill chemical abusers' in *Evaluation and Programme Planning* Volume 21, No. 2 pp 137–198

Glaser, A. (1983) 'Therapeutic communities and therapeutic communities: a personal perspective' in *International Journal of Therapeutic Communities* Volume 4, No. 2 pp 150–162

Goethals, I., Soyez, V., Melnick, G., DeLeon, G. and Broekaert, E. (2011) 'Essential elements of treatment: a comparative study between European and American therapeutic communities for addiction' in *Substance Use and Misuse* Volume 46 pp 1023–1031

Gosling, H. (2015) *An Invitation to Change? An Ethnographic Study of a Therapeutic Community for Substance use.* Unpublished PhD Thesis. Liverpool John Moores University

Hannah-Moffatt, K. (2001) *Punishment in Disguise* Toronto: University of Toronto Press

Farrall, A. (2000) 'Testing the effect of therapeutic communities' in *Women, Crime and Drugs. Women and Criminal Justice* Volume 11, No. 1 pp 21–48

Illich, I. (1977) *Limits to Medicine: Medical Nemesis — The Expropriation of Health* Harmondsworth: Penguin Books Ltd

Kennard, D. (1998) *An Introduction to Therapeutic Communities. Therapeutic Communities* London: Jessica Kingsley Publishers

Kooyman, M. (1986) 'The psychodynamics of therapeutic communities for treatment of heroin addicts' in DeLeon, G. and Ziegenfuss, J. (1986) *Therapeutic Communities for Addictions. Readings in Theory, Research and Practice* USA: Springfield pp 29–41

Kooyman, M. (1993) *Therapeutic Communities for Addicts. Intimacy, Parent Involvement and Treatment Outcome* The Netherlands: Swets and Zeitlinger

Lamb, H.R. and Goertzes, V. (1974) 'Ellsworth House: a community alternative to jail' in *American Journal of Psychiatry* Volume 131, pp 64–68

Lipton, D. (1998) 'Therapeutic community treatment programming in correction' in *Psychology, Crime and Law* Volume 4, No. 3 pp 213–263

Lipton, D. (2010) 'A therapeutic distinction with a difference: comparing American concept-based therapeutic communities and British democratic therapeutic community treatment for prison inmates' in Shuker, R. and

Sullivan, E. (eds) *Grendon and the Emergence of Forensic Therapeutic Communities: Development in Research and Practice* Chichester: Wiley-Blackwell

Mathiesen, T. (1974) *The Politics of Abolition* Oxford: Martin Robertson

Messina, N. Buldon, W. Hagopian, G. and Prendergast, M. (2000) 'Predictors of prison-based treatment outcomes: a comparison of men and women participants' in *American Journal of Drug and Alcohol Abuse* Volume 32, No. 1 pp 7–22

Moloney, P. (2013) *The Therapy Industry* London: Pluto Press

Nemes, S. Wish, E. and Messina, N. (1999) 'Comparing the impact of standard and abbreviated treatment in a therapeutic community. Findings from the district of Columbia treatment initiative experiment' in *Journal of Substance Abuse Treatment* Volume 17, No. 4 pp 339–347

Perfas, F. (2004) *Therapeutic Community. Social Systems Perspective* Lincoln: iUniverse, Inc.

Rapley, M., Moncrieff, J. and Dillon, J. (2011) 'Carving nature at its joints' in Rapley, M., Moncrieff, J. and Dillon, J. (eds) (2011) *De-Medicalising Misery* London: Palgrave

Rawlings, B. and Yates, R. (2001). *Therapeutic Communities for the Treatment of Drug Users.* London: Jessica Kingsley

Scott, D. (2008) *Penology* London: Sage

Scott, D. (2013) 'Visualising an abolitionist real utopia: principles, policy and practice' in Malloch, M. and Munro, B. (eds) (2013) *Crime, Critique and Utopia* London: Palgrave

Scott, D. (2015) 'Eating your insides out: interpersonal, cultural and institutionally-structured violence in the prison place' in *Prison Service Journal* No. 201, pp 68-72

Scott, D. and Codd, H. (2010) *Controversial Issues in Prison* Buckingham: Open University Press

Scott, D. and Gosling, H. (2015) 'Counterblast: thinking beyond the punitive rationale — promoting TCs as a radical alternative to prison?' in *Howard Journal of Criminal Justice* September, 2015

Small, D. (2011) 'Psychotherapy: illusion with no future' in Rapley, M., Moncrieff, J. and Dillon, J. (eds) (2011) *De-Medicalising Misery* London: Palgrave

Stevens, A. (2013). *Offender Rehabilitation and Therapeutic Communities. Enabling Change the TC Way* United Kingdom: Routledge

Sugarman, B. (1984) 'Towards a new, common model of the therapeutic community: structural components, learning processes and outcomes' in *International Journal of Therapeutic Communities* Volume 5, No. 2 pp 77–98

Sugerman, B. (1986) 'Structure, variations and context. A sociological view of the therapeutic community' in DeLeon, G. and Ziegenfuss, J. (1986) *Therapeutic Communities for Addictions. Readings in Theory, Research and Practice* USA: Springfield

Vanderplasschen, W., Vandevelde, S. and Broekaert, E. (2014). *Therapeutic Communities for Treating Addictions in Europe. Evidence, Current Practices and Future Challenges.* European Monitoring Centre for Drugs and Drug Addictions. Available online at: http://www.emcdda.europa.eu/attachements.cfm/att_226003_EN_TDXD140 15ENN_final.pdf (consulted 10 October 2014)

Waldorf, D. (1971) 'Social control in therapeutic communities for the treatment of drug addicts' in *The International Journal of Addictions* Volume 6, No. 1 pp 29–43

White, W. (1998). *Slaying the Dragon. The History of Addiction Treatment and Recovery in America* Bloomington: Lighthouse Institute

Wilson, S. and Mandelbrote, B. (1985) 'Reconviction rates of drug dependent patients treated in a residential therapeutic community: 10 year follow-up' in *British Medical Journal*, Volume 291, pp 105

Yates, R. (1981) *Out from the Shadow* London: NACRO

Yates, R. (2002) *A Brief History of British Drug Policy: 1950–2001. Scottish Drugs Training Project.* University of Stirling. Available online at: https://dspace.stir.ac.uk/bitstream/1893/1135/1/1950-2001.pdf (consulted 22 January 2014)

Yates, R. (2003) 'A brief moment of glory: the impact of the therapeutic community movement on the drug treatment systems in the UK' in *International Journal of Social Welfare* Volume 12, pp 239–243

Yates, R. (2012) 'In it for the long haul: recovery capital, addiction theory and the inter-generational transmission of addictive behaviour' in Adan, A. and Vilanou, C. *Substance Abuse Treatment: Generalities and Specificities* Barcelona: Marge-Medica Books pp 35–51

Zarkin, G. Dunlap, L. Belenko, S. and Dyna, R. (2005) 'A benefit-cost analysis of the Kings County District Attorney's Office Drug Treatment Alterative to Prison (DTAP) program' in *Justice, Research and Policy* Volume 7, No. 1 pp 1–24

12.

Playing the 'Get Out of Jail Free' Card: Creating a new abolitionist-based consensus?

This chapter was first delivered as a conference paper at the inaugural conference of the European Group, 'Working Group on Prisons, Punishment and Detention' in Liverpool on 22 March 2013 and was published in Canning, V. (ed.) Sites of Confinement *in October 2014.*

> [W]henever experiences shows that certain things do not answer the purpose for which they were intended, then the right to continue ceases. That is, whenever it becomes apparent that certain acts done for the purposes of punishment do not serve the purposes for which they were intended — i.e. do not tend to protect society — then the right to repeat them ceases, and any further repetition of them will be simply a wrong done by society to one of its members, an injury inflicted by the strong on the weak.

So wrote John Peter Altgeld (1884: 50) nearly 130 years ago in his book *Our Penal Machinery and its Victims*. In this classic text, Altgeld raised major objections to both the imprisonment of children and women and the use of remand, and his critique of the 'penal machinery' is all the more interesting because, at the time of writing, he was a serving American judge. Previous chapters have pointed to numerous limitations facing contemporary sites of confinement, indicating that time has once again come to recognise, as Altgeld did, that their repetition is "simply a wrong done by society" by the "strong on the weak".

The case against prisons' 'right to continue' (Ibid.) seems all the more pertinent in our time of "hyper-incarceration" (Wacquant, 2010). Indeed, the recent growth in the average daily population (ADP) of prisoners in England and Wales is staggering. At the end of 1992, for example, the ADP stood at around 40,600 prisoners, yet by October 2011, the daily population had surpassed 88,000. Although the ADP has declined in recent months — on Friday 15 March 2013, there were 84,501 people in prisons and young-offender institutions in England and Wales, and a further 366 children held in secure children's homes and secure training centres — prisoner populations are out of control.[1] Despite such exponential growth, it remains all too clear that prison does not work, at least when measured against its official aims (Sim, 2009). Forty-seven per cent of adults are reconvicted within one year of release. This figure increases to 60% for ex-prisoners who served sentences of less than twelve months, and to as high as 70% for those who have served more than ten prison sentences (Ministry of Justice, 2009).

When challenging hyper-incarceration, abolitionists must advocate strategies and tactics that can be adopted in our historical conjuncture and thus be immediately influential. This should not mean compromising abolitionist values or abandoning utopian visions or radical alternatives, but rather being politically astute and having a clear strategy of engagement. The most important question, I think, for penal abolitionists today is 'what can we do right now to challenge hyper-incarceration and yet, at the same time, leave open the possibility for radical change?'

Our escape from hyper-incarceration begins by reversing the tide, making small steps towards penal abolition and the creation of a society rooted in the principles of social justice and the acknowledgement of common humanity. Any successful intervention must be abolitionist, for it is only by adopting abolitionist principles and values that we can hope to avoid 'co-option' (Mathiesen, 1974) and 'carceral clawback' (Carlen, 2002). Yet abolitionists cannot achieve this alone. We need a broad-based alliance that draws upon penal pressure groups, the liberal penal lobby — penal minimalists, reductionists and moderates — as well as progressive politicians, practitioners and members of the general public. Further, both penal and social transformation can only be achieved through alliances with other radical social movements committed to social justice, anti-violence and human dignity for all. We need a strategy and consensus consistent with abolitionist values and sensibilities if we are to effectively dismantle the penal apparatus of the Capitalist State.

I have referred elsewhere to how an abolitionist real utopia (Scott, 2013a, 2013b) would aim to challenge hyper-incarceration whilst, at the same time, promote radical social and penal transformation. Such an abolitionist real utopia would be grounded within the immanent real-world conditions of our historical moment, and its strategy for the radical

---

[1] The numbers of prisoners in England and Wales has remained at a similar level between 2013-2016. In June 2016 there were just under 86,000 people in prison.

reduction in prison populations would draw upon the 'attrition model' and its associated stance of the 'selective abolition'. Let us consider this further.

The writings of John Peter Altgeld and William Nagel both espoused embryonic versions of the attrition model, but it is the writings of Faye Honey Knopp and colleagues in their abolitionist handbook *Instead of Prisons*, first published in 1976, that laid down the principles of this approach. In short, the attrition model aims to gradually reduce imprisonment:

> 'Attrition' which means the rubbing away or wearing down by friction, reflects the persistent and continuing strategy necessary to diminish the function and power of prisons in our society. (Knopp, 1976: 62, emphasis in the original)

In the last thirty-five and more years, the attrition model has been promoted by abolitionists such as Thomas Mathiesen, Stan Cohen, Joe Sim and Julia Oparah, and I believe it remains the most plausible abolitionist strategy yet devised. The associated model of selective abolitionism, which has been advocated by abolitionists such as Pat Carlen, Phil Scraton, Barbara Hudson, Barry Goldson and Deb Coles, is rooted in the assumption that certain categories of lawbreakers must not be sent to prison because of (1) the relative harmlessness of the offence, (2) the vulnerabilities of the person who has broken the law, or (3) that imprisonment has unnecessarily harmful consequences that should, if at all possible, be avoided. Such lawbreakers, albeit perhaps on different grounds, should be deliberately excluded from imprisonment. Alongside Helen Codd, I brought a number of these groupings of prisoners together to present a holistic case for selective abolitionism in our book *Controversial Issues in Prisons* (Scott and Codd, 2010).[2] The book maintained that selective abolitionism could be immediately adopted by politicians and penal campaigners who wished to lobby the government for major reductions in the prison population.

It was recognised that such an approach must be conscious of the contradictions and the dangers generated by this strategy. Attrition and selective abolitionism are not enough on their own. They must be

---

[2] On average, in 2016 a prisoner in England and Wales attempts to take their own lives every five hours.

understood as part of a wider abolitionist critique of prisons and criminal processes, and as the first step on a path to a socially just society. On this assumption, I believe the seven well-debated 'tactics' detailed below may lead us in the right direction and help generate a new abolitionist consensus. Collectively, they entail, to use a metaphor from the popular board game *Monopoly*, playing the 'get out of jail free' card.

1. Moratorium on all prison building

I would like to suggest that an anti-prison activist's first priority should be to organise international, national and local campaigns challenging the moral, economic and political viability of building more prisons. Indeed, stopping the building of new prisons is essential for the success of penal reduction. Moratoriums directly challenge the prison-building programmes and are a crucial intervention for the following eight reasons:

i) There is recognition that the level of financial investment in prison building deters politicians from calling for penal reduction later on.
ii) It provides an opportunity to draw attention to the direct costs of penal incarceration and may allow some discussion of its hidden costs — both human and financial.
iii) It recognises that the inherent harms and pains of penal incarceration cannot be removed by improved physical conditions.
iv) It can facilitate discussion of how money allocated to prison building could be reinvested in new employment possibilities in the community which do not deliberately inflict pain on other humans.
v) Political pressure is created to develop alternative policies and indicates to politicians that they can no longer simply expand the penal apparatus to deal with pressing social problems.
vi) It directly challenges privatization and companies such as Serco and G4S that build prisons, focusing attention on the limitations of private finance initiatives and engendering the support of the penal practitioners and the liberal penal lobby opposed to privatisation.
vii) It provides a focused campaign against new prisons, and there is a strong possibility that such an intervention could generate new alliances.
viii) It is something that can be achieved in our historic conjuncture. In the current economic climate, economic expenditure is clearly an area of vulnerability and one that can be exploited.

2. Targeting existing prisons for immediate closure

A moratorium may help to create the political will to do something about our large prison populations, and this can be enhanced by calls to close existing prisons. Lists of the 'worst prisons' can be drawn up in a number of different ways, but perhaps the greatest immediate influence comes from those prisons highlighted in 'official' discourse, such as reports by Her Majesty's Chief Inspectors of Prisons (HMCIP). On such a basis, the following three prisons could be earmarked for immediate closure:

i)   HMP Wandsworth has recently been described by the *Guardian* (13 March 2013) as "Britain's worst jail". A 2011 HMCIP report highlights how the prison was "demeaning, unsafe and indecent", where some prisoners were kept locked up for twenty-two hours a day, whilst others had no access to showers for months on end. An authoritarian officer culture pertained and there were serious concerns about "unnecessary and disproportionate" prison officer violence. In March 2013, HMP Wandsworth was the fourth most overcrowded jail, exceeding capacity by 448 prisoners (at 167% capacity).

ii) The third most overcrowded prison in England and Wales in March 2013 was HMP Lincoln, which was at 170% capacity. In the December 2011 report, the HMCIP found Lincoln Prison "unsafe", with unacceptable levels of bullying, victimisation and assaults. Prisoners lived in "filthy conditions" and were kept locked up for most of the day. Prison officers appeared morally indifferent to the painful realities of prisoners.

iii) In a damning HMCIP report from July 2010, HMP Dartmoor was described as having a "pervasive negative culture" grounded in the antiquated principles of less eligibility. Dartmoor Prison was unsafe, violent and there was strong evidence of prison officer racism, homophobia and other forms of discrimination.

The Prison Service in England and Wales has closed thirteen prisons in the last four years, with seven prisons closed in March 2013 — Bullwood Hall, Camp Hill, Canterbury, Gloucester, Kingston, Shepton Mallet, Somerset, and Shrewsbury.[3] Abolitionists need to call for similar clusters of closures, without new prisons being opened. In the first instance, the targeting of the 'worst prisons' (with the recognition that there may well be much

---

[3] There have been further closures of prisons announced since 2013. These include HMP Holloway in London in 2015. Two concerns have been raised about recent prison closures. The first is that some old prisons are being closed because of the property value of the land and that after demolition new and exclusive housing for the rich will be built in their place. The second is that there is a major prison building programme underway which will expand rather than reduce overall capacity of the prison service, partly through building new 'super prisons' larger than the ones which have been closed.

worse jails than Wandsworth) may prove most persuasive to penal authorities and gain support from other constituents in the penal lobby.

3. Virtual end of remand in custody

The prison has been a place of custody, holding people awaiting trial for more than 1,000 years (Pugh, 1968). In March 2013, there were 13,000 people in prison on remand. The limitations of pretrial/preventive detention have long been identified, and have been central to the liberal penal lobby in the UK since at least the publication of A Taste of Prison (King and Morgan, 1976) some thirty-seven years ago. Remand prisoners today continue to face significant difficulties, including experiencing more impoverished living conditions than sentenced prisoners (HMCIP, 2012). People on remand have less access to facilities, basic 'entitlements' and preparations for their legal proceedings are likely to be greatly inhibited. Each year, 29,400 people remanded in custody are not given a prison sentence (Ibid.). It is now widely recognised that remand is not necessary to ensure a person's return to court for trial (Ibid.). One way, therefore, of immediately reducing the prison population is to abolish pretrial detention for all but the very small number of accused that genuinely present a threat to public safety. Such an initiative could reduce the prison population by around 10,000 in as little as three months.

4. Decriminalisation of 'victimless' or 'harmless' acts

One way to 'reduce the flow' of people into prison is to stop imprisoning individuals who have undertaken 'victimless' or 'harmless' petty offences. I will briefly consider the substance users and drug takers here. Abolitionists have argued that it is important to suspend our judgement on drug taking, arguing that whether we morally approve of them or not, such victimless acts cannot be effectively regulated by the criminal law (Knopp, 1976). There are estimated to be more than 400,000 illegal drug users in the UK (Seddon, 2006) and over 250,000 drug takers have been officially defined as 'problematic drug users' (PDUs). It is estimated that 75,000 PDUs pass through the prison system annually and that 45,000 PDUs are currently in prison (NOMS, 2005). Prisons are designed to contain, punish and deliver blame through pain rather than facilitate the care or positive transformation of individuals. In Portugal, drug taking and the possession of drugs has been decriminalised and drug problems are now considered a public-health issue. Money that would have been spent on penal incarceration is spent on health care, which is around 75% cheaper than the previous penal strategy. As a result, there has been a reduction in both heroin usage and drug-related property offences in Portugal. Extensive evidence from the UK suggests that treatments of drug takers are more likely to be successful in the community than criminal justice interventions (Bennett and Holloway, 2005). This implies that if treatment is a genuine aspiration it would be more sensible to decriminalise drug taking. Adoption of a public-health agenda for drug taking would reduce the prison population by tens of thousands in a very short period of time.

5. Raise the age of criminal responsibility

Criminal processes control and regulate the behaviour of children and young adults. Official data indicate that lawbreakers reach peaks in offending rates in the mid teens — although such data can and should be problematised, as they are based on officially recorded 'crimes', and they negate much adult crime undertaken in private spaces. Penal custody seems grossly inappropriate for children and young adults, for they are unlikely to have the life experience or coping skills required to deal with either punitive environments or the loss of close personal relationships. Most children who are imprisoned are not persistent offenders — with many having only one or two previous offences — and they are most likely to have committed petty property offences. Imprisoned children are characterised by poverty; family instability; emotional, physical and sexual abuse; homelessness; isolation; loneliness; self-harm; and disadvantage (Goldson, 2005; Goldson and Coles, 2005). Many children in custody have learning difficulties; have been placed on the child-protection registry; have self-harmed in the past; and have grown up in state care homes. Raising the age of criminal responsibility, initially to fourteen and later to sixteen, would allow for alternative ways of dealing with children in trouble who come to prominence. For those people under the age of eighteen, the courts should be asked to restrict interventions to police warnings, suspended sentences or unconditional discharges, and thus denaturalise the idea that confinement is suitable for any child. Human rights and children's charities would be natural allies and would broaden the basis of an abolitionist consensus.

6. Diversion of vulnerable people from criminal processes

There are a number of people with vulnerabilities imprisoned today who should be diverted from the criminal process, but here I focus exclusively upon people with mental-health problems. Mental-health problems are often linked with homelessness, poverty and unemployment, and *The Social Exclusion Report* (2002, cited in Scott, 2008: 116) notes that:

- 80% of prisoners have mental-health problems (66,000 people)
- 20% of male and 15% of female sentenced prisoners have previously been admitted to a mental hospital
- 95% of young prisoners aged fifteen to twenty-one suffer from a mental-health problem.

Prolonged passivity leads to isolation and the prison place presents a serious danger to the mental health of those confined. Numerous aspects of the daily prison regime are potentially damaging: crowding; frustrations experienced in dealing with the minutiae of everyday life; lack of mental or physical stimulation; the preponderance of negative relationships rooted in fear, anxiety and mistrust; physical, emotional, sexual or financial exploitation; and inadequate care with an overemphasis on medication.

Political momentum for the diversion of people with mental-health problems reached a new crescendo as recently as March 2011, when the then Justice Secretary Ken Clarke called for enhanced diversion schemes. There are currently over 100 adult *Criminal Justice Liaison and Diversion* schemes (established 1999) in England, which assess and advise on mental-health needs of offenders, sometimes referring offenders for treatment rather than punishment. From April 2013, *Health and Wellbeing Boards* will commission health and social-care services, including for those with mental-health problems. Abolitionists should try and influence the new Health and Wellbeing Boards to enhance provision for diversion. Whilst conscious of the problems of "net widening" (Cohen, 1985) and recognition that detention in a mental-health institution may be just as problematic as being confined in a penal one, highlighting the inappropriateness of punishing people with mental-health problems could mean that tens of thousands of people are diverted from prison.

7. Decarceration of vulnerable and harmless people from custody
Finally, we turn to the immediate removal of people from prison. As detailed above, there are a number of prisoners with vulnerabilities that have undertaken relatively harmless acts, but I will focus here only on women prisoners. Over a third of all adult women in prison have no previous convictions, and most women sentenced to imprisonment are sentenced for non-violent offences, with the largest group being

sentenced for drug offences (Ministry of Justice, 2008). The number of women prisoners has slightly fallen in recent times and, on 15 March 2013, there were 3,968 women in prison. Women are not imprisoned for the seriousness of the act perpetrated, but rather because of *who* they are: women who do not conform to a particular expectation of womanhood are those most likely to find themselves in prison (Scott and Codd, 2010). Most women offenders are not dangerous and approximately 3,000 of the women in prison could be released in a matter of weeks via early release, probation, home monitoring, and amnesties. Sentencers could also pilot the introduction of waiting lists for women offenders.

Not only, but also...

The above seven tactics must not be deployed in isolation of wider critiques of criminal processes or the introduction of social reforms rooted in social justice. Abolitionists must constantly guard against the possibility of the arguments of the attrition model/selective abolition being co-opted or used to justify the responsibilisation of offenders and subsequent negation of their care post-release (Hannah-Moffat, 2001). Abolitionists must also ensure that this strategy is not used to obfuscate the inherent harms and pains of imprisonment. The concern can perhaps be best illustrated through a consideration of 'suicidal ideation'. Prisons are deadly. One prisoner takes their own life every week in prisons in England and Wales, and the likelihood of a prisoner taking their own life is between four and eleven times higher than that of the general population (Scott and Codd, 2010). Coping is a tenuous, relative and fluid concept that ebbs and flows over time. Somewhere between one third and one half of the prison population have suicidal thoughts, and many have thought recently about taking their lives. If such figures are accurate, this would involve somewhere in the region of 42,000 people (Ibid.). The prison place is a toxic environment and all humans placed in such a degrading and damaging place are vulnerable to its structured harms. Abolitionists must therefore continue to question the core assumptions of the penal rationale and not focus exclusively upon prisoners who can most easily be defined as 'vulnerable', whatever its political utility.

Abolitionists recognise that the law reflects the interests of those who hold power rather than upholding a widely accepted moral code. Most people are regular lawbreakers yet most 'criminal acts' are not penalised. For every 100 serious crimes reported, twenty-five people are arrested, twelve are convicted and three end up in prison (Knopp, 1976). Those who are imprisoned are disproportionately from working-class, poor and impoverished social backgrounds. Abolitionists must keep at the forefront of the debate the problems of economic and social inequalities, and strive to develop alliances with social movements promoting human rights and social justice. Undoubtedly we must, somehow, try to create a new 'abolitionist consensus' that can make a difference here and now. Yet, at the same time, abolitionists and anti-prison activists must also continue to aspire to live in, and fight for, *a world without prisons*.

References

Altgeld, J.P. (1884) *Our Penal Machinery and its Victims* London: Leopold Classic Library

Bennett, T. and Holloway, K. (2005) *Understanding Drugs, Alcohol and Crime* Berkshire: Open University Press

Carlen, P. (2002) 'End of Award Report: Funding report ECHR: L216252033 ECHR' unpublished document

Cohen, S. (1985) *Visions of Social Control* Cambridge: Polity Press

Goldson, B. (2005) 'Child Imprisonment: A case for abolition', *Youth Justice* Volume 5, No.2 pp 77–90

Goldson, B. and Coles, D. (2005) *In the Care of the State?* London: INQUEST

Hannah-Moffat, K. (2001) *Punishment in Disguise* Toronto: University of Toronto Press

HMCIP (2010) *Inspection of HMP Dartmouth* London: HMCIP

HMCIP (2011a) *Inspection of HMP Wandsworth* London: HMCIP

HMCIP (2011b) *Inspection of HMP Lincoln* London: HMCIP

HMCIP (2012) *Thematic Review of Remand Prisoners* London: HMCIP

King, R. and Morgan, R. (1976) *A Taste of Prison* London: Routledge & Kegan Paul

Knopp, F.H. (1976) *Instead of Prisons* California: Critical Resistance

Mathiesen, T. (1974) *The Politics of Abolition* Oxford: Martin Robertson

Ministry of Justice (2008) *Offender Management Caseload Statistics 2008* London: The Stationery Office.

Ministry of Justice (2009) *Re-Offending of Adults: Results from the 2007 Cohort* London: The Stationery Office

National Offender Management Service (NOMS) (2005) *Strategy for the Management and Treatment of Drug Users within the Correctional Services* London: NOMS

Pugh, R.B. (1968) *Imprisonment in Medieval England* Cambridge: Cambridge University Press

Scott, D. (2008) *Penology* London: Sage

Scott, D. (2013a) 'Visualising an Abolitionist Real Utopia: Principles, policy and praxis' in Malloch, M. and Munro, W. (eds) *Crime, Critique and Utopia* Basingstoke: Palgrave

Scott, D. (2013b) 'Unequalled in Pain' in Scott, D. (ed) *Why Prison?* Cambridge: Cambridge University Press

Scott, D. and Codd, H. (2010) *Controversial Issues in Prisons* Buckingham: Open University Press

Seddon, T. (2006) 'Drugs, Crime and Social Exclusion: Social context and social theory in British drugs-crime research' in *British Journal of Criminology* Volume 46, No. 4 pp 680–703

Sim, J. (2009) *Punishment and Prisons* London: Sage

Wacquant, L. (2010), 'Class, Race and Hyper-incarceration in Revanchist America' in *Daedalus* Volume 139, No. 3, Summer 2010, pp 70–80

Epilogue

The *European Group for the Study of Deviance and Social Control* (European Group) today is an international organisation uniting critical thinkers all over the world. People now regularly attend European Group annual conferences from South America, North America and Australasia and, through social media, the newsletter and journal, the European Group is connecting with the daily lived experiences of activists, practitioners and academics across the globe. In terms of membership — whether measured through those people subscribing to the journal, members who are on the group mailing list, conference attendance, or members of social media such as Facebook and Twitter — the European Group has never been so successful. And perhaps, given the regressive changes taking place in the 'corporate university' in many countries, and the horribly disfigured nature of inequalities under neoliberal capitalism, the European Group has never been so important.

The European Group works best when it adheres closely to its values of mutual support, collegiality and friendship. Such an informal atmosphere enhances the possibilities for deep engagement with the core issues under discussion and the promotion of critical scholarship and learning. It is important that, at every level, the group lives up to its principles and there are opportunities for personal as well as professional development. In this sense, the European Group should and does stand out from other criminological forums. It is not in competition with the *European Society of Criminology* or mainstream criminology. Rather, the European Group offers a radical alternative based on a non-hierarchical ethos and genuine democratic participation in decision-making processes. This is not to say that the European Group will not face some very stern tests in its immediate future. The increasingly international nature of the group means there are new challenges in ensuring fairness and equity between those in the global north and global south. Irrespective of the level of commitment and scholarship, financial and time constraints impact differentially on members in different parts of the world (and, indeed, in different parts of Europe). Old problems around the superficiality of comparative criminologies have diminished somewhat, but structured power relations shaping the dominance of one voice over another have not been eradicated. Consciousness of the subaltern voice is now deeper than ever before in the European Group, but problems preventing the subaltern from being able to speak continue. Being

215

conscious of, and moving away from, Anglo dominance of the European Group will continue to be a major challenge. This is not to call for a weakening of the membership of the European Group in the UK, but to suggest that more should be done to help facilitate and grow membership and participation across countries in Europe and, indeed, across the globe.

The ethos of the European Group is that all members are equal, but in a world shaped by social fault lines around 'race', class, gender, sexuality, (dis)ability, age and language, some members are more equal than others. A commitment to equity and attempting to mitigate (as well as the broader commitment to transform) existing inequities in power relations should also be central to the organisation of the group. As part of its emancipatory politics and praxis, the European Group should be prepared to try and address some of the imbalances confronting members. This historically has meant promoting 'solidarity' prices for those who can afford it and reduced costs/bursaries for those who need them, such as activists without institutional affiliations. Where possible, the group must look to express its inclusionary philosophy by helping those who could not otherwise attend conferences — supporting PhD students with subsidised places; supporting members from countries with assisted places in times of economic and political troubles; recognising that the travel costs are much higher for some than others and, therefore, offering bursaries and travel assistance to help bridge the gap between the global north and global south. With a political commitment to social and transformative justice should come organisational commitment of the group to do what it can, when it can — given, of course, its own budget restrictions — to facilitate conference attendance and critical scholarship.

Another important way of building and consolidating membership is through the work of the National Representatives (national reps). Their role is to build networks, and the national reps are undoubtedly the lifeblood of the organisation. There are no easy ways of measuring the success of national reps — time served, numbers of members in a given country, influence in terms of shaping the direction of the group — these are all important indicators and each in turn is influenced by the historical development of critical criminology, current socio-economic context, political climate and recognition of critical scholarship in a given country. One further significant way of boosting membership is through the working groups. Since 2012, there has been the re-establishment of working groups on prisons, detention and punishment; social harm/zemiology; harms of the powerful; and the global north/global south, and more new working groups are being developed in the coming months and years. While the national reps build around geographical ties, working groups provide opportunities for members from different countries to connect through common research interests. Both networks are invaluable for future success. Both require a combination of knowledge and experience alongside opportunities for new people with lots of energy and enthusiasm to become involved. Openness and non-hierarchy should permeate all roles within the group and ensure as much as is feasible that there is a good balance between commitment, dynamism and familiarity with the workings of the group.

That those involved in organising annual conferences, events and publications keep costs to a minimum has historically been part of the ethos of the group. The real strength of European Group conferences is the engagement with other like-minded people involved in struggles for justice, not the 'frills' associated with conference meals and accessories. The lower the costs, the higher the uptake. When money is generated it is ploughed back into the group to help members. Budgets have always been tight because the European Group has never had a membership fee: historically, membership was renewed by attending the conference each year and any profits from the conference would go to the European Group. In recent times, only a small amount of income has been generated via conferences, and many conferences lose rather than make money. With the establishment of the European Group Journal, *Justice, Power and Resistance*, it may be possible to generate some further funds for the group. The journal's costs are low, but if those members who can afford to do so pay the solidarity subscription, it may be possible in the future to keep conference fees down to the bare minimum.

Further, it is important that members write *about* the current and historical importance of the European Group. No matter how influential the group has been in shaping critical criminologies in Europe and elsewhere, unless we write about its significance over time its place in facilitating and enhancing critical analysis will be lost. Contemporary critical criminological texts now tend to downplay the role of the European Group. Whilst there are some notable exceptions (Swaaningen, 1997; Gilmore et al., 2013), often the group is ignored or relegated to a footnote. There has, over the last few years, been talk of a 'history project' which aims to encourage memoirs of the group and the undertaking of interviews with established members. Only a few interviews have thus far been collated, and it is very important that over the next couple of years more reflections on the European Group are recorded. If undertaken, they could become one of the key legacies of the group itself.

The *European Group for the Study of Deviance and Social Control* must learn from its past: it must ensure that, in all its workings and organisation, it retains a commitment to dialogue, participatory democracy and non-hierarchical relations. It must also retain its commitment to emancipatory politics and praxis. Undoubtedly, the group will have its ups and downs in the future. It will face new and unexpected troubles, as well as encountering some now familiar difficulties and dilemmas. What it must not forget is that the best way forward will always be through adhering to its founding vision and its core political and ethical values. The European Group is always bigger than any one individual or even a small group of active people. The story of the group and its success are down to group members collectively wanting the group to survive and prosper. Let us hope, nay anticipate, that people will still be telling this story in many decades to come.

Appendix 1:
Working Group on Prison, Detention and Punishment: 2013 Manifesto[1]

1. This European working group provides a network and database for teachers, researchers, students and activists across Europe (and beyond) who have an interest studying prisons, detention and punishment. The working group will provide an opportunity to share our knowledge of sites of confinement and the operation of the penal rationale, and help establish new links with activists and academics worldwide who engage critically with the current forms, extent and nature of detention and punishment. The working group will thus provide an opportunity to connect local campaigns with a wider global network through which we can collectively provide solidarity and support. The working group also aims to foster a greater understanding of contemporary penality, offer possibilities for collaborative research, and work towards emancipatory change. We recognise that, since the inception of the confinement project in the eighteenth century, the boundaries between different sites of detention have become increasingly blurred: prisons house foreign nationals and recalcitrant mental-health patients; high-security hospitals hold the 'criminally insane'; immigration centres are run like prisons. The working group is committed to the abolition of penal confinement and other sites of involuntary detention. We also aim to challenge the logic and assumptions of the penal rationale and propose the development of non-repressive means of handling social problems and conflicts.

2. In many countries around the world there has been a proliferation of sites of confinement. More than ten million people are confined in prisons and many more millions are housed in other forms of detention. However, the rise of global hyper-incarceration and the

---

[1] This manifesto was a synthesis of the article 'Detention' (Scott, D. (2008) *Criminal Justice Matters*), the chapter 'Playing the "get out of jail free" card: creating a new abolitionist-based consensus?' (Scott, D., see Chapter 12 of this volume) and the 1975 European Group Manifesto (see Gilmore et al. (2013) *Critique and Dissent* Ottawa: Red Quill Books). The Working Group Manifesto was first published in the *European Group Newsletter* in 2013 and later in Gilmore et al. (2013).

analytical frameworks that underscore its assumptions have been challenged by a growing number of academics in their teaching and research, and also by social workers, anti-prison activists, social justice-inspired social movements, members of the radical penal lobby, progressive members of the public, socialist politicians and students. An increasing number of organisations all around the globe are now directly challenging hyper-incarceration. The European working group aims to contribute to the development of abolitionist and anti-prison activism, and to highlight the limitations of the current application of confinement. We acknowledge that the mobilisation of grass-roots activists is absolutely necessary for any sustained radical transformation of current penal and social realities.

3. The working group aims to encourage members to formulate intellectual interventions and direct activism that can systematically expose the brutal realities of detention, penal confinement and community punishments, and facilitate a reduction in the stigmatising effects and collateral consequences of the application of the penal rationale. We recognise that it is essential that the experiences and voices of detainees are given a platform to air their views and that the brutal and inhumane realities of sites of confinement are brought to the attention of the wider public and those in positions of power. The working group supports the rights of activists and citizens, including those sections of the voluntary sector that are pursuing social justice and penal reductionism, to pursue their goals without domination by governmental or profit-making interests.

4. The working group prioritises critical scrutiny of the justifications of the punitive rationale; punishment in the community, semi-penal institutions and probation hotels; and the wider moral and political contexts of the deliberate infliction of pain. The justification of detaining people in the interests of others should be critically scrutinised and located within its given social, economic, political and moral context. This does not mean we believe that nothing should be done, or that all forms of detention or deprivation of liberty are necessarily unjustified (especially those forms of detention provided for the best interests of the detainee), but rather that imprisonment and many forms of detention are illegitimate responses to wrongdoing, social harms and social problems. Sites of confinement

fail to uphold human rights, meet the demands of social justice or provide transparent or accountable forms of state governance. The increasing reliance upon involuntary detention, prisons and other forms of detainment in recent times also draws attention to its very real threat to democracy. All forms of detention have faced consistently high death rates and intentional self-injury, institutionalisation and disculturalisation, bullying and sexual violence, staff's moral indifference, institutionalised racism, masculinist hierarchies of power, and broader vulnerabilities to systemic abuses through torture and inhuman and degrading treatment. What the different institutions also seem to share is a historically broad inability to satisfy the duty of care owed to those whom they detain. We also acknowledge that detainees are predominantly poor, in bad physical and mental health, unemployed, and badly educated. It is the less fortunate, vulnerable and needy who are disproportionately detained and this fact draws direct connections with the need for a more socially just world.

5. The organisation of the European working group on prisons, detention and punishment is undertaken by a steering group that will consist of at least the following: a working-group coordinator, the coordinator of the *European Group for the Study of Deviance and Social Control*, and the secretary of the *European Group for the Study of Deviance and Social Control*. Members of the working group may also be invited to join a steering group. The working group will meet every year at the annual conference of the *European Group for the Study of Deviance and Social Control*, and members are encouraged to organise other events, meetings and conferences throughout the calendar year to help generate ideas, networks and direct interventions. Such events may be full meetings for the whole working group or specially convened meetings of local activists in one given region/nation. A separate mailing list will be maintained and other European Group media sources, such as Facebook, YouTube and Twitter, will be used to disseminate information about the working group and its activities. The working group coordinator will be elected at the European Group's annual conference and full details of the membership of the working group will be detailed on our website www.europeangroup.org.

6. Members of the working group are committed to the reversal of the proliferation of sites of confinement, and the utilisation of strategies drawing upon direct action and abolitionist praxis, in order to facilitate radical penal and social transformations. Though strategies of engagement will vary from place to place, depending upon local circumstances, we believe that to achieve our aims we must propose a number of direct interventions that are feasible here and now and that can exploit contradictions in the operation of penal power. We call for the following general interventions as a means to facilitate a long-term and radical reduction in the populations of those detained in sites of confinement.

i) An international moratorium on building new sites of confinement (prisons/asylums/immigration centres) and on the allocation of existing buildings and spaces as locations of involuntary detention.

ii) An end to the privatisation of sites of confinement and the insidious expansion of the carceral state via the voluntary and private sector.

iii) A detailed and critical interrogation of existing state detention, followed by a systematic call for governments to close the most inhumane, degrading and torturous sites of confinement without opening new houses of detention.

iv) A virtual end to pretrial detention and the abolishment of the antiquated notion of bail, except for those who present a serious threat to society.

v) The safeguarding and expansion of the legal rights of detainees. Post incarceration, ex-detainees must be recognised as full citizens and given full and uninhibited access to employment, housing, other social and financial services and full access to political and civil society.

vi) The decriminalisation of victimless and harmless acts, such as alcoholism, deviant sexualities between consenting adults, substance misuse and drug taking. The criminalisation of sex workers (who are often from working-class backgrounds) is harmful and victimising, and we propose alternative responses that protect and prioritise the safety of the men and women who engage in this work.

vii) The decriminalisation of infringements of migration laws.

viii) To raise the age of criminal responsibility in all countries in the world to the age of at least sixteen.

ix) To divert people with mental-health problems, learning disabilities, severe physical disabilities, the profoundly deaf and people with suicidal ideation from the criminal process, whilst at the same time ensuring any alternative interventions are both 'in place' of a penal sanction and are not merely forms of 'trans-incarceration' to other sites of confinement.

x) To immediately remove those people most vulnerable to the inherent harms and pains of confinement from places of detention.

xi) To formulate and advocate radical alternatives to the criminal process and social injustices for individual and social harms that are feasible and could be implemented immediately or within a short period of time.

xii) To propose that all governments prioritise meeting human need, recognising common humanity and facilitating social justice as the most effective means of preventing/dealing with human troubles, conflicts and problematic conduct.

Appendix 2:
G4S 2014 Annual General Meeting

This appendix was originally published in the European Group Newsletter *in July 2014.*

A number of us from the 'Reclaim Justice Network'[1] are shareholders in G4S (we have one share each). Six of us were present yesterday (5 June 2014) at the G4S Annual General Meeting (AGM) and this account is a way of bearing witness to what happened. The AGM was situated in the ExCel — a location well off the beaten track and difficult to find, at least for those not familiar with London. This did not stop a large number of protestors gathering outside the ExCel AND a very significant number of protestors — who were either shareholders or acting as proxy — from attending the AGM. The six of us from Reclaim Justice left our meeting place near to the venue about half an hour before the AGM was due to start — we all left separately and we agreed that we would have no contact with each other once inside the building — this is about as close as I think I'll get to 'espionage' and I felt like I was in a 'Mission Impossible' movie. We all got in and sat well apart.

The AGM was attended by the twelve board members of G4S — ten white middle-aged men and two women: one at either end. None of them spoke as we individually entered the room and took our seats. They looked directly at us with very stern and serious faces. They did not even look at each other or attempt to communicate among themselves. The room filled: there were perhaps as many as eighty sitting in the seats allocated for shareholders, and all around us were around fifteen security guards. I suspect there were also security guards sitting among us, and as the afternoon went on, one very burly man spent a considerable amount of time staring at me.

The AGM was opened by the chair and there were disruptions by shareholders almost from the start. A large number of protestors were focused on the role of G4S in the detention of Palestinians. There was clearly a very organised and large number of people from the charity 'War

---

[1] The *Reclaim Justice Network* is a collaboration of individuals, groups, campaigners, activists, trades unionists, practitioners, researchers and people most directly affected by criminal justice systems, who are working together to radically reduce the size and scope of criminal-justice systems and to build effective and socially just alternatives. https://downsizingcriminaljustice.wordpress.com/

on Want'. Their group used codings (hums and coughs for key words) and at regular intervals there were attempts to make statements condemning G4S policies in Palestine/Israel. The reaction of G4S security guards to these protests was appalling. Protestors were pulled from their seats, dragged kicking and screaming out of the room, with sometimes attempts by security staff to muffle their protests. Two people sitting directly next to me were part of this protest group and were manhandled very badly. The feeling of unease and anxiety engendered when another human being is being dragged away directly next to you left me shaken, and my emotions stirred.

Ashley Almanza, current CEO of G4S, gave his presentation (disrupted by numerous protestors: the most effective of which was when around seven people from different parts of the room all protested at once — this lasted for a couple of minutes for, despite the size and numbers of the security guards, they seemed reluctant to engage protestors on a one-to-one basis). At this point, shareholders started to call for an adjournment and, to appease us, the security guards were asked to not remove anyone else but simply ask them to be quiet. However, the damage was done. G4S, in its daily work, practices, invokes and deploys violence, and now they were doing so with their own shareholders. As a number of shareholders noted, the whole meeting was a 'disaster for G4S'.

Then came questions (there were still around 50 or 60 people in the room at this point). In the main, the first part of the questions (which lasted about two hours) were all focused on Palestine and directed at members of G4S; however, I was the second person allowed to ask a question. I asked Ashley Almanza who he thought the 'customers' of G4S were — the annual report is riddled with the word and he also mentioned the 'customer' as a priority on a number of occasions in his talk. He seemed unprepared and gave a vague answer which did not really give a clear picture (he seems to think that his employees are his customers!). He did not mention prisoners/detainees, so I then followed up my question by pointing this out. He again was unable to give a satisfactory account. Then followed around ten or twelve questions on G4S and its relationship to Israel which revealed (among other things) that one of the 'independent and impartial' academics commissioned to provide a human-rights audit of its practices in Israel (which actually simply responsibilised detainees and prisoners) was a Zionist! Further egg on the face of the board.

The chair then requested other questions not related to the topic, and discussion started to focus on a number of more 'domestic issues', and prisons and 'care and justice' services in the UK. Following a discussion of deaths in custody, I was given the opportunity to once again have a dialogue with Ashley Almanza — this time concerning self-inflicted deaths, parasuicide and self-harm. The 'chief executive' claimed that he was not allowed to publish materials without government approval! I challenged this and asked him for a public commitment from G4S that they would next year ensure that all data on self-harm and attempted self-inflicted deaths (including those who tragically succeed in the act) be made publicly available via their website. My understanding is that he made that commitment, which at least is one step towards greater democratic accountability.

Colleagues from Reclaim Justice Network were also then invited by the chair to ask questions, including points on G4S management; Oakwood Prison inspectorate reports; a letter published only on Wednesday in *Inside Time* which indicates mass resignations of prison officers from Oakwood; and questions about prisoners working forty-hour weeks and if G4S made profits from these work contracts. Ashley Almanza stated on a number of occasions in response to this that G4S did not make profits from prison labour.

Finally, concerns were expressed about the claims made by G4S in its annual report and the conduct of the meeting. A vicar raised some important concerns about the limitations of G4S and how it handled the meeting. I then added (with a sense of humour here) that 'My advice to Ashley Almanza and the G4S board is that they take "independent and impartial advice" on how best to conduct their security'.

Appendix 3:
G4S and Human Rights

A number of members of the Reclaim Justice Network *[RJN] hold one share in G4S. This allows those members to attend the G4S Annual General Meeting every year and raise questions regarding human rights violations and democratic accountability. According to the 2015 Annual Report "G4S is the world's leading global, integrated security company specialising in the delivery of security and related services to customers across six continents". It is also a multinational corporation that is regularly steeped in scandal and controversy. There were 16 protestors at the 2016 G4S AGM, six of which were members of RJN. This letter was sent to Ashley Almanza, G4S Chief Executive Officer and John Connolly, Chair of the G4S Board of Directors on 27th May 2016 following a discussion with themselves and other board members at the close of the 2016 AGM.*

I am writing to you following our conversation at the G4S Annual General Meeting [AGM] on the 26th May 2016. Our discussions focused on ethics and human rights. The G4S 2015 *Annual Report and Accounts*[1] emphasises the values underscoring the company as an "ethical organisation" (page 20) and the 2015 *Corporate Social Responsibility Report*[2] [CSR] highlights the "G4S ethics code" (page 32) and its commitment to "an open approach to addressing human rights issues" (page 29). In the two hours of questions at the AGM this year, however, nearly every question focussed on the failure of G4S to meet such commitments. In this letter I would briefly like to highlight three specific points regarding this commitment to human rights and offer some ways in which you could work towards enhancing this.

My first point concerns the manner of the removal of peaceful protestors from the AGM. For example, in one case the shirt of a women protestor was ripped by G4S guards and afterwards she had marks on her arms. The reputation of G4S is not well served through such treatment. It is imperative that G4S find a more human rights compliant way of responding to such democratic encounters in the future.

My second point is more substantial. During the AGM I highlighted the 'human rights leitmotif' expressed in the meeting and suggested that G4S

---

[1] G4S (2016a) *Securing Your World: Integrated Report and Accounts 2015* London: G4S / Park Communications
[2] G4S (2016b) *Securing Your World: Corporate Social Responsibility Report 2015* London: G4S / Park Communications

undertake a 'human rights audit' of their work. This suggestion was accepted as a recommendation by the chair. Such a human rights audit should expand upon the current understanding of human rights in the 2015 *CSR report*. On page 20 of the 2015 *CSR Report* it is stated that "our respect for human rights is core to the sustainable success of our business and continue to be an important part of our risk assessment and mitigation process." The language of human rights means more than 'business risks' and should be understood as a commitment to legal covenants and arising ethical responsibilities. Most notably human rights entail the recognition of the inherent human dignity of other human beings and a culture of respect. G4S would benefit enormously from an independent review drawing upon a range of external experts in the field of human rights. I would also encourage G4S to cultivate an aspiration, from top downwards, of becoming a world leader in the promotion of human rights. This means striving to not only meet human rights standards but to also transform the organisational culture so that the G4S slogan of 'securing the world' becomes synonymous with the protection of human dignity. The scope of your human rights audit could then entail local and global action plans on how human rights policies and outcomes can be enhanced; human rights training of staff and how good practice in recognition of the dignity of others can be best rewarded; the development of human rights champions within different parts of the organisation to create cultural change and the formation of a new 'Human Rights Committee' dedicated to promoting human rights governance; a strengthening of the 'speak out' whistle-blower policy documenting human rights violations across the organisation, its subcontractors and other partners; and open, democratic and transparent processes which allow the voices of staff, service users, shareholders and other stakeholders to be heard in a way that is compliant with respect and dignity.

My third point relates to existing practice in HMP Altcourse, Liverpool, regarding the treatment of prisoners who have attempted to take their own lives. Six prisoners have died at the prison since 2013, including the high profile deaths of Connor Smith and Andrew Bain, and there were 900 reported incidents of self-harm in 2013, up from 290 in 2009. At the AGM it was noted that self-harm figures in prisons run by G4S are now to be included in annual reports. I welcome this announcement. There is, however, a tragic pattern emerging of a significant failure of the duty of care. Lessons need to be learnt from such terrible events to ensure the safety and well-being of all those currently being held in the care of G4S.

At one public meeting in Liverpool, attended by myself and more than 80 other people in February 2016, a prison custody officer detailed the alleged response of other staff to a prisoner who attempted to take their own life at HMP Altcourse. The allegation is that a prisoner who attempted to burn themselves alive by lighting matches in their clothing was mocked by prison custody officers. This is a serious allegation and I would like to request that G4S undertake a thorough investigation into the treatment and response of staff to prisoners who self-harm, experience mental health problems and / or experience or have acted upon suicidal ideation. Here I think G4S would benefit from engaging with experts in the field, such as INQUEST, who can work with you to help you identify new policies and practices that meet the requirements of human rights covenants and aspirations.

I look forward to learning more about this at the AGM next year.

Appendix 4:
Critical Criminology Survey Institutions

University

1 Cardiff*
2 Chester
3 Edge Hill
4 Essex
5 Greenwich
6 Huddersfield
7 Lincoln*
8 Liverpool JMU*
9 Liverpool
10 London Metropolitan
11 Manchester Metropolitan
12 Middlesex
13 Open University*
14 Sheffield Hallam
15 Stafford
16 Sunderland
17 Teesside
18 Ulster
19 West England
20 York

* Indicates that at this institution, there were two respondents

Twenty out of 124 universities in the UK

Appendix 5:
Critical Criminology Survey Respondent Details

Respondent No.	Length of Time Working in University	Current Position
1	6–10 years	Senior Lecturer
2	10–15 years	Professor
3	20 years or over	Professor
4	20 years or over	Principal Lecturer
5	6–10 years	Senior Lecturer
6	20 years or over	Professor
7	15–20 years	Senior Lecturer
8	20 years or over	Senior Lecturer
9	1–5 years	Senior Lecturer
10	1–5 years	Lecturer
11	6–10 years	Reader
12	15–20 years	Senior Lecturer
13	1–5 years	Senior Lecturer
14	20 years or over	Professor
15	15–20 years	Professor
16	6–10 years	Lecturer
17	1–5 years	Lecturer
18	10–15 years	Research Fellow
19	20 years or over	Principal Lecturer
20	1–5 years	Lecturer
21	1–5 years	Lecturer
22	Less than one year	Research Student
23	6–10 years	Principal Lecturer
24	20 years or over	Senior Lecturer

Twenty-four questionnaires returned between 14th March and 12 May 2014

Appendix 6:
Critical Criminology Survey Questionnaire

CRITICAL CRIMINOLOGY PROGRAMMES IN BRITISH UNIVERSITIES
Open Questionnaire March 2014

REF:

Length of time you worked as a full-time member of staff in the university sector:
- Less than one year
- 1–5 years
- 6–10 years
- 10–15 years
- 15–20 years
- 20 years or over

Current position:
- Part-time/Sessional
- Research Student
- Lecturer
- Senior Lecturer
- Principal Lecturer
- Reader
- Professor

Part A: The Critical Criminology Programme

1. Would you characterise the criminology programme you teach at your university as a 'critical criminology programme'? Why?
2. What do you understand by the term 'neoliberal university'? In what ways may this enhance or encroach upon critical pedagogy?
3. Have you encountered institutional opposition to implementing a critical criminological teaching curriculum?

4. Can you give any examples of recent policies at your university that have enhanced the development of critical criminology programmes at your institution?

5. In what ways do you think that current university managerial priorities are impacting upon the critical criminology curriculum?

6. In what ways do you think that the current university emphasis on employability is impacting upon the critical criminology curriculum?

Part B: Teaching Critical Criminology

7. What do you consider to be some of the main obstacles/difficulties confronting teachers of critical criminology today in the UK?

8. In what way, if at all, do you think that broader educational policies (in schools and colleges) are impacting upon the teaching of critical criminology at universities?

9. How do you think that the idea that students are 'customers' has impacted upon your experience as a university lecturer?

10. Do you think that students have become more or less engaged with contemporary political and socio-economic issues? If you think the latter is true, can you think of any strategies that could be deployed to overcome student disengagement?

11. Do you think students are specifically attracted to critical, as opposed to positivist, criminology courses?

12. In what ways, if at all, do you think that the 'academic profession' is being 'deprofessionalised'?

Part C: Doing Critical Research

13. Do you think that the focus on income generation has curtailed or enhanced space for independent critical criminological research?

14. What do you consider to be some of the main obstacles/difficulties confronting researchers in critical criminology today in the UK? Can you think of any strategies that could be shared with other members of the European Group to overcome them?

15. In what ways do you think there is space and opportunity for critical criminologists to engage with the media? What strategies

concerning media engagement could be deployed that could be shared with other members of the European Group?

16. Have you personally encountered difficulties with having critical criminological research funded or published?

Part D: Moving Forward

17. Do you think that the problems and possibilities shaping the critical criminological curriculum today are significantly different to those of the past?

18. In what ways do you see new openings, sites of contestation and resistance in the academic workplace?

19. Where do you think that the teaching of critical criminology in universities in the UK will be in ten years?

20. In what ways do you think that the *European Group for the Study of Deviance and Social Control* can help us overcome current obstacles/support the critical criminological curriculum?

21. Are there any other points or issues you think should be raised regarding the current role and future prospects for critical criminology programmes in the UK?

Made in the USA
Charleston, SC
08 August 2016